IMAGES of America

DEMING

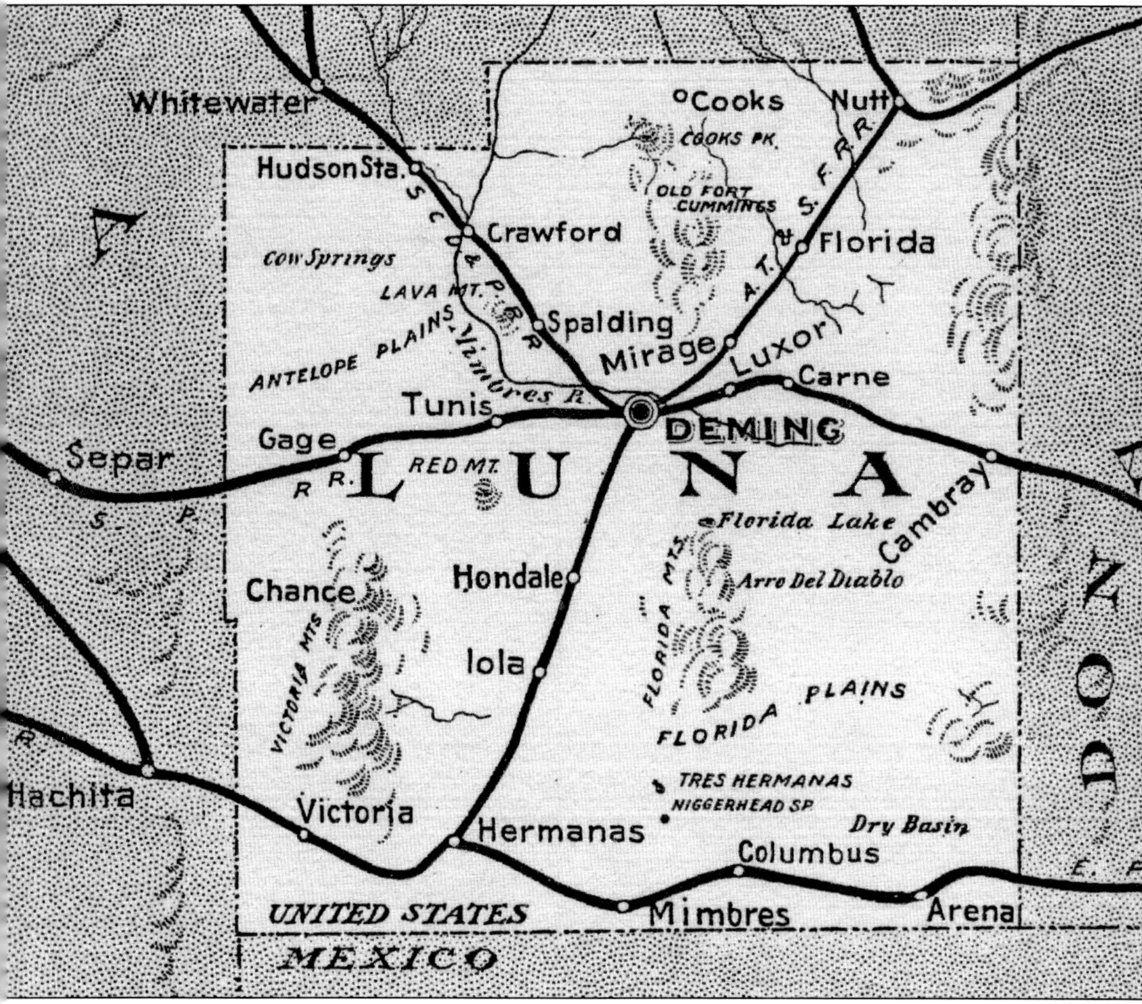

This map shows how Deming's creation revolved around the railroad. Each place marked along the railroad was a water stop for the steam locomotives. Separ, Gage, and Tunis were stops along the Southern Pacific Railroad, while Mirage, Florida, and Nutt were beside the Atchison, Topeka & Santa Fe Railway. The other thick black lines represent other railroads that came after Deming's establishment with the second transcontinental railroad. (Courtesy of Deming Luna Mimbres Museum Archives.)

On the Cover: North of the Southern Pacific Railroad's main line in Deming, New Mexico, stood Union Depot. Southern Pacific Railroad built and owned the large structure and occupied its west end. It housed railroad and telegraph offices, a waiting room, an Adams Express Company office, and a Wells Fargo Express office, which is featured on the cover. The east end was occupied by the Atchison, Topeka & Santa Fe Railway. The middle section of the building was occupied by a Harvey House, one of Fred Harvey's popular eateries. (Courtesy of Deming Luna Mimbres Museum Archives.)

IMAGES
of America

DEMING

Laura V. Krol

ARCADIA
PUBLISHING

ISBN 978-0-7385-8537-6

Published by Arcadia Publishing
Charleston, South Carolina

Printed in the United States of America

Library of Congress Control Number: 2011937472

For all general information, please contact Arcadia Publishing:
Telephone 843-853-2070
Fax 843-853-0044
E-mail sales@arcadiapublishing.com
For customer service and orders:
Toll-Free 1-888-313-2665

Visit us on the Internet at www.arcadiapublishing.com

To my grandfather Edward Krol, who uprooted his devoted wife, Victoria, and handsome sons, Richard and Steve, from Chicago and moved to Deming in 1962.

Contents

Acknowledgments

Being a hometown girl, there are many people to whom I am indebted for their assistance with this project. My mother and father cultivated a passion for history at a very young age. Long car trips down bumpy roads led me to this moment. My sister Katie and I would whine about needing the restroom, while our brother Christopher sat quietly looking out the window. The ultimate destination was not a restroom, but a historical marker, monument, or museum. This book could be considered a product of all of that whining, Dad.

I have a newfound appreciation for all of my teachers after sprinting into the field of education. Each of them is remembered for his or her kind and inspiring words.

Without the Luna County Historical Society granting permission to use its archives at the Deming Luna Mimbres Museum, this book would not be possible. Sylvia Ligocky, dedicated volunteer and retired teacher, spent many hours with me in the archives looking for "just one more photograph" to add to my ever-growing collection. William Bayne Anderson, president of the Luna County Historical Society, was kind enough to be my fact-checker. They are both great assets to the historical community.

Maria Rudloff of the Luna County Clerk's Office assisted me in endless treasure hunts at the courthouse for information about the people and places in this text.

I would be remiss not to mention my mentor as I completed my graduate thesis on Camp Cody. Dr. Scott E. Fritz is a devoted economic historian at Western New Mexico University. He has assisted me in many projects and is a historical inspiration.

I wrote this text as a memorial to the great people who resided and raised families in Deming. My desire is that the history of my hometown continues to live on through this book. Whether you have a connection to Deming or are just passing through, Happy Reading! May your journey be historical.

All of the images appear courtesy of the Deming Luna Mimbres Museum Archives unless otherwise noted.

Introduction

The Deming area was traversed long before the railroad company established the town in 1881 and had been along a transcontinental route for many travelers over the years. Native Americans, both Mimbres and Apache; Spanish explorers; American and immigrant settlers and stagecoach drivers; US Army men; and health-seekers were all a part of the early history of the American West in the Deming area. Each of these groups of people told a unique segment of Deming's lively history and has created the town's atmosphere today.

The first group that left evidence of its presence was the Mimbres Indians. They created petroglyphs at a location known today as Pony Hills, which is northeast of Deming. Since there is no oral or written history of these people, the carvings cannot be fully interpreted. The petroglyphs remain at this site, though much vandalism and erosion have occurred over the years.

Governor of New Mexico Juan Bautista de Anza led an expedition in 1780 to discover a route between Santa Fe, New Mexico, and Arizpe, Sonora. While Anza headed south, Don Joseph Antonio de Vildosola and Don Franciso Martinez left Sonora headed north. They were all to meet in the "Sierra de los Mimbres." Anza explored Cooke's Peak, Vildosola went to Mimbres, and Martinez traversed the Florida Mountains. All three groups experienced scuffles with the Apaches and never made contact with the other parties. It was believed that due to the intensity of the Apaches, this area was never inhabited.

Cooke's Spring, located at the base of Cooke's Peak north of Deming, was an important water stop for stagecoaches before and after the Civil War. In 1846, Lt. Col. Philip St. George Cooke led the Mormon Battalion to the spring in search of a new wagon road to California. The Mormon Battalion was a part of Brig. Gen. Stephen Watts Kearny's Army of the West, sent by Pres. James K. Polk to occupy upper Mexico during the Mexican-American War. The men began their journey at Council Bluffs, Iowa Territory, on July 16, 1846, and took 194 days to march almost 2,000 miles to San Diego. The trail that they followed would be known by travelers as Cooke's Wagon Trail. It was recognizable to travelers after the battalion because over 500 men and dozens of women walked the road and created a solid path for others to follow.

After the Mormon Battalion, the Military Appropriations Act of 1853 authorized a large expenditure. It allowed the government to conduct explorations and surveys for a practical route for a railroad from the Mississippi River to the Pacific Ocean. Lt. John Grubb Parke, a topographical engineer, surveyed the area of present-day Deming against Secretary of War Jefferson Davis's orders. Davis felt that the area was explored thoroughly earlier. When Parke reached Cooke's Wagon Trail, he decided to follow the road to Mesilla. He returned to Cooke's Spring and surveyed a more southerly line to the Rio Grande. Parke felt that this was a practical route to Fort Fillmore near Mesilla. (This would be the route the railroad companies chose in the 1870s and 1880s.)

The spring continued as a known stop to livestock drivers, immigrants, and gold-seekers. In 1857, it was a water stop for George Henry Giddings's San Antonio–San Diego Mail Company, which provided stage and mail service between those two stops in Texas and California. The mail company route followed Cooke's Wagon Trail, which marked the way to the West. After Giddings provided service to the area for a mere year, the Butterfield Overland Mail route went through the area from St. Louis, Missouri, on its way to San Francisco, California. The company, run by John Butterfield, was awarded the mail contract by the US government. The first mail carried through the area by this company was in the early morning of October 1, 1858. A Butterfield station was soon established near the spring. Mail continued to be carried through the area until the government ordered the closure of the line in March 1861, when Texas seceded from the Union.

Not too long after, on October 2, 1863, Brig. Gen. James H. Carleton established Fort Cummings, near Cooke's Spring. Prior to the fort's establishment, Apaches from the Warm Springs and Chirihuahua tribes killed many travelers along the Butterfield Trail. It could be argued that this area, Cooke's Canyon, was the second most dangerous point on the southern route to California (the first being Apache Pass, near Fort Huachuca, Arizona). During the Civil War, there were many accounts that numerous graves and skulls were scattered along the roadside near the spring, where the people had died at the hands of the Apaches. Some believe that at least 800 travelers were killed. Fort Cummings was constructed near the spring for protection of the wagon trains and officially established on October 2, 1863. As the Indian fighting reduced, Fort Cummings was abandoned in August 1873. After a large massacre near the old fort, it was reopened in January 1880. The fort continued to protect travelers until it was abandoned for the final time in October 1886.

The railroad companies became interested in the area, especially after Parke's survey in 1853. Leland Stanford (a Republican politician), Collis Huntington, Charles Crocker, and Mark Hopkins were known as the "Big Four," and they created the Central Pacific Railroad. These men saw to it that the Southern Pacific Railroad Company of New Mexico was incorporated in 1879 for the purpose of building the main railroad line from San Diego, California, through Lordsburg, New Mexico, and then to Deming. While the Southern Pacific Railroad was being constructed from the west, the Atchison, Topeka & Santa Fe Railway (Santa Fe) was being extended from the northeast. At a point that was to be called "Deming," the two railroads were to meet.

It has been suggested that Stanford may have recommended that the junction of the two railroads be named Deming after Crocker's wife's maiden name. It was unknown in November 1880 where Deming would be located, as the Southern Pacific continued building east from Lordsburg and the Santa Fe left the Rio Grande Valley at Rincon heading southwest. One thing was certain: water was the principal resource that influenced the selection of the Deming junction. George E. Gray of the Southern Pacific Railroad Company of New Mexico and A.A. Robinson of the Atchison, Topeka & Santa Fe Railway met 10 miles east of the Mimbres River in December 1880 to discuss the location. Near this place, a tent city called New Chicago sprang up with people anticipating the joining of the railroads in the area. It was believed that the junction would become a new gateway to the American West. Gray and Robinson agreed to the site where the two railroads would meet. Everyone who was living in New Chicago moved his belongings to the area of the junction (present-day Deming).

Southern Pacific's main line reached Deming on December 15, 1880. Train engineers who passed through the area bringing construction materials to build the railroads claimed that in December 1880, there was not one dwelling in the vicinity. Three months later, in early March 1881, the Atchison, Topeka & Santa Fe Railway's tracks arrived, which linked the two railroads and created the second transcontinental railroad. A silver railroad spike was driven in the track as a commemoration of the event. Santa Fe's first through train from Kansas City to Deming departed on March 17, 1881, headed west with engine no. 85 and eight cars following. Within one year of the railroads' arrival, there were at least 28 businesses in Deming.

Deming steadily grew as the years continued. The Mexican Revolution began only 30 miles south of Deming in 1910. Many leaders were struggling for power after longtime president Porfirio Diaz's reign. One rising leader, Francisco Pancho Villa, would significantly impact this area. The United States knew the threat that Villa posed, so in July 1914, the New Mexico National Guard moved its regular two-week summer training camp to Deming. It set up Camp Brookes north of the railroad tracks on a large piece of land. The US Army from Fort Bliss also joined it. This joint maneuver had very loose plans, since they believed that they would lead an armed intervention into Mexico. The training continued with no incident. After two weeks, the camp closed. But Villa's impending threat loomed.

Villa ordered a raid on United States soil in Columbus, New Mexico, 25 miles south of Deming, on March 9, 1916. His 500 followers (many of whom were forced to serve), known as *villistas*, killed 17 Americans and lit the small town on fire. This greatly changed the dynamics in southwestern New Mexico. Gen. John J. "Black Jack" Pershing led an expedition into Mexico searching for Villa. Many young men volunteered for the Border Service and were stationed in camps along the boundary. Camp Deming was established on the same piece of land that was occupied by Camp Brookes two years prior and housed about 500 men. Villa was never captured, but several villistas were. Six men were hanged in Deming.

Soon after the end of the Pershing expedition, the United States entered World War I, and Deming yet again played a significant role militarily. The town was selected to be the site of a National Guard training camp that housed 28,000 soldiers. Camp Cody was erected in July 1917 on the same land that was used for previous camps—though on a larger scale. The camp was completed with all of the necessities to train and entertain the troops, who came mostly from the Midwest. A group of men was sent to France from the camp but did not fight in the war, since they arrived after the armistice was in effect. Camp Cody was only a part of the local economy for 18 months. Most of the buildings on the site were moved to other military locations, but the large base hospital remained on the site.

After the war, Deming was seeking a group to take over the old base hospital. At the same time, Americans with tuberculosis were looking for a place that would benefit their health. Joseph A. Mahoney, representing the Deming Chamber of Commerce and president of the Holy Family Catholic Church Parish Council, worked with the Sisters of the Holy Cross Hospital Association of Indiana and served as a successful bidder at an auction to purchase the 480 acres of land from the government. The sanatorium was a large draw for the area and brought many patients and their families to Deming until it was destroyed by a fire on March 12, 1939.

In the 1930s, Pres. Franklin D. Roosevelt recognized the need for relief, recovery, and reform for the United States and its citizens—especially during the Great Depression. He created many agencies to put citizens to work. The Works Progress Administration (WPA) made a significant impact in Deming. A post office, public library, city hall and fire station, two-room addition to the hospital, park, and numerous road, curb, and sidewalk improvements were among larger projects taken on locally. Additionally, the Civilian Conservation Corps (CCC) established a work camp nine miles northeast of Deming at Mirage. Through the CCC, 175 men worked in the area of Cooke's Peak and the Florida Mountains maintaining the land through revegetation and soil erosion, flood, and rodent control. At least $514,009.60 was invested in Deming from 1933 to 1940.

Around the time Deming was beginning to get back on its feet, another military establishment arrived after the American entry into World War II. Deming Army Air Field was built in 1943 southeast of town in what is known today as Industrial Park. The airfield was a training school for 8,000 bombardiers. While the bombardiers were training, other Deming residents were fighting the war in the Philippines as part of the 200th and 515th Coast Artillery, New Mexico National Guard. The men were taken captive and were part of the Bataan Death March. There were 83 men from Deming in the 200th (which suffered a 43-percent casualty rate) and nine local men in other units (three of whom died); a total of 39 Deming men died during the Bataan march.

The rest of Deming's history lies mostly in highway traffic and proximity to the United States–Mexico border, which has stimulated the economy for years. In 1963, construction began on Interstate 10 through Deming. It has become the major west-east arterial interstate between California and Florida. Transportation continues to bring people to Deming, especially for its largest event to boost tourism. The Great American Duck Race is held annually on the fourth weekend in August. People gather to "rent" a duck to race down an eight-lane track. Beginning in 1980, it has grown to include a large group of vendors, a hot-air balloon rally, outhouse race, duck pageant, tortilla toss, carnival, and parade, in addition to duck racing.

There are many firms that successfully employ numerous residents, who will become the heart for future histories written about Deming. Deming is the home of the world's largest processor of green chili peppers, Border Foods, Inc. Wal-Mart Stores, Inc., held a grand opening for its local store in 2003. Deming Public Schools is the largest employer in Luna County. Nearly 800 employees educate Luna County's youth. The second-largest employer is the US Department of Homeland Security, with over 400 agents. Through these firms and the continued influence of the interstate, the citizens of Deming will continue to build on their colorful legacy, which has become the story of their beloved town.

One

Wild Southwest before 1881

Before Deming was officially founded, people had roamed the area for hundreds of years. A site uncovered in 2001 revealed that over 40,000 years ago, a Columbian mammoth died in the area. Giant, well-preserved tusks were unearthed by 20 volunteers and researchers who used paintbrushes to whisk dirt off the area. One tusk was eight feet long, while the other was 10 feet long. A Deming man, Dr. Frederic G. Haessly, found the site in November 2000 while looking for minerals to use in his jewelry.

Petroglyphs located at Pony Hills, a US Bureau of Land Management (BLM) site about 20 miles northeast of Deming, can be dated back to the Mimbres culture. The petroglyphs cover a large area on a group of hills and were dated back between AD 900 and AD 1150. This site is located near a natural spring near the base of the 8,404-foot Cooke's Peak. Cooke's Spring had the US Army's protection as early as August 22, 1863.

At that time, a company of 5th Infantry California Volunteers was posted there to protect the spring from the Apache Indians who traversed Cooke's Canyon. The canyon was also known to many as Massacre Canyon, which reflects its history. At least 800 people died traveling through the canyon. The place where the Army was stationed was known as Fort Cummings, which was officially established on October 2, 1863. It was the only walled fort in the Territory of New Mexico. A 90-trooper expedition was housed there in April 1864, when the government sent men to nine posts on Apache lands in New Mexico.

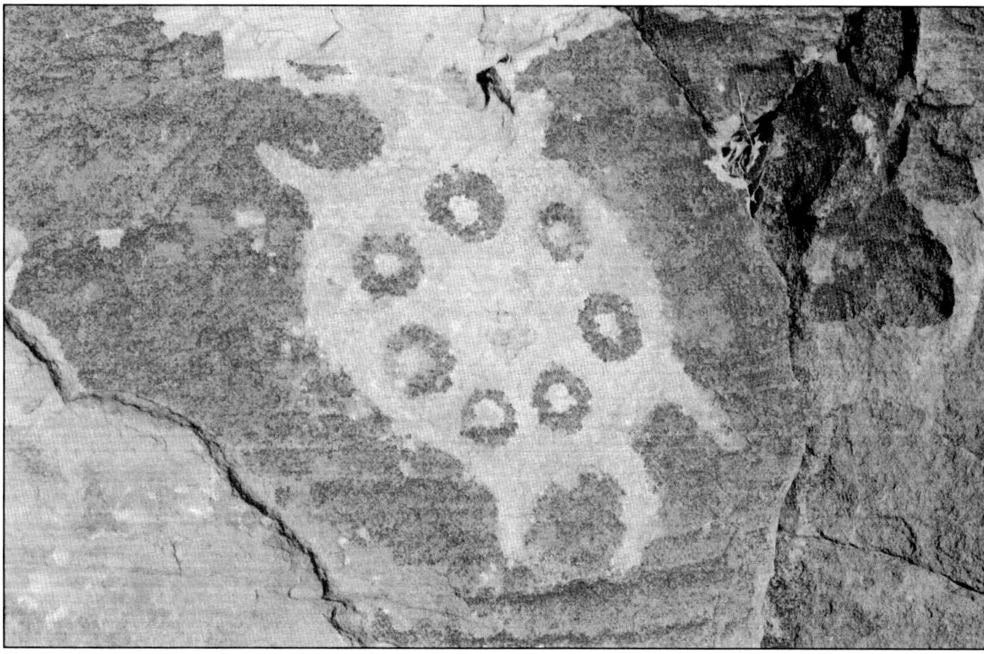

These modern photographs reveal some of the most pronounced petroglyphs at the Pony Hills site outside of Deming. While it is common to hear visitors to the site describe the petroglyphs as a person or thing that resembles something in modern times, anthropologists are careful how they describe them. Petroglyphs that look like recognizable objects are called morphoglyphs. People are described as anthropomorphs, and other living things or animals are called zoomorphs. Above, the carving seems to resemble a turtle, which would be labeled a zoomorph by an archeologist. Below, the image reflects a bighorn sheep and is also a zoomorph. (Both, courtesy of Joshua E. Williams.)

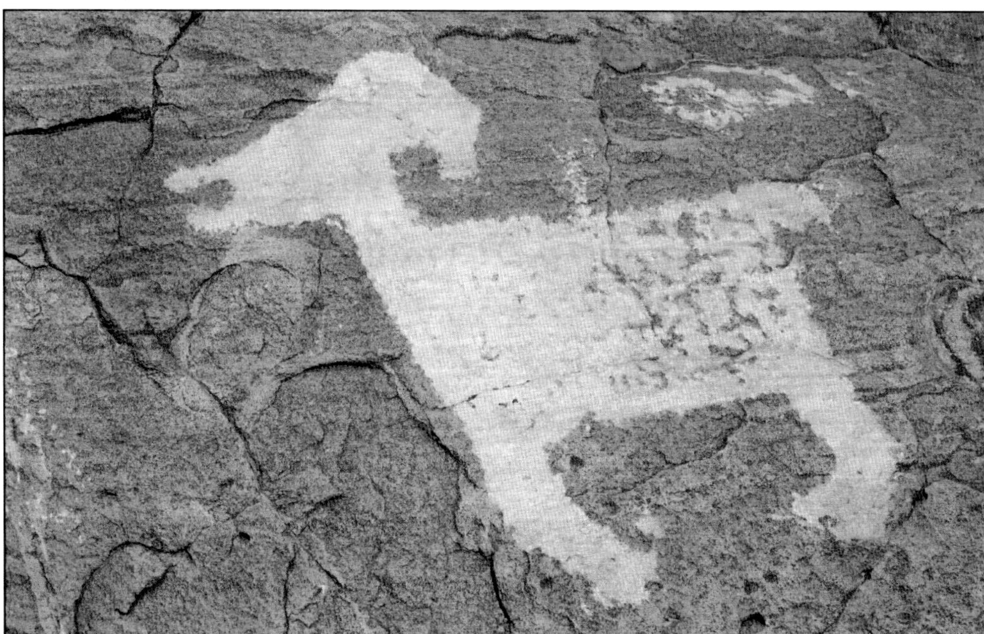

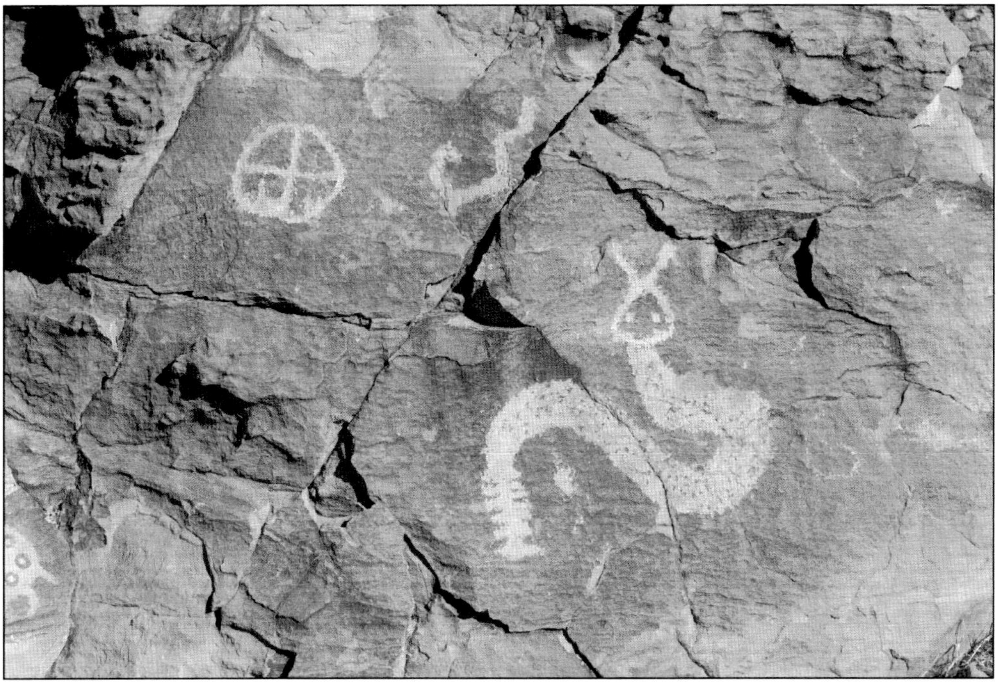

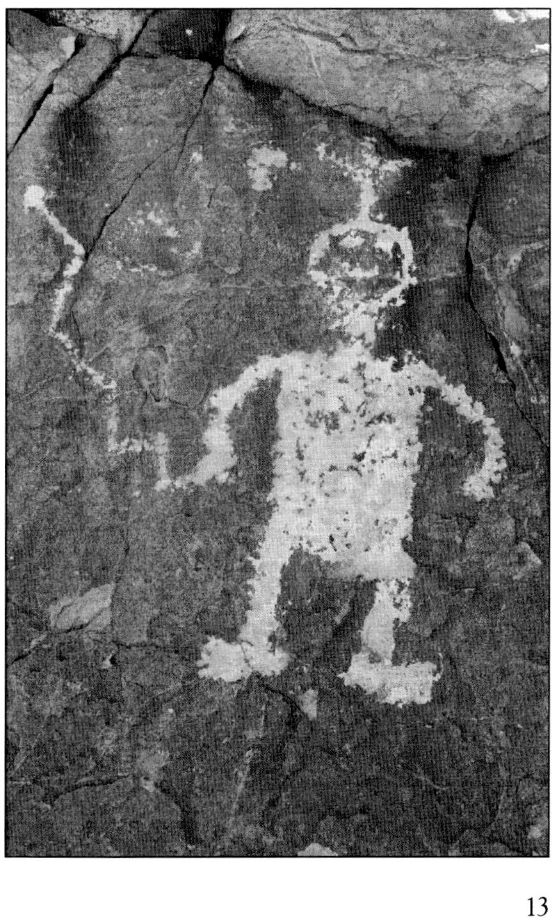

In the image above, carvings of people, animals, and symbols are found scattered across the large outcropping of rocks at Pony Hills. On the left side of the photograph, the zoomorph resembling a turtle can be seen. A circle cut by two lines into fourths and a wavy line (morphoglyphs) can be seen to the upper left. A very defined rattlesnake (zoomorph) is seen as the main object in this photograph. At right, one of the more pronounced anthropomorphs appears to be a person. The inlay of this petroglyph is carved out completely. (Both, courtesy of Joshua E. Williams.)

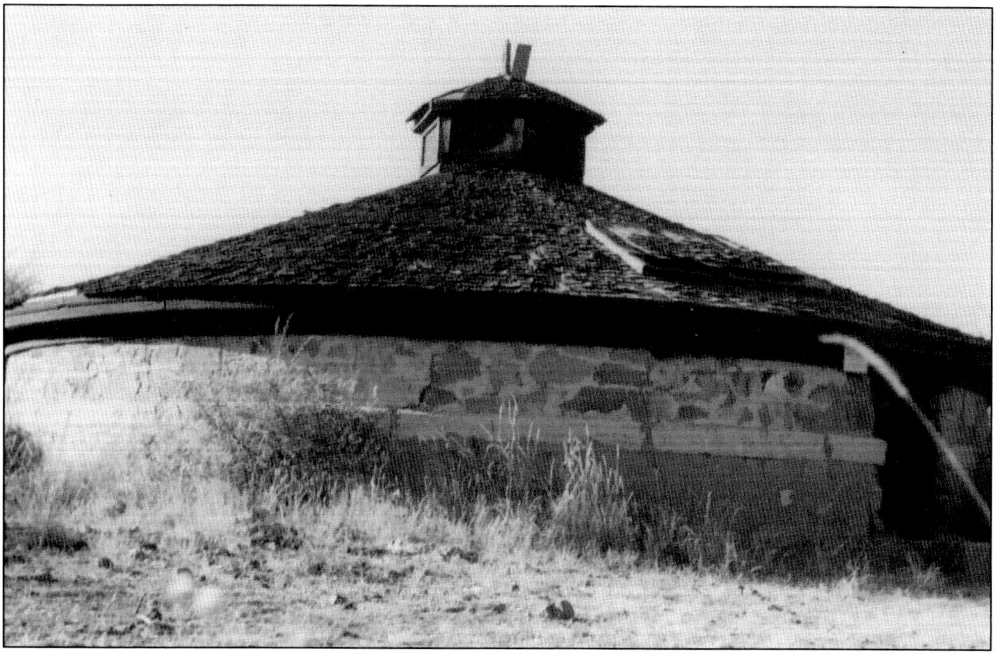

Cooke's Spring was an important water stop for stagecoaches. The Cooke's Spring House shown was built by the Atchison, Topeka & Santa Fe Railway in 1881, the same year the railroad was established in Deming. The roof of the springhouse was reconstructed in 1987. Water flowed by the force of gravity from the springhouse to the railroad's Florida Station.

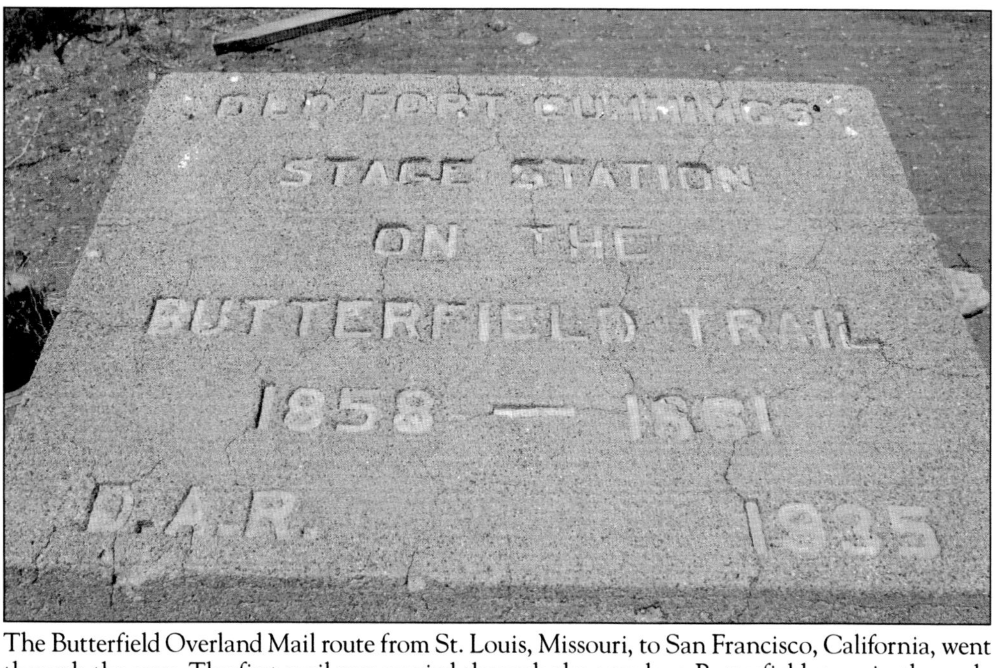

The Butterfield Overland Mail route from St. Louis, Missouri, to San Francisco, California, went through the area. The first mail was carried through the area by a Butterfield stage in the early morning of October 1, 1858. A Butterfield station was established at the spring as a designated stop on the route until the government ordered the closure of the line in March 1861. (Courtesy of Joshua E. Williams.)

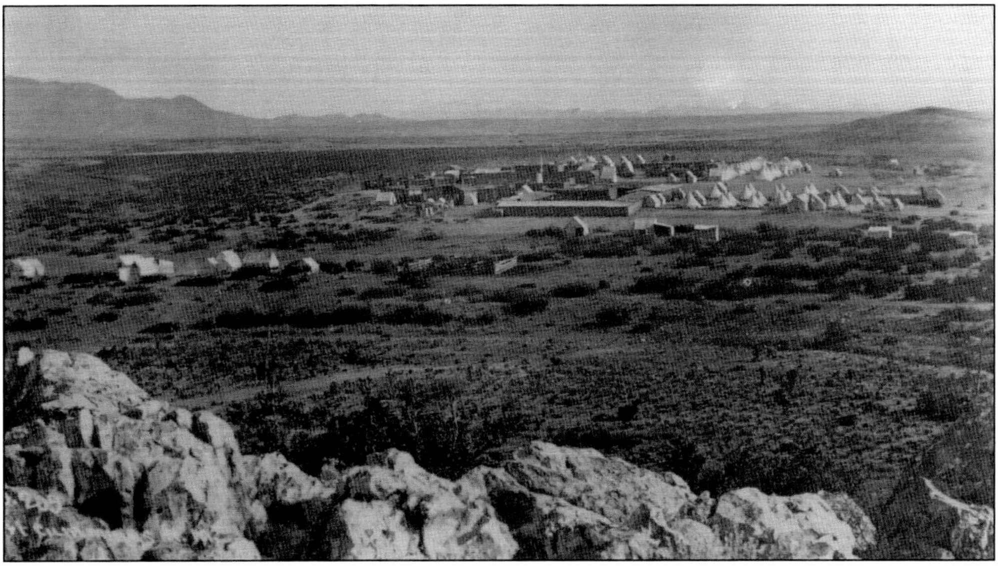

Fort Cummings was established on October 2, 1863, to protect travelers along the Butterfield Trail from Native Americans who were becoming dangerous and deadly in their attacks. This vintage photograph was most likely taken in 1882, as there are numerous buildings seen here that were not present prior to that date.

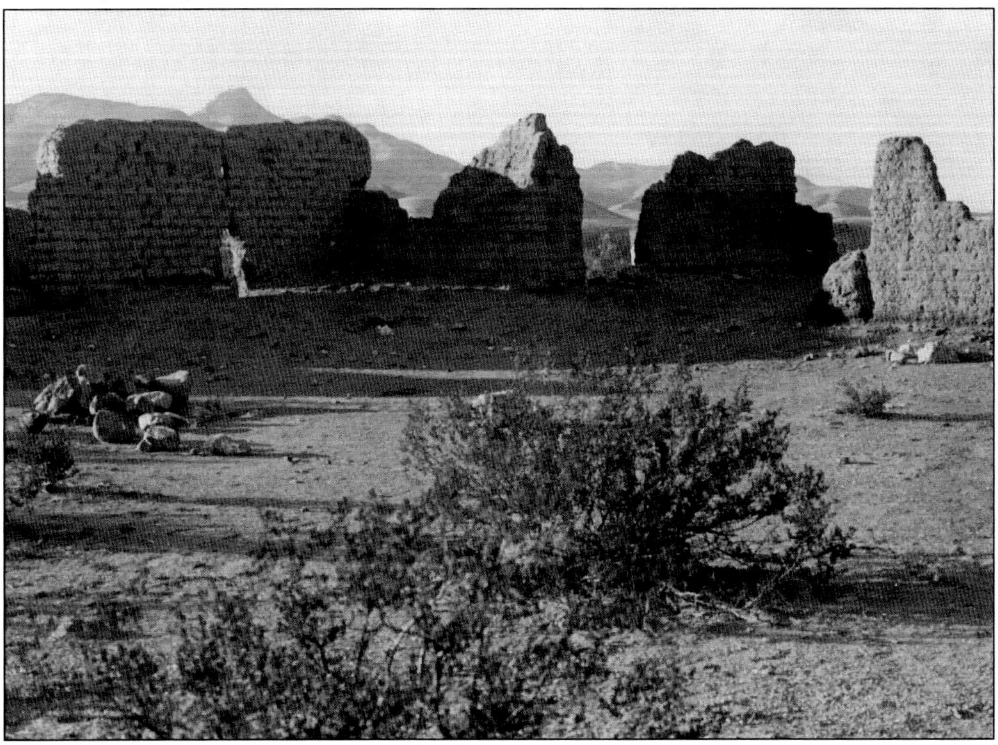

This photograph, taken almost 100 years after the establishment of Fort Cummings, shows what remains. The fort was constructed of adobe and wood, with 10-foot walls measuring 320 feet from east to west and 360 feet from north to south. Many records show that while there were many buildings, the fort was overcrowded.

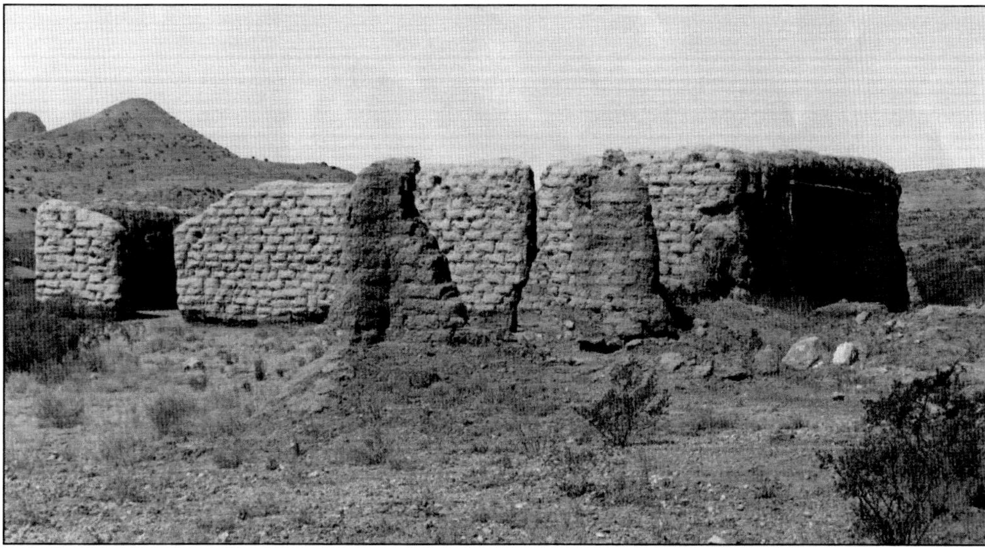

This is another view of the remains of Fort Cummings, most likely taken in the 1970s. There were quarters for the troops, five sets of officers' quarters, a hospital, guardhouse, and storehouses on the site at its prime. The storehouses held two years' worth of supplies for 100 men. Also, corrals were established for 65 horses. Mexican females were listed as laundresses and domestic servants in the 1870 census.

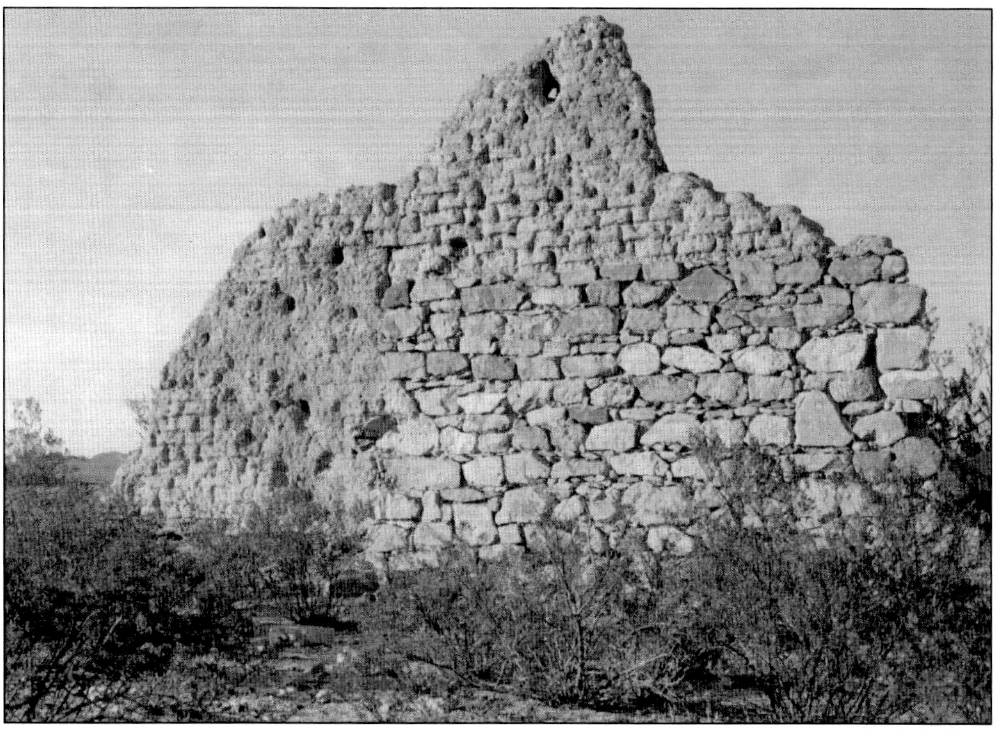

This is the only remaining rock wall at the site. This photograph was probably taken in the 1970s. Fort Cummings was named after Maj. Joseph Cummings, 1st New Mexico Cavalry, who was killed by Navajos in northeastern New Mexico in the summer of 1863. The entire site of Fort Cummings could fit inside two football fields placed side by side.

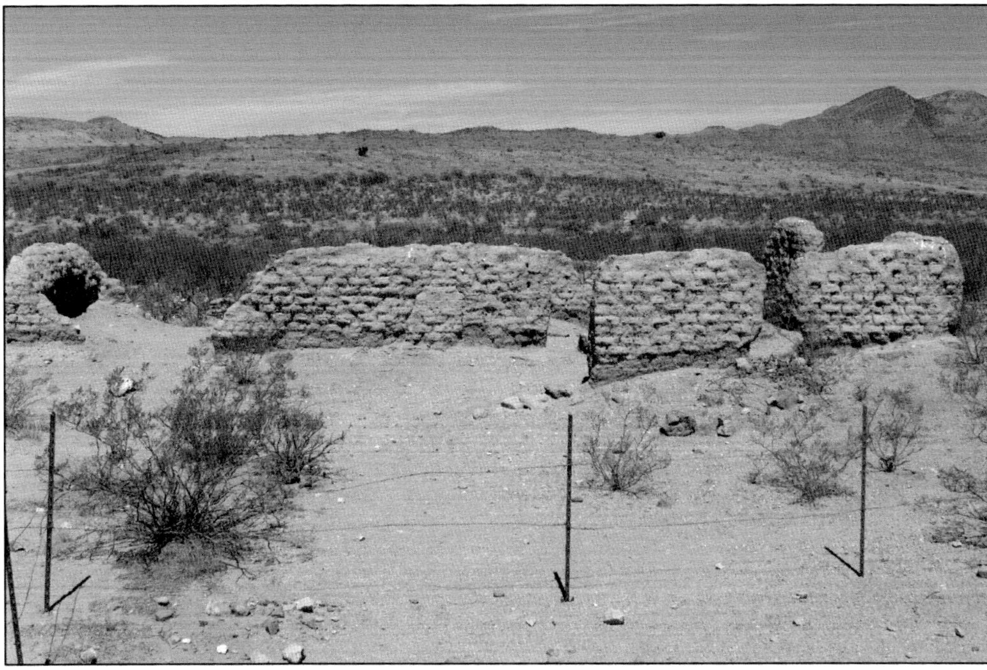

Today, weathering and erosion have affected the preservation of this historical site outside of Deming. This photograph was taken in June 2011. Each time visitors make a trip to the site, there is less to see, as it is disappearing into the sands of time. (Courtesy of Joshua E. Williams.)

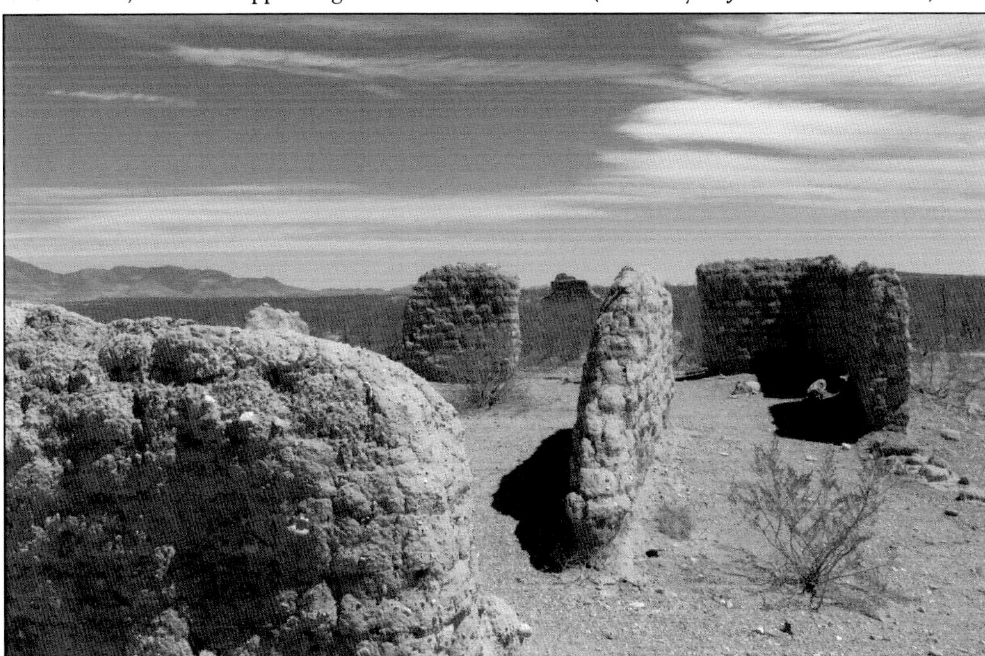

On this day in June 2011, the footing of Cooke's Peak is seen on the left and smoke from the Wallow Fire, Arizona's most devastating fire to date, is shown in the upper right. Creosote bushes have grown in much of the area where the fort once stood to protect travelers. (Courtesy of Joshua E. Williams.)

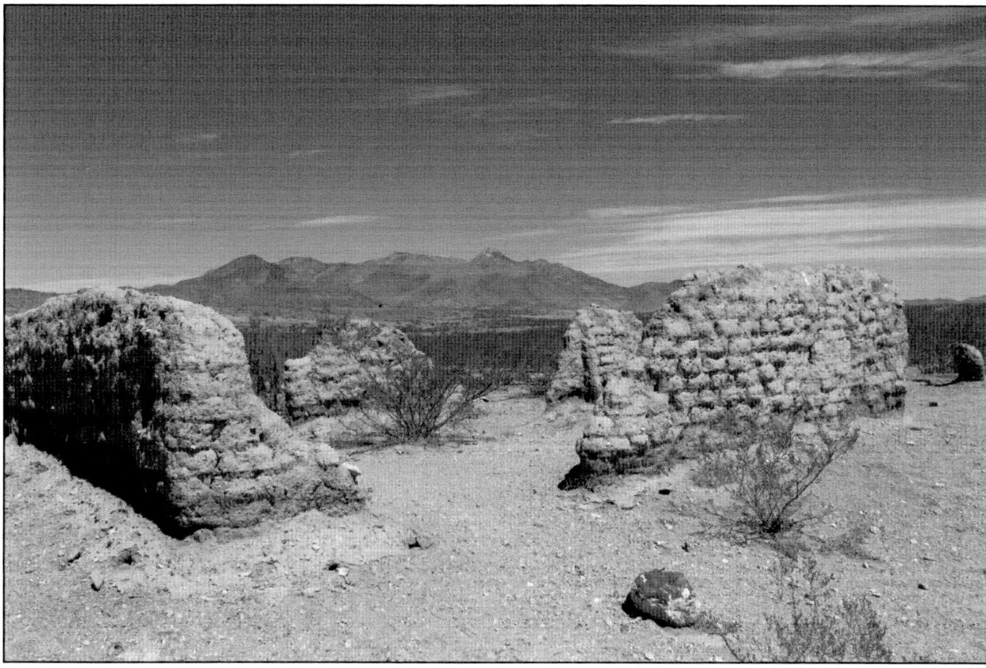

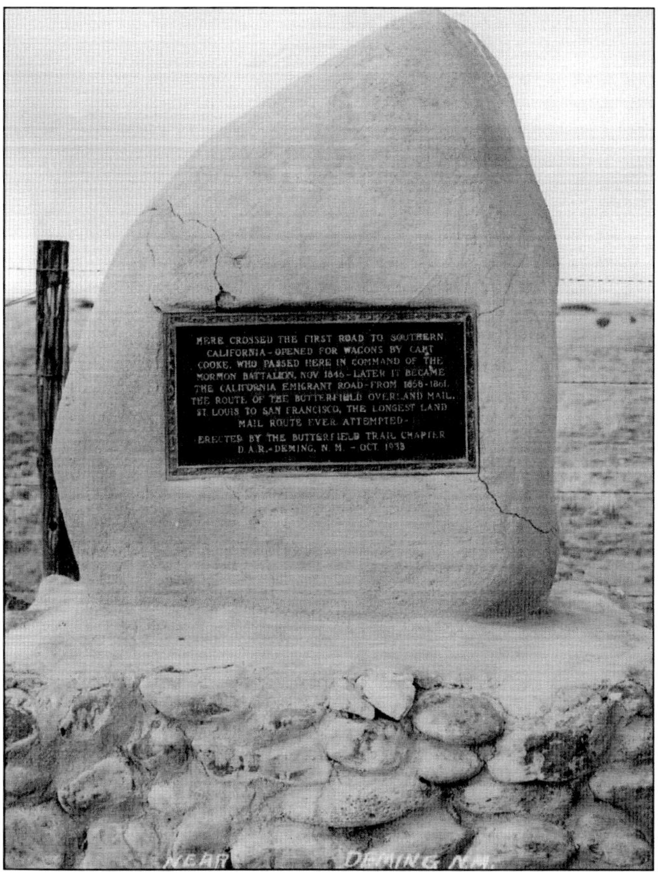

Cooke's Peak overlooks the ruins of Fort Cummings (above). The Daughters of the American Revolution erected a plaque in 1933 about 15 miles north of Deming off of US Highway 180 (left). The plaque states: "Here crossed the first road to southern California—Opened for wagons by Capt. Cooke who passed here in command of the Mormon Battalion, Nov. 1846—Later it became the California Emigrant Road—from 1856–1891, the Route of the Butterfield Overland Mail, St. Louis to San Francisco, the longest land mail route ever attempted. Erected by the Butterfield Trail Chapter D.A.R.—Deming, N.M.—October 1933." (Above, courtesy of Joshua E. Williams.)

Two

Second Transcontinental Railroad

Deming marked the junction of the Southern Pacific Railroad and Atchison, Topeka & Santa Fe Railway. Local residents gathered and drove a commemorative silver railroad spike in Deming at 3:45 p.m. on March 8, 1881. Among those present at the ceremony were R.R. Coleman, manager of the construction of the Atchison, Topeka & Santa Fe Railway; A. Longstreet, J. H. Bates, and J.F. Kilales, all from Southern Pacific Railroad; and Ira M. Bond, *Mesilla News*. This gave the Territory of New Mexico its first access to markets from coast to coast. A congratulatory telegram was sent by New Mexico governor John C. Frémont.

While the junction was completed in March 1881, the first Southern Pacific train traffic came to Deming on December 15, 1880. The first train operating on the second transcontinental railroad occurred on March 28, 1881. At the time of the connection made in Deming, reports swarmed national newspapers that the new town was completely lawless. The *Daily Globe* (St. Paul, Minnesota) reported on April 3, 1881, that "Deming is perhaps the worst place of its size on the continent." As in any new settlement, discord was common due to the lack of rules or order enforced by a government.

Deming was not officially founded until November 1881 and was named after the wife of railroad man Charles Crocker, Mary Ann Deming. Before Deming's founding, a tent city named New Chicago sprang up 10 miles from the present town. People came from all over, as they knew the junction would be a significant point for travelers in the American West. Once the railroads agreed on the spot for the junction, tents were moved from New Chicago to Deming, the "Gateway to the West."

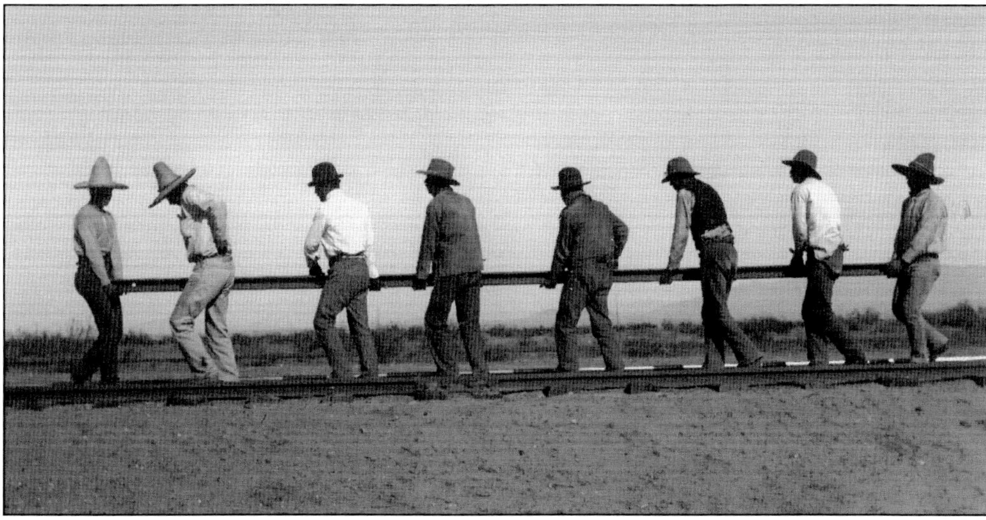

Mexican laborers are photographed carrying a rail to be placed near Deming, New Mexico (above). The men who were responsible for driving the railroad spikes are shown photographed in front of a train, which was most likely a construction train (below). Construction trains were used to hold the supplies. It is unknown what percentages of workers were Chinese or Mexican. About 1,000 Chinese laborers camped in Old Steins, located 80 miles west of Deming, while building the rails near Lordsburg, New Mexico. About 3,000 Chinese laborers stayed in El Paso, Texas, while the rails were built in that area. It could be inferred from surrounding towns that there were anywhere from 1,000 to 3,000 Chinese laborers in Deming.

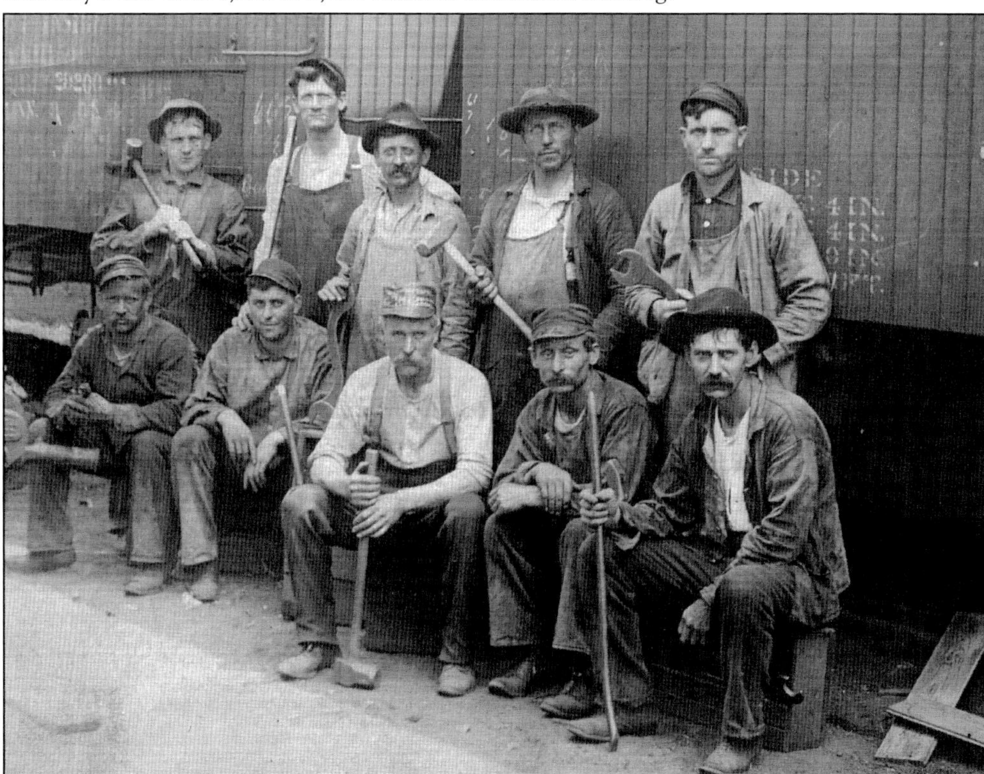

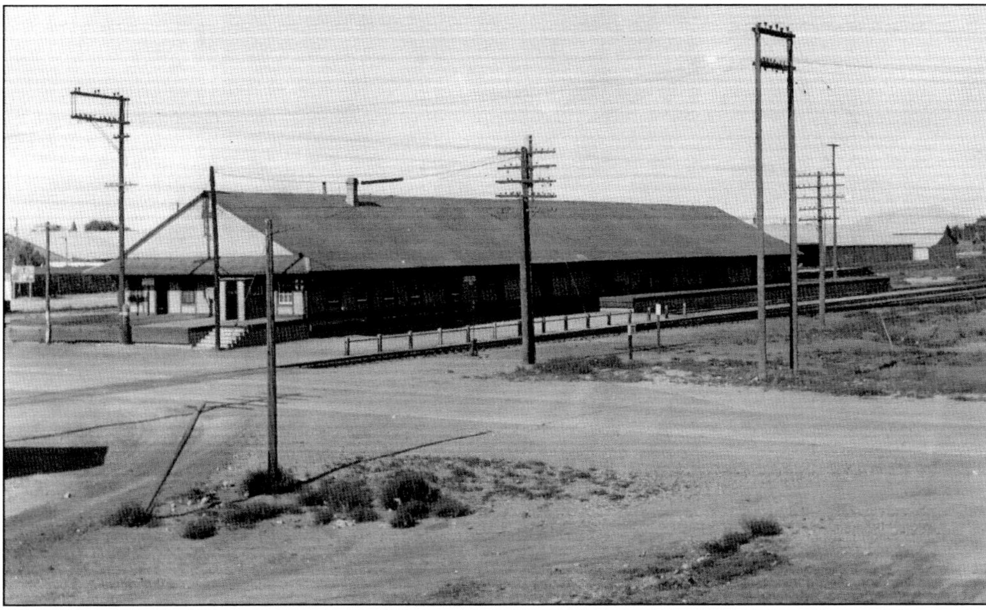

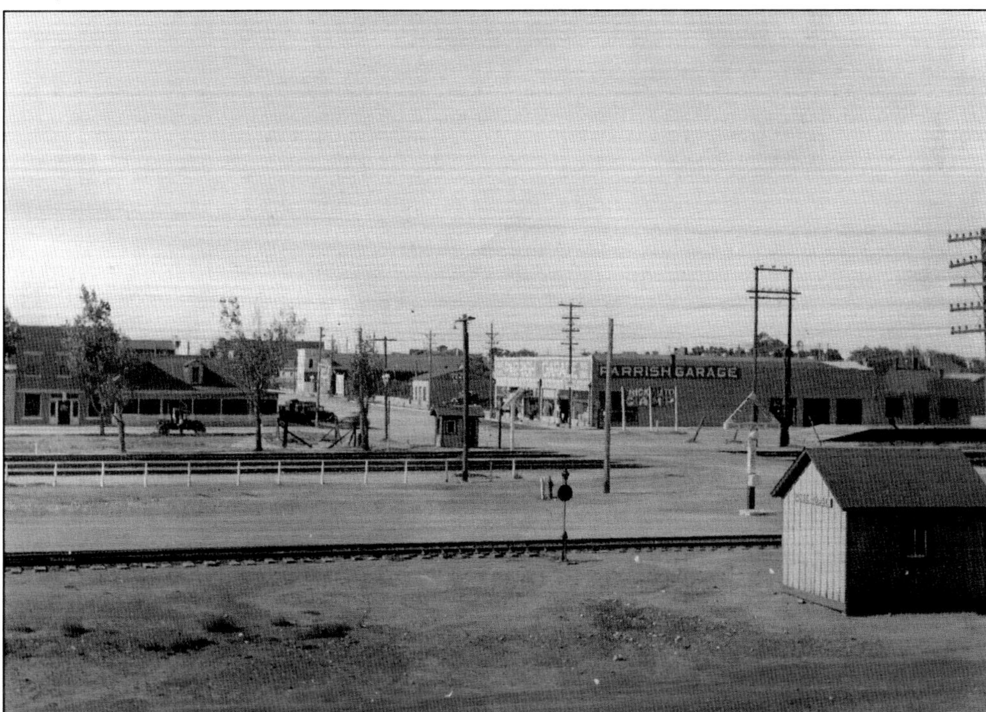

The Southern Pacific Railroad's freight depot is depicted above. In the growing town of Deming, the business district was close to the railroad, which made moving supplies easy for businessmen (below). This photograph was taken in the late 1920s, as automobiles are present. The extensive power line system can also be seen. The power company, Deming Ice and Electric, was located very close to the railroad. Its plant had two 125-horsepower engines with a small auxiliary 75-horsepower engine and two generators, a large 25-ton ice machine, two large cold storage areas, and an office.

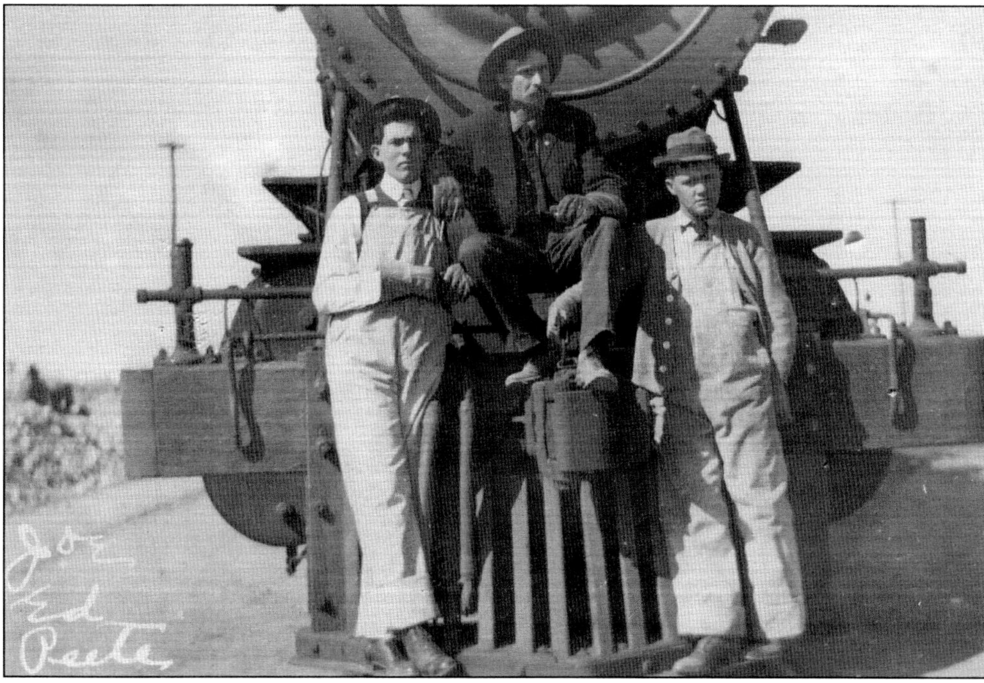

Joe ?, Ed ?, and Pete ? are photographed in front of a steam locomotive (above). Other unidentified men can be seen in front of an 1880 locomotive on the rails (below). The first train robbery in the Territory of New Mexico took place 13 miles outside of Deming on November 24, 1883, on a similar train. Six masked gunmen killed the engineer and escaped with cash taken from passengers and the express car. The six were found about four months later and were imprisoned without bond in the Grant County Jail in Silver City, New Mexico. They escaped but were later caught; two of the men were hanged.

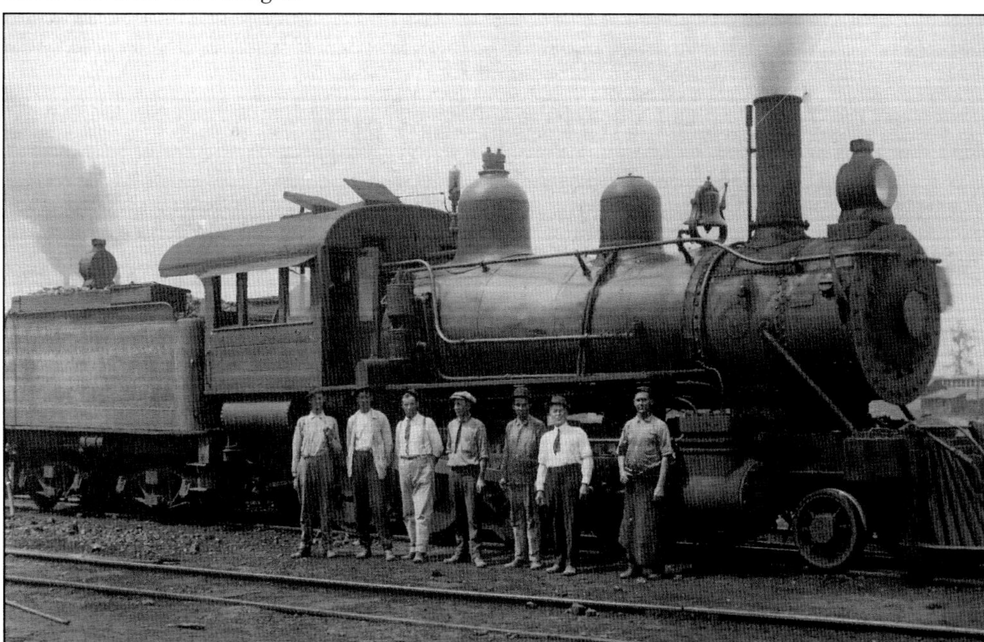

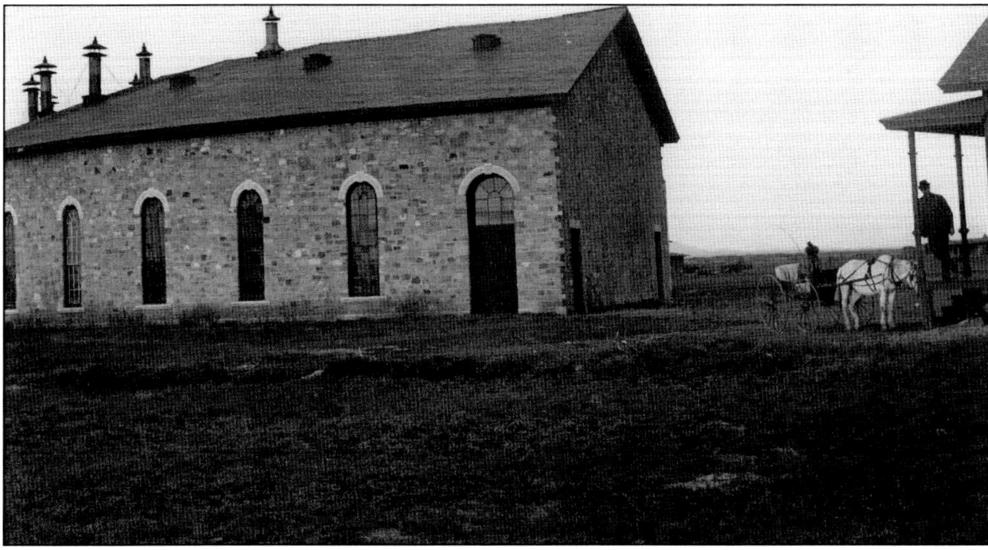

The Atchison, Topeka & Santa Fe Railway's roundhouse (above) was built in 1880 and was used by the railroad until 1933. The roundhouse caught fire on August 24, 1945, and was completely gutted. In addition to the dozens of Danish Prize Milk boxes, the photograph indicates that 12,000 pounds of groceries were packed on one large mail parcel headed out of Deming, New Mexico (below). The parcel post rate on a 45-pound article from Deming to Silver City, 50 miles north, was 49¢, so the post office would have received over $130 to ship this load to the neighboring town.

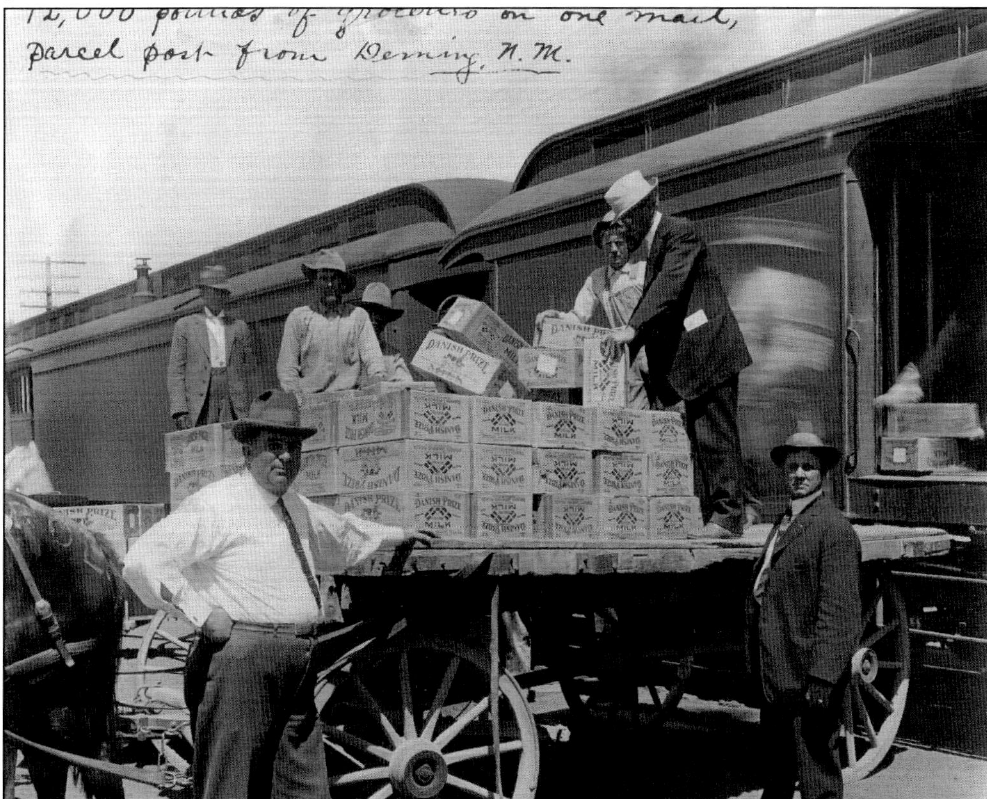

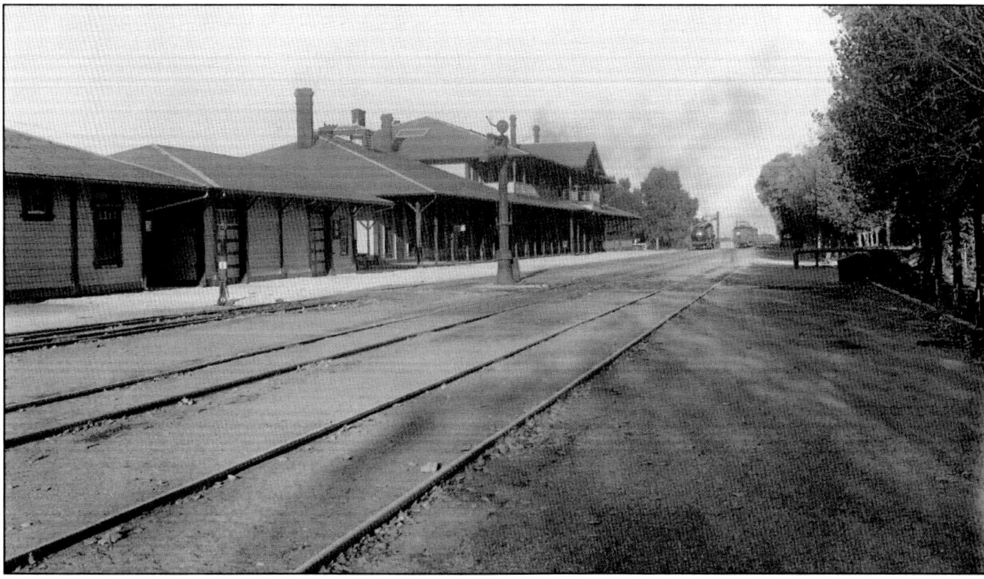

Union Station and Park in Deming, New Mexico, were surrounded by large trees and a wide street (above). It can be inferred that the station received its name because it was the junction where the two rail lines—Atchison, Topeka & Santa Fe and Southern Pacific—met in 1881. Union Station and Park were accompanied by one of Fred Harvey's eateries. A Harvey Girl waits for hungry customers at the Harvey House's lunch counter in 1905 (below). The Harvey House was a welcome addition for the railroad station, since patrons could wait there until they caught their next train. Deming residents also used the Harvey House as a meeting place for large groups.

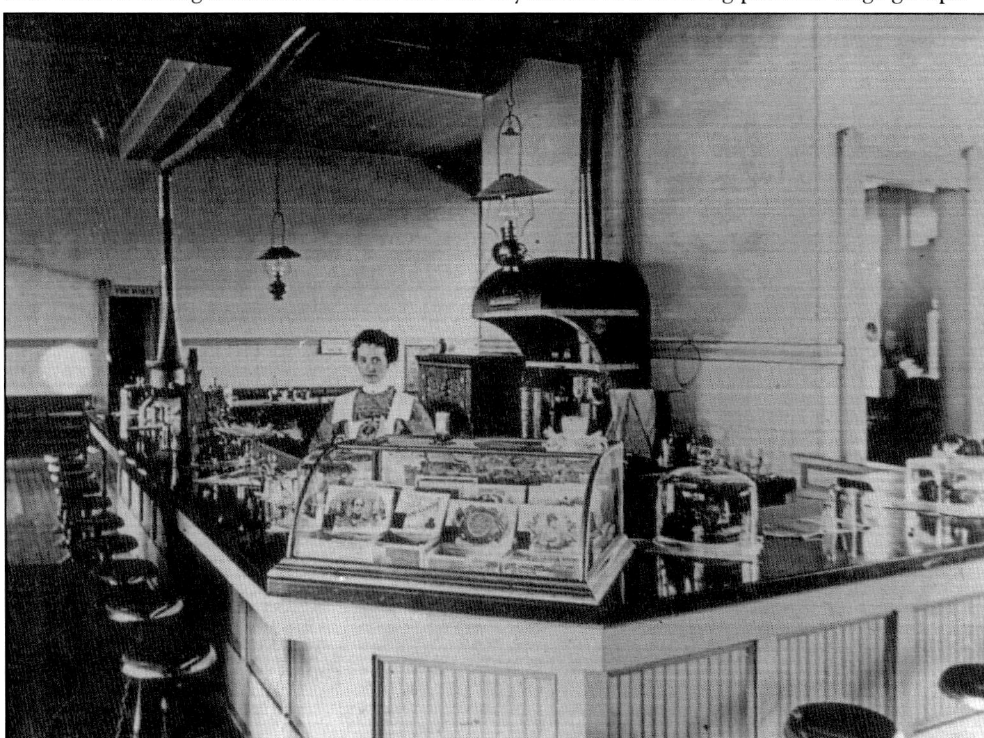

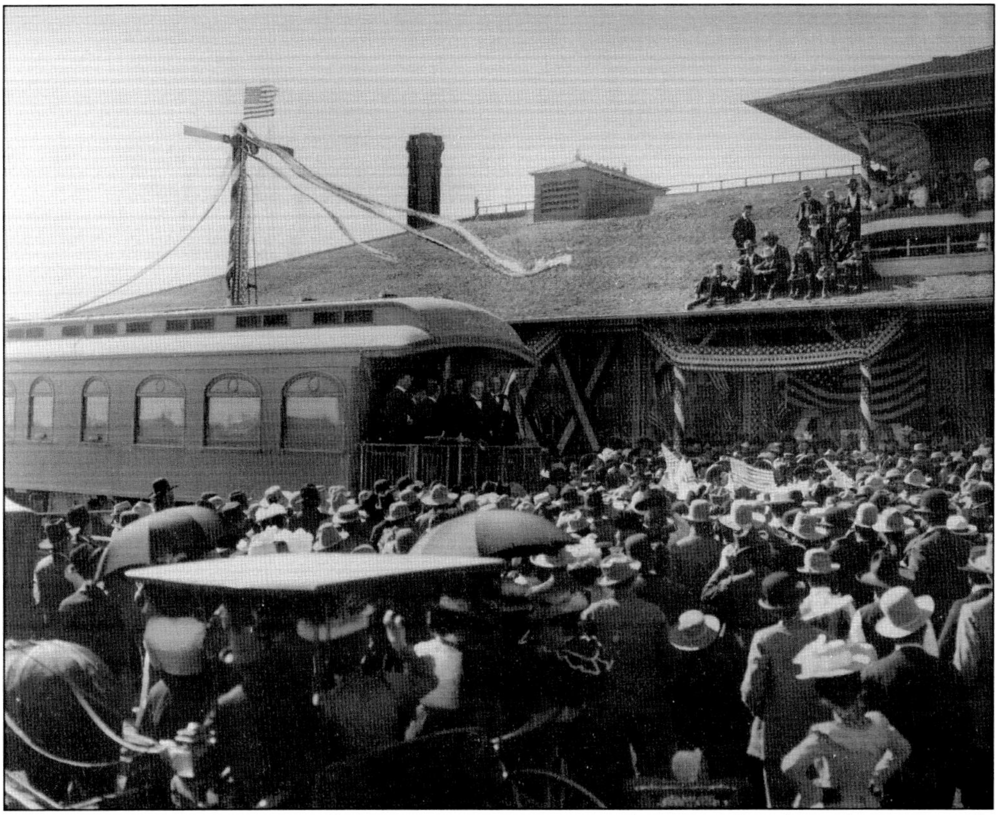

Pres. William McKinley stopped in Deming on May 6, 1901, but never left the railcar. First Lady Ida McKinley was with him but stayed inside since she was ill. A large crowd held signs asking for the Territory of New Mexico to become a state, as territorial governor Miguel Otero was also in the party.

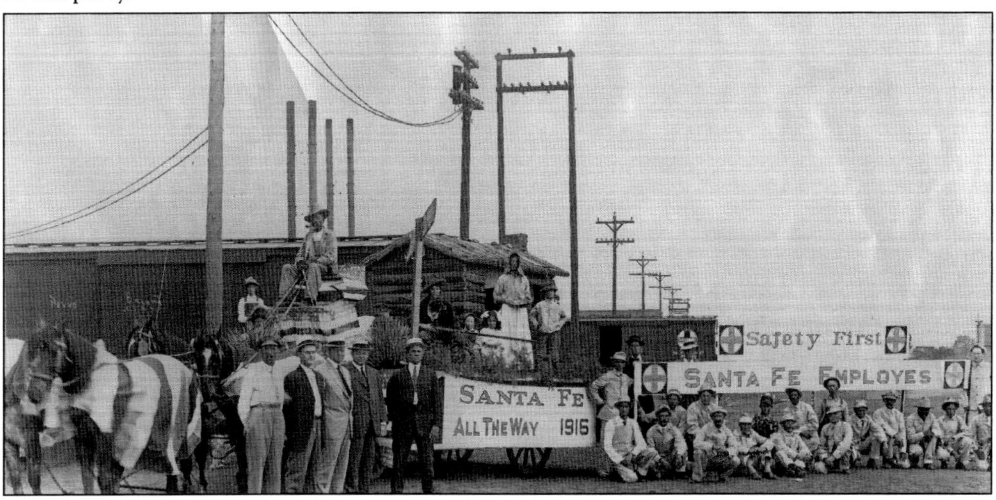

Shown are the Santa Fe Railway employees after a large parade in the streets of Deming in 1915. In 1924, within 10 years of this photograph, the Santa Fe Railway employed an average of 140 employees at Deming. These dedicated employees earned a total monthly payroll between to $16,000 and $17,000.

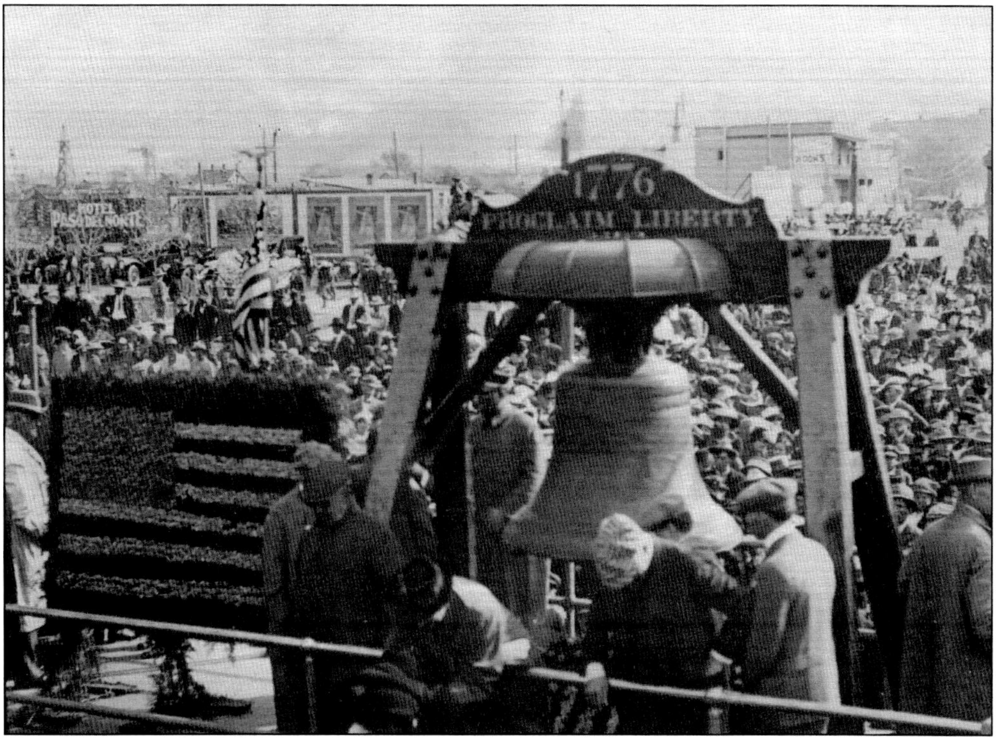

The Liberty Bell traveled through Deming on a railroad car on November 16, 1915, after being displayed for five months at the Panama-Pacific International Exposition at San Francisco, California. As the bell traveled back to Philadelphia, Pennsylvania, it made stops in many towns along the way. The longest stop in New Mexico was in Deming. The bell was displayed along the railroad for 25 minutes.

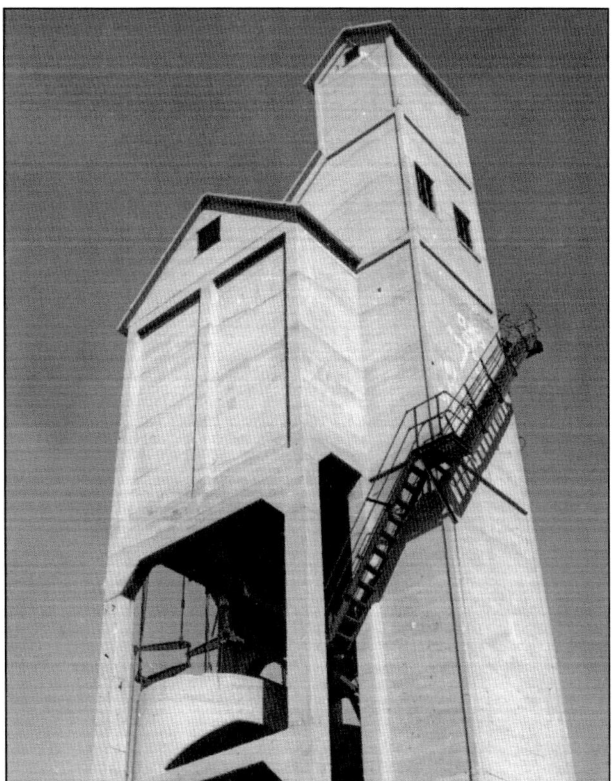

This Southern Pacific Railroad coal chute was built in the latter part of 1925 by DeOgle Construction of Chicago. During the construction phase, one worker, C.P. Dasen, fell off the chute to his death in November 1925. The chute was used until 1948 or 1949. An implosion demolished the structure on January 23, 1998.

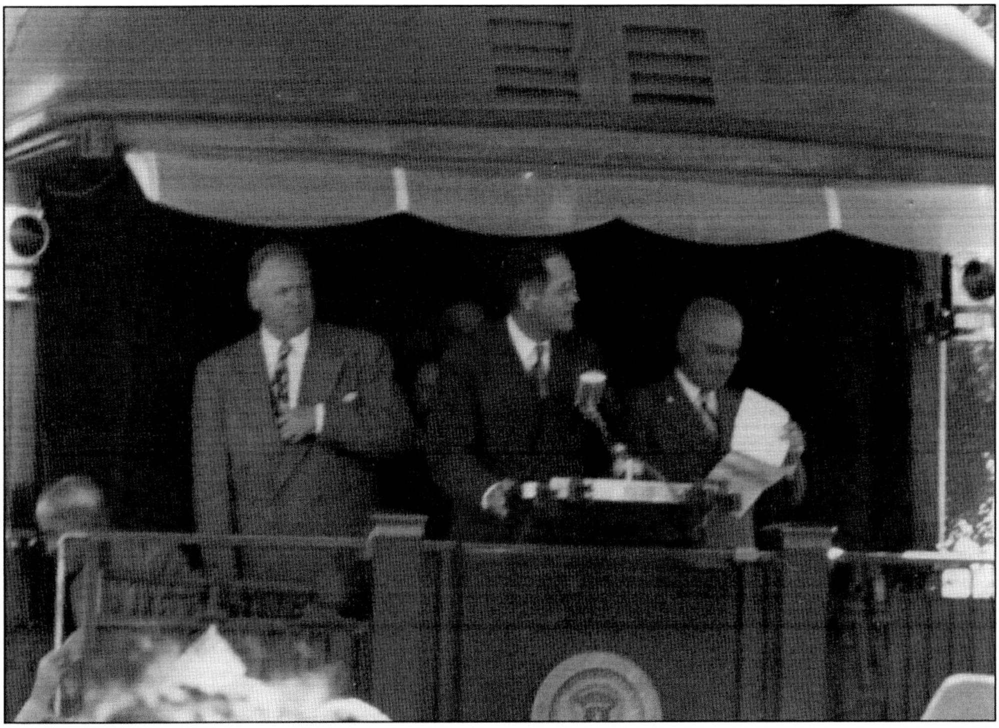

Pres. Harry S. Truman, his wife, Bess, and daughter, Margaret, made a whistle-stop in Deming on September 25, 1948. Truman was passing through Deming on his way to confer with former vice president John Nance Gardner in Uvalde, Texas. President Truman was also accompanied by New Mexico governor Thomas J. Mabry and Clinton P. Anderson, a Democrat running for the US Senate that November. Businesses were closed from 8:30 a.m. to 10:00 a.m. in order for citizens to attend his 20-minute address. A special space was created for 2,000 schoolchildren from Deming and surrounding communities to attend as was additional space for 300 invited guests.

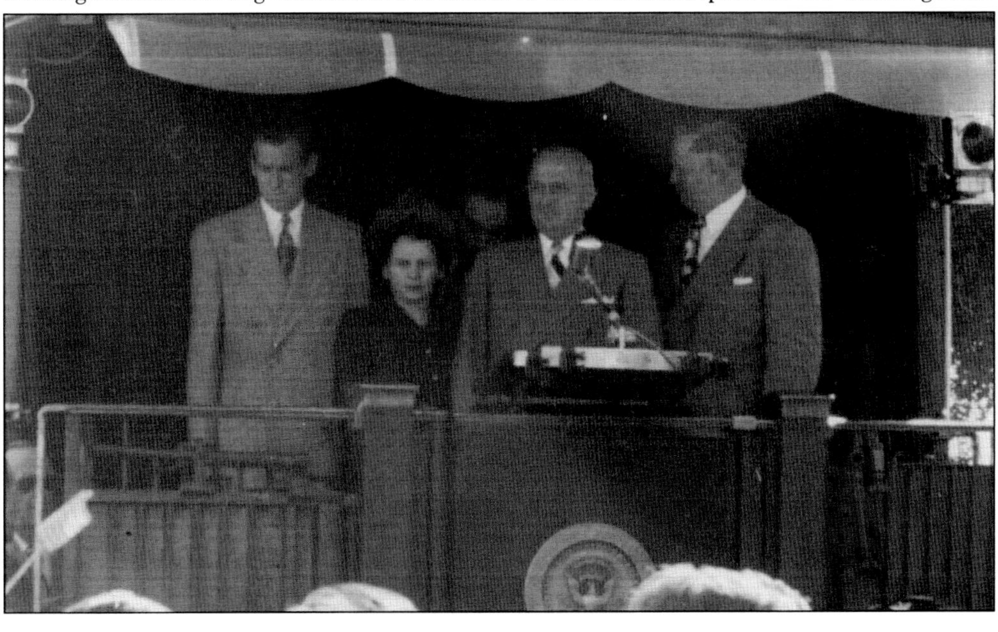

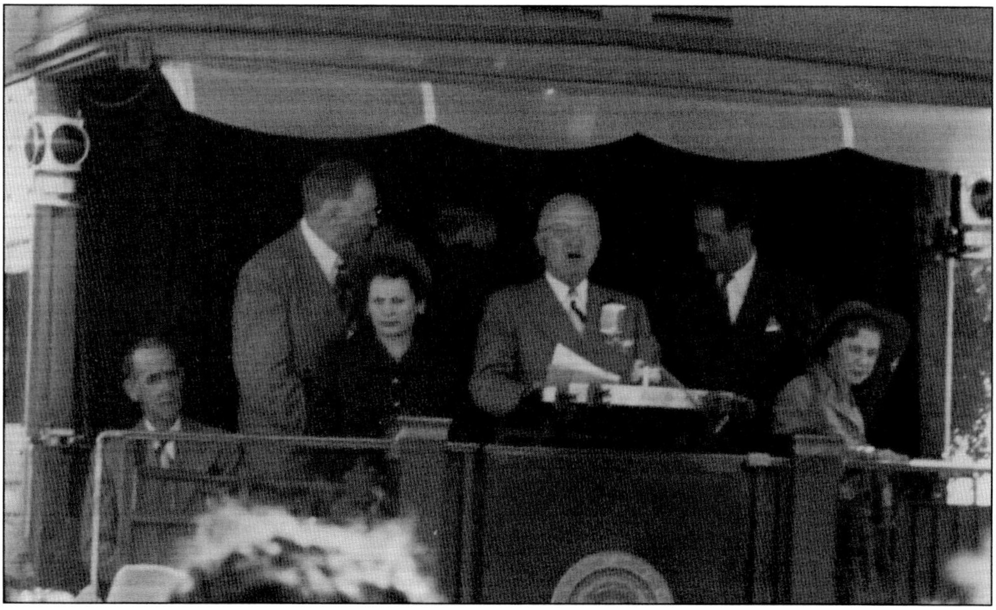

Deming resident Hubert H. Ruebush, of Ruebush Brothers Saddlery, crafted some fine leather goods as gifts from Deming to the president. A hand-tooled leather belt and necktie were the main items held by the president (below). After he received the gifts, Truman said, "I appreciate this very highly, this belt and this necktie. I need a pair of leather lungs and that will just exactly fit. Yesterday, in Yuma, Arizona, they gave me some sterling silver spurs engraved with my name on them, just the same as this belt is. Now, when I get this belt and that leather lung necktie and that pair of spurs on, I can certainly take the Congress for a ride!"

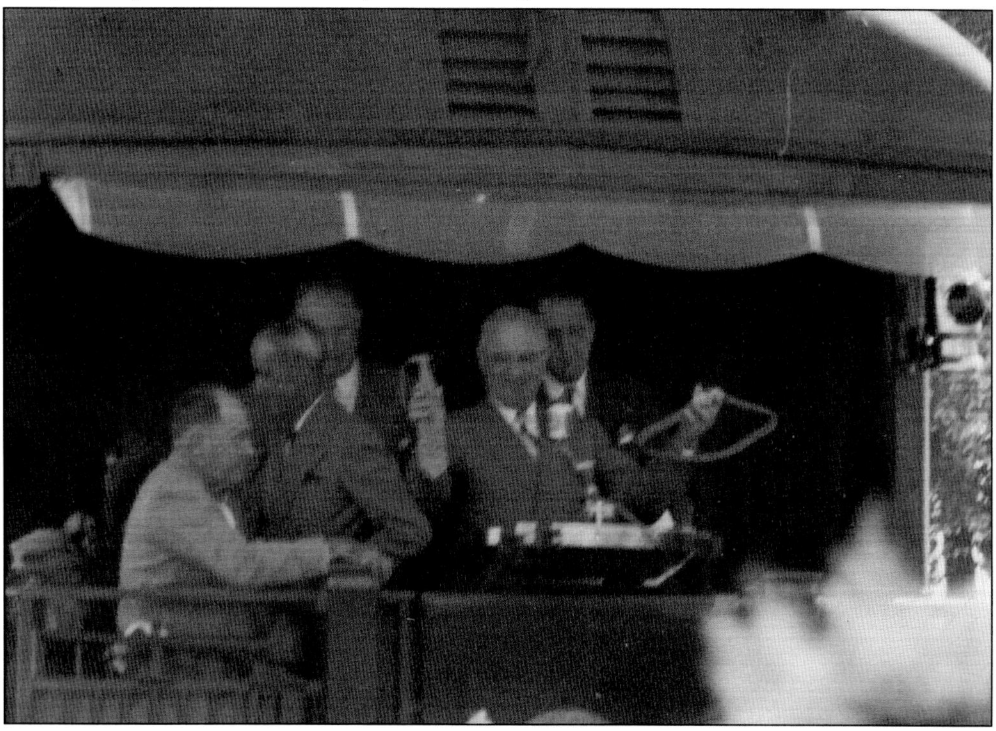

Three

Young Deming and the Creation of Luna County

Deming, at its founding, became a part of Grant County, which was established in 1868. Grant County's seat was in Silver City. For many years, Deming was said to be treated unfairly. Many businessmen and politicians fought for Deming and the surrounding area to separate itself from Grant County. As early as 1888, letters were being written to the territorial government.

Luna County was carved out of portions that were originally Grant and Doña Ana Counties in 1901. Luna County was created by an act of the Territory of New Mexico Legislature adopted on March 16, 1901. There were many who could be credited with the successful creation of the new county. Local leaders in the movement secured support from Don Solomon Luna, Republican politician, and it was in his honor that the county was named. Other names including Logan and Florida were discussed prior to Luna's assistance. Taking office on April 8, 1901, the following men headed up Luna County's first government: Newton A. Bolich, District I commissioner; William M. Taylor, District II commissioner; James P. Byron, chairman and District III commissioner; Burrage Y. McKeyes, clerk; Edward Pennington, assessor; C.J. Kelly, treasurer; Cipriano Baca, sheriff; and William R. Merrill, probate judge.

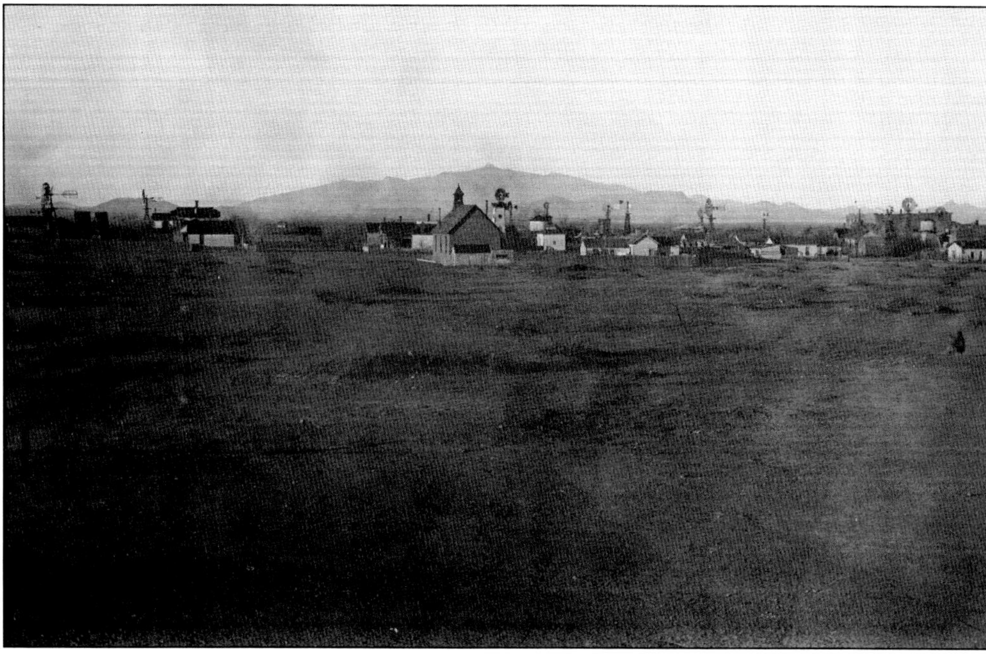

Cooke's Peak rises north of the growing village of Deming (above). In this photograph, 13 windmills can be seen throughout the town. This is what many accounts credit as the source of the nickname "Windy City." The Methodist church, the first brick building in Deming (center), is shown here, as is a school (right). A different view of Deming is seen (below) with the Florida Mountains to the southeast. Deming became incorporated as a village in 1902, and its first trustees were Seaman Field, T.A. Carr, Louis H. Brown, Albert Beals, and Anthony J. Clark.

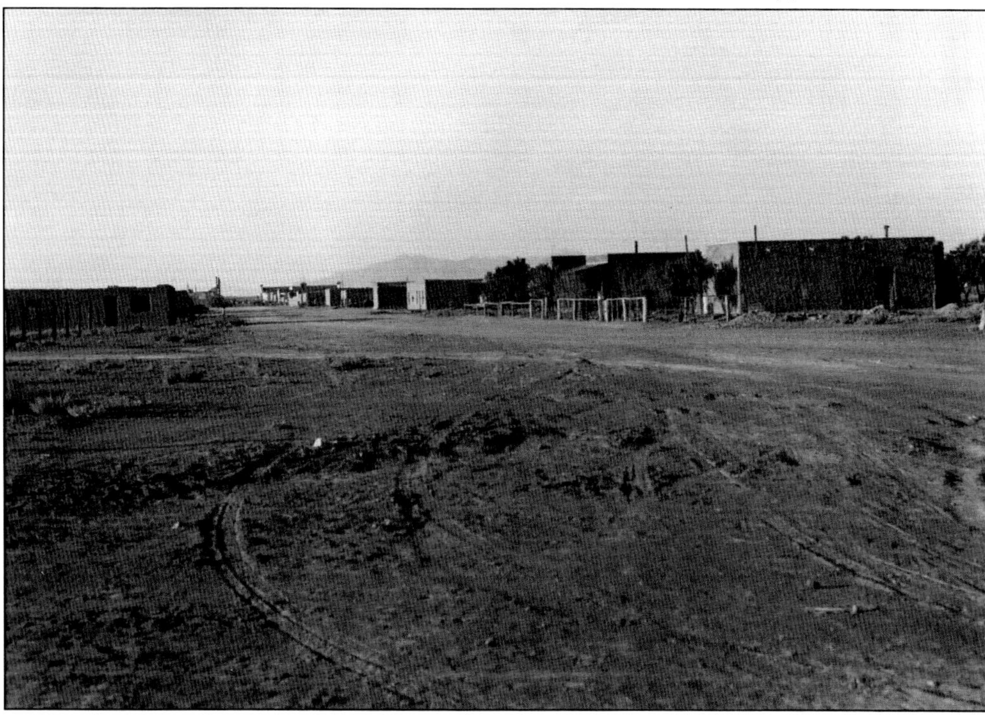

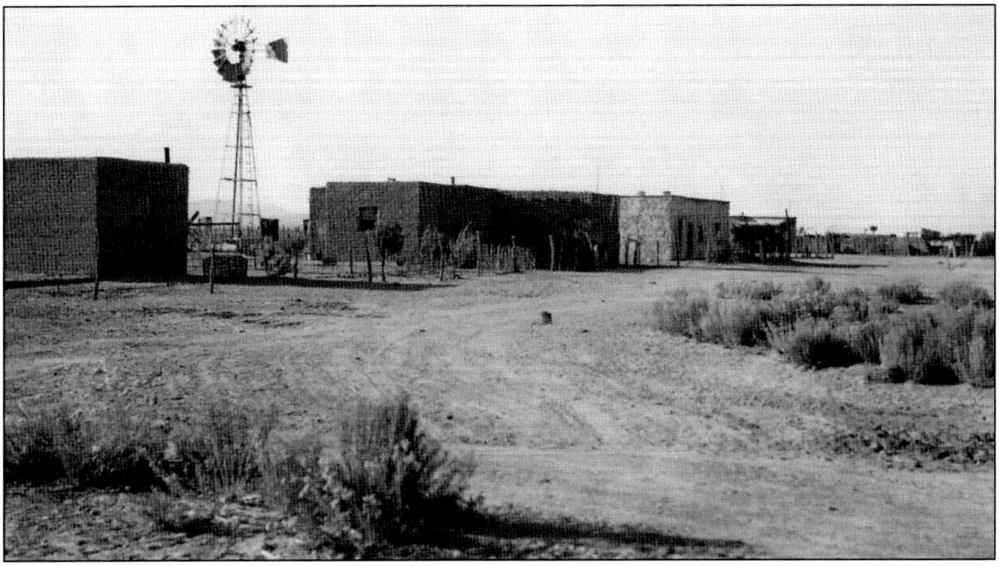

Most of the first houses in Deming were constructed out of adobe (above). Adobe is a natural building material that is made from sand, clay, water, and an organic material, usually straw. The mixture is shaped into bricks using frames and left to dry in the sun. Houses that are constructed out of adobe are very durable and can last for centuries. Adobe bricks are seen drying in the sun (below). This photograph was taken in 1884. This block lies between Silver Avenue (left) and Gold Avenue (right). The blacksmith's shop is the darker building to the right of the photograph. A Wells Fargo bank currently stands on the old blacksmith's property. On the left side of the photograph, a varnish and wood staining business is shown.

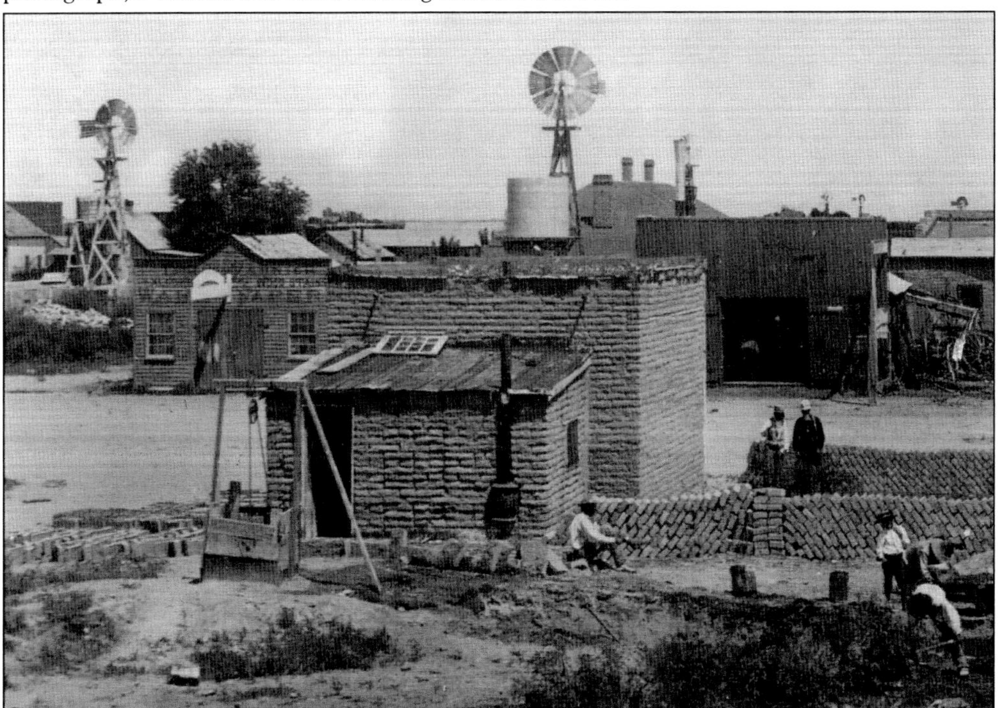

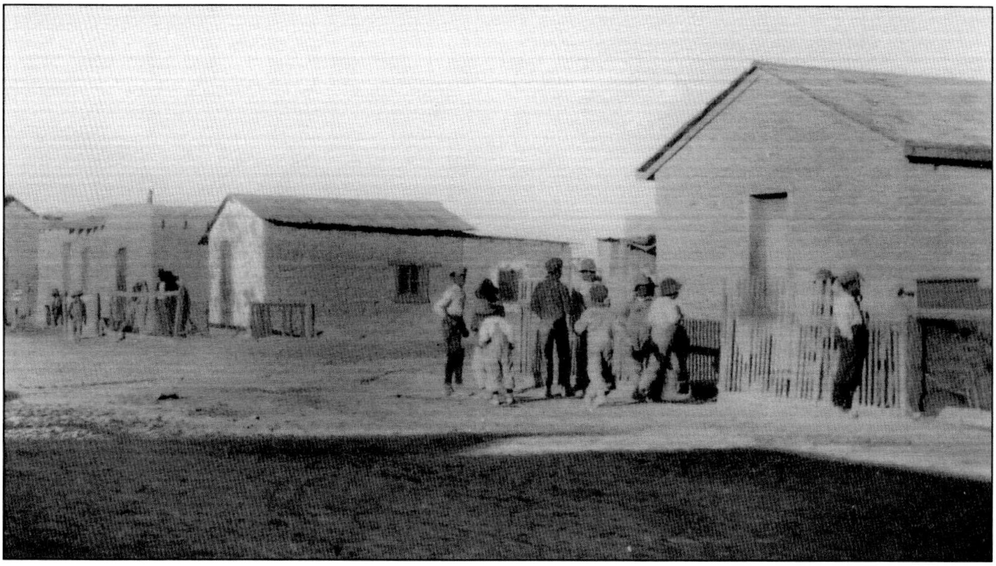

By 1901, Deming had two newspapers, the *Deming Headlight* and the *Deming Herald*. There were four churches that empowered residents weekly. The Bank of Deming was operational, with about $50,000 in deposits. The Santa Fe Roundhouse and shops gave residents something to do, while the Union Depot was always a focal point for the community. Many homes were erected at this time (above). The town jail was located on the corner of East Pine Street and Platinum Avenue (below). This photograph was taken in the late 1880s. The jail was turned over to the county when Luna County was formed in 1901.

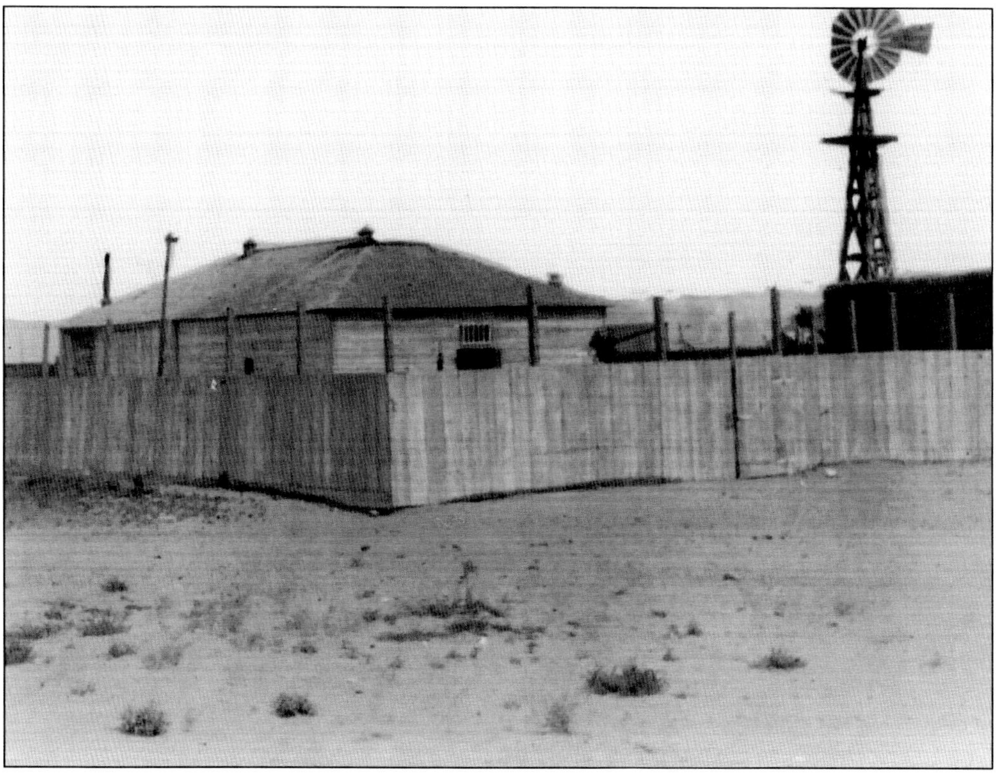

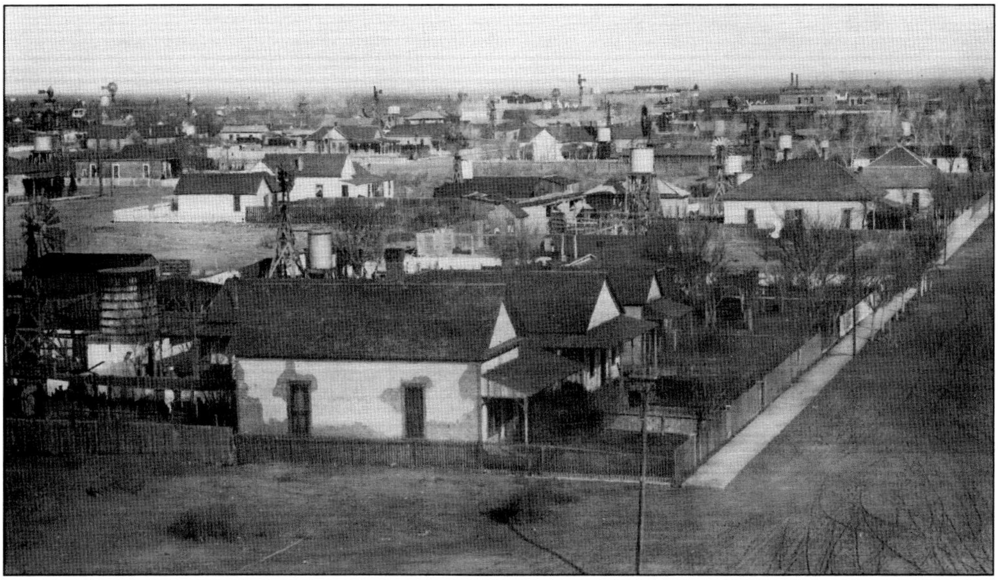

Deming is shown in the early 1900s. Where the town ends toward the back of the photograph, two stacks that belong to Deming Ice and Electric rise above the town. Those stacks mark the north boundary of Deming. This photograph was taken at a northwestern angle, perhaps from the Luna County Courthouse.

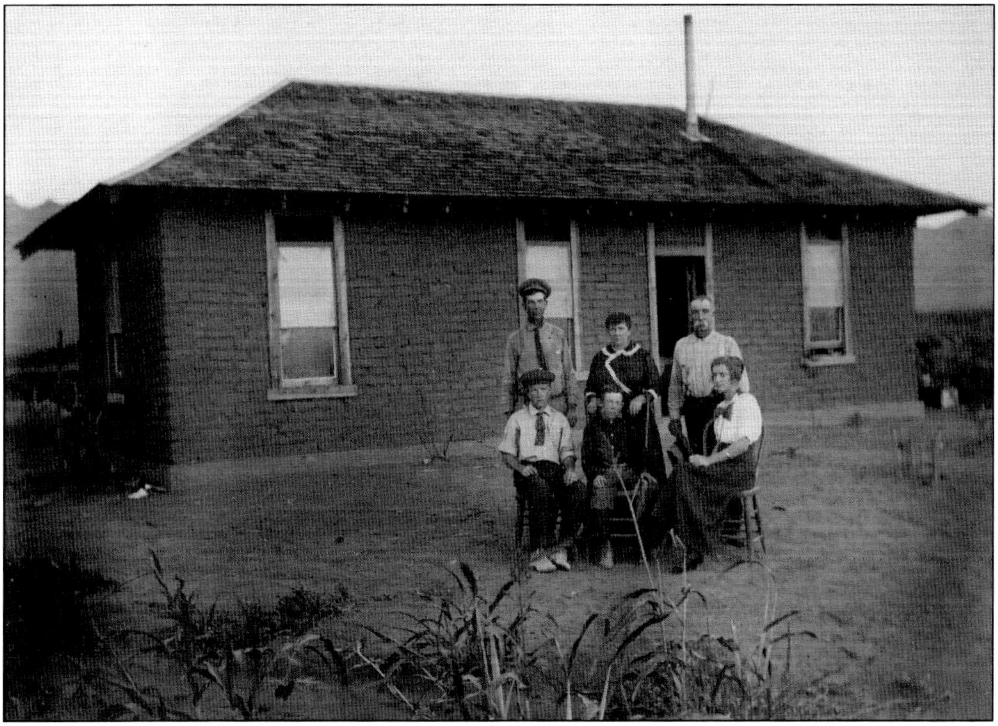

The Edward H. Bell family homesteaded at the foot of the Florida Mountains, southeast of Deming. This photograph was taken in 1914 and shows, from left to right, (standing) Roy, Katherine, and Edward Bell; (sitting) George, Francis, and Elizabeth Bell. Ruins of the original homestead are still present but are only accessible by horse. (Courtesy of the Jim Bell family.)

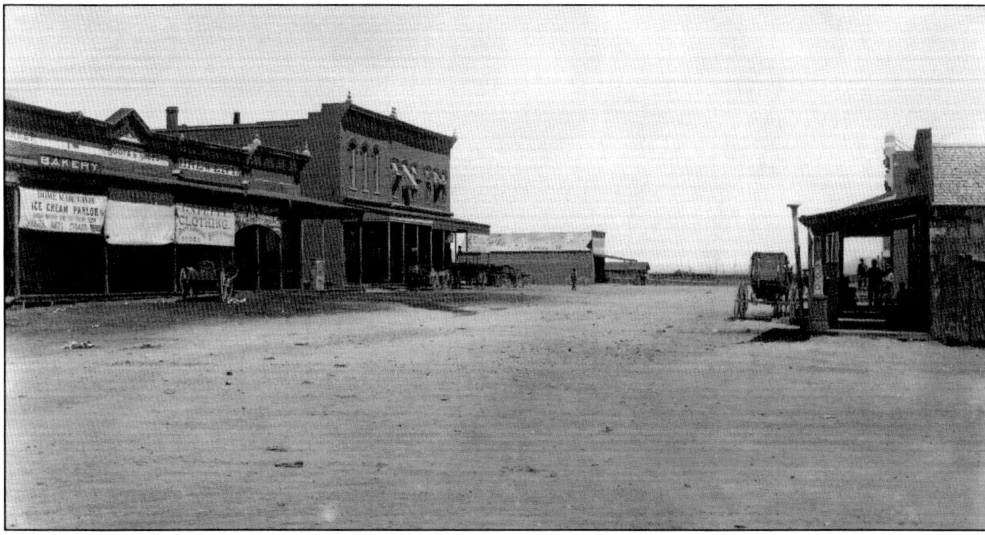

These two photographs show the same block but at different times, as evident by the wear on Gold Avenue, the businesses, and the type of wagons. The John Deckert Building (left) housed several enterprises. A bakery, Hodgon Emporium, G.N. Petty Clothing, and a German restaurant and brewery are all featured with visible advertising (above). These are some of Deming's earliest businesses. The Fleishman Beals Company and German Beer Hall are in the next taller building. Last on that side of Gold Avenue is H.H. Kidder's grocery business. A store featuring paint, Mimbres Valley Realty Company, a brewery, and groceries are all contained in the John Deckert Building in the early 1900s (below).

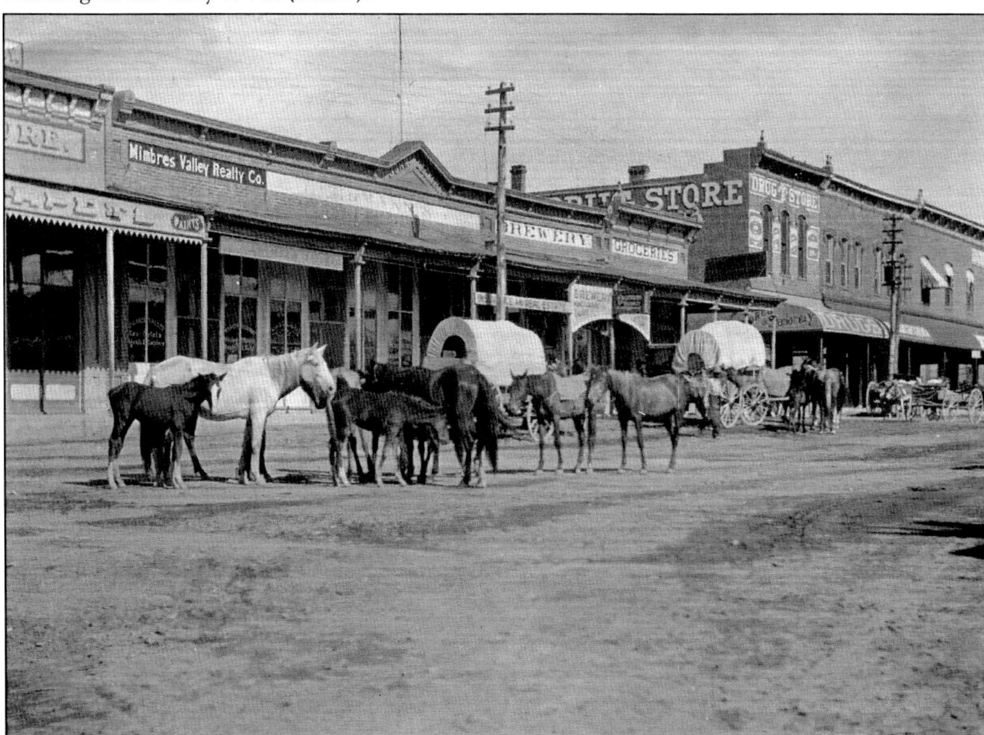

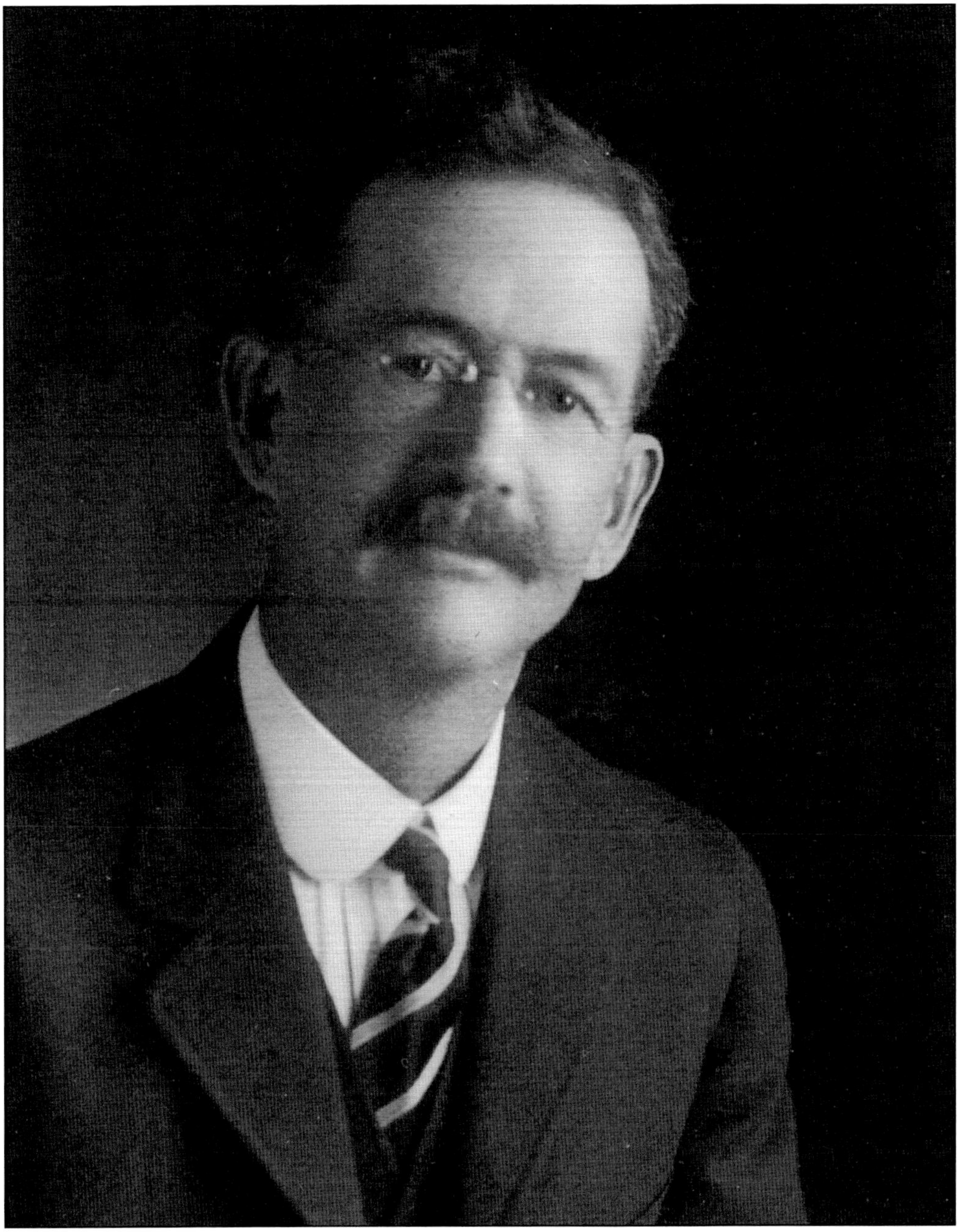

At age 18, Joseph A. Mahoney came to Deming in May 1882 from Lagoda, Indiana. He worked for his brother-in-law Anthony J. Clark before opening his own grocery business in 1885. Mahoney married Ella Broderick of Indiana and had a daughter, Mary. He became very involved in the new community, his business, mining, real estate, the local school system, the New Mexico Normal School Board of Regents, and the creation of a new county, among other activities. It can be argued that if not for Mahoney's ingenuity, Deming would not have progressed as quickly as it did.

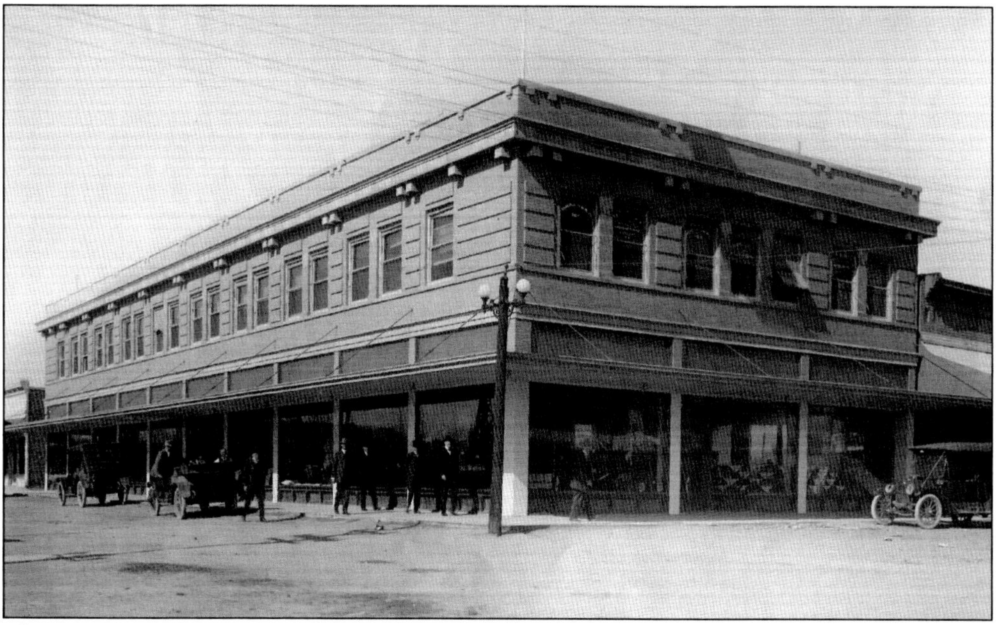

The Mahoney Building is located on the northeast corner of Gold Avenue and Spruce Street. It was erected in 1912, after Joseph A. Mahoney expanded his business. He operated his dry goods business for several years before this building was erected. In 1885, his store suffered damage from a fire, and he reopened his business the next day, never missing a beat. He expanded his business to include hardware and furniture after 1889.

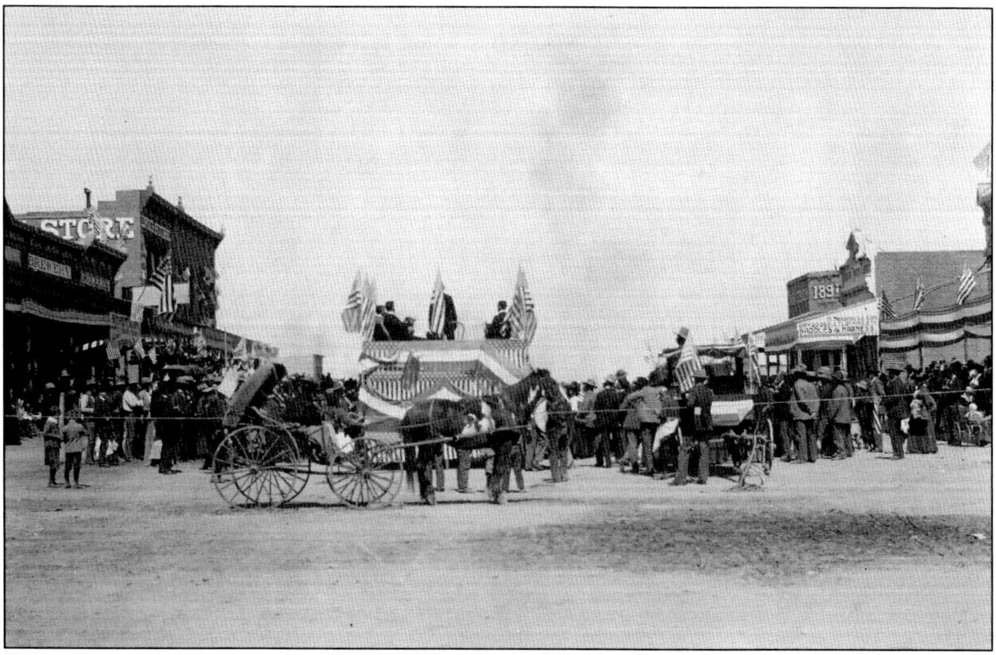

April 1, 1901, was declared Mahoney Day in Deming, which began with a parade. Mahoney Day celebrated the creation of Luna County. Prior to March 16, 1901, Deming was part of Grant County, for which Silver City was the county seat. Joseph A. Mahoney was a local leader in the movement to create a separate county.

Newton A. Bolich (left) and Nate Beals (right) stand before a photographer with their pronounced top hats at right. Bolich, known to many as Newt, became the first District I county commissioner on April 8, 1901. William M. Taylor, District II, and James P. Byron, District III, also served on the first Luna County Commission. Bolich owned a dry goods store in Deming, which is pictured with other stores in 1906 (below). Bolich's is the most distant store shown here on Pine Street. Near the flagpole is Gallup Saddles and Harness. The Lindauer Mercantile Company advertises its tents, tarps, pistols, guns, and ammunition—all of the things someone needed in early Deming: protection from weather and people.

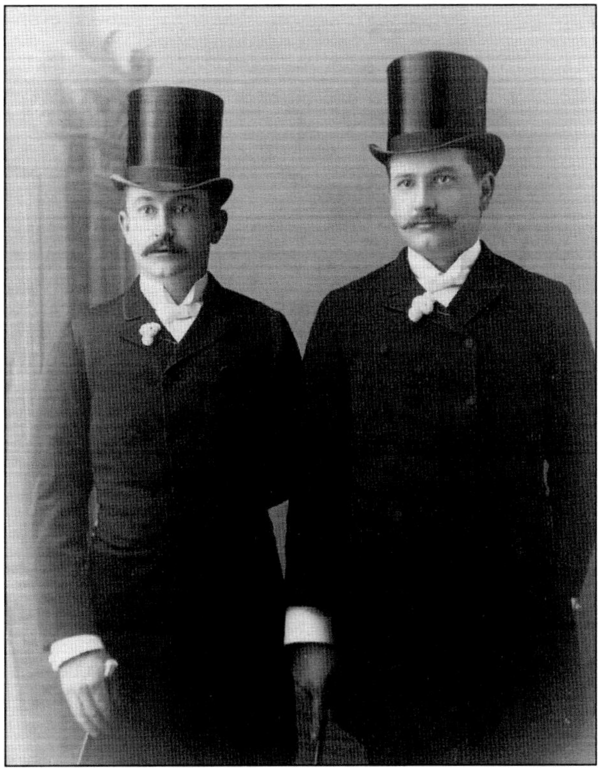

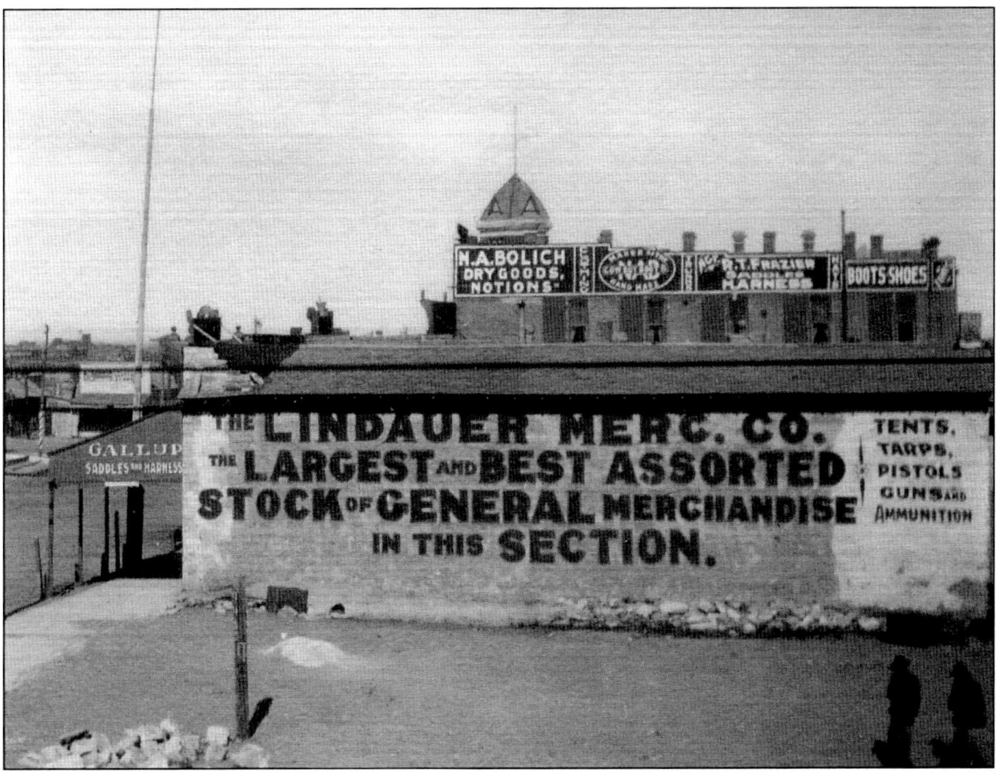

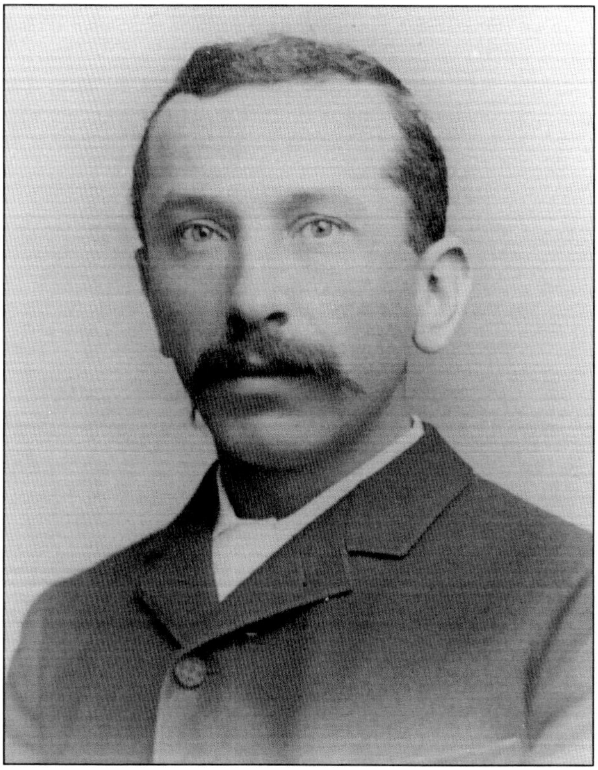

Sigmund Lindauer, pictured a few years after his arrival in Deming and near the end of his life, owned the largest general merchandising establishment in town, Lindauer Mercantile Company. His business began as Lindauer & Wormser, a partnership with Gustavo Wormser in 1883 that soon dissolved. Both German men began their own businesses in Deming. Lindauer traded with large Mexican caravans four times per year in 1883. The caravans used ox-drawn wagons. Everyone knew when the Mexican traders were in town. They would stay for several days and boost the local economy. Lindauer continued managing his business until he passed away in 1935. His son, Herman, took over the store, which continued for years.

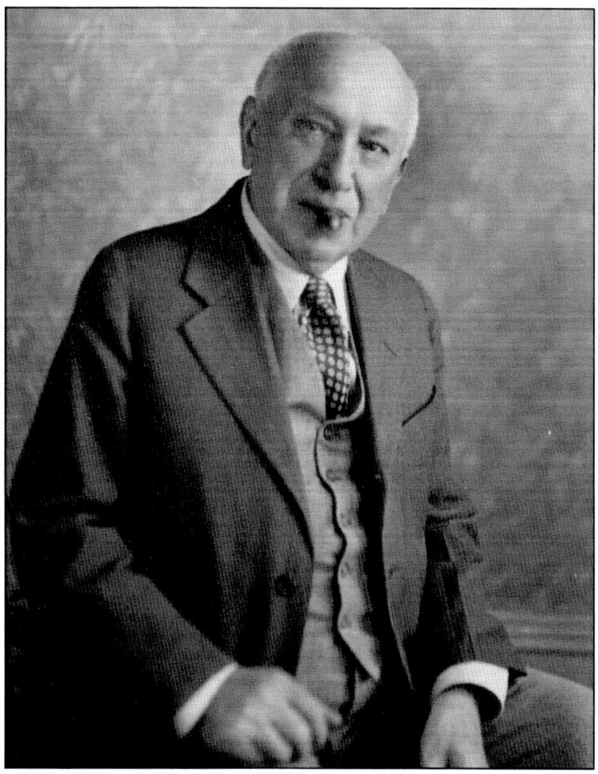

Arthur A. Temke (right) moved to Deming in December 1901 after practicing law in Wisconsin. Temke was the village attorney from 1904 to 1911 and the village clerk from 1905 to 1911. Upon the death of U. Francis Duff, in May 1906, the governor appointed Temke the county superintendent of schools. Julius Rosch (below, right), dubbed the founder of the Old Timers Association, is shown here with his son Herman. Rosch's wife was delighted when her new house was built and wanted to invite her husband's friends over to show it off. Rosch decided to only invite people who had been in Deming for 30 years or more, which was how long he had been in town. A total of 28 men attended on March 7, 1913, and signed an autograph album with their names, ages, and years of arrival.

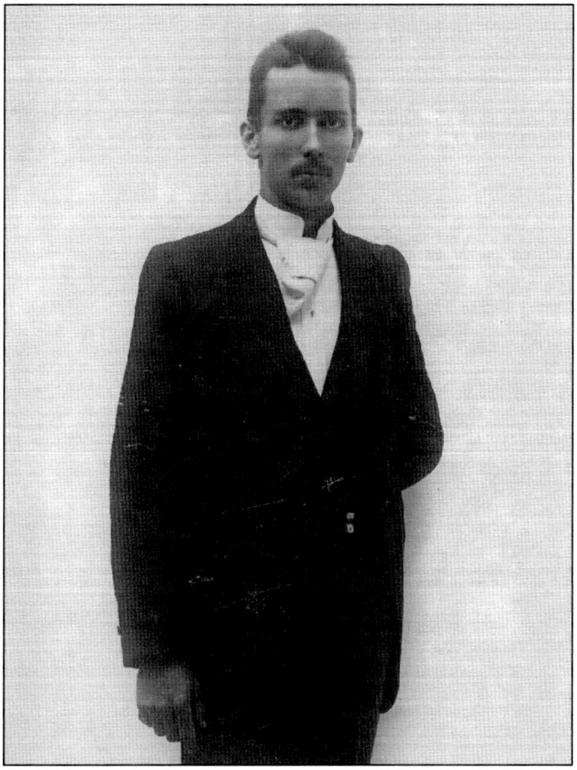

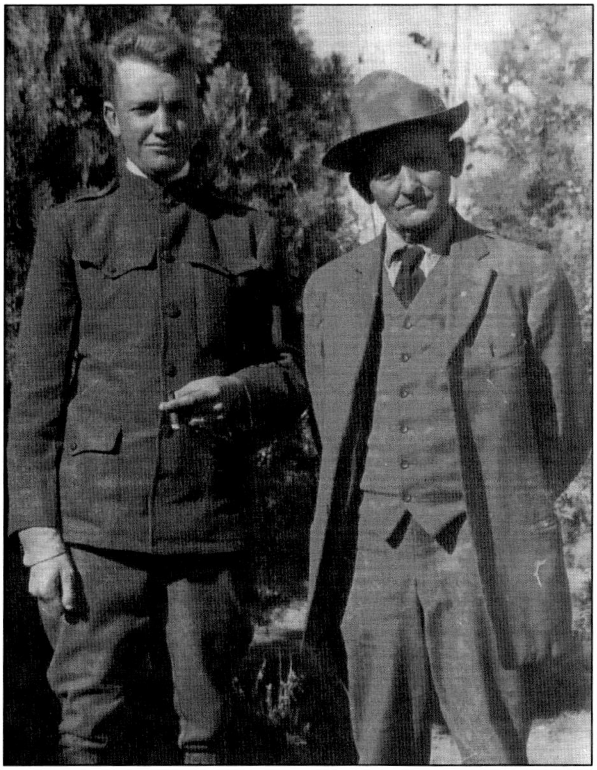

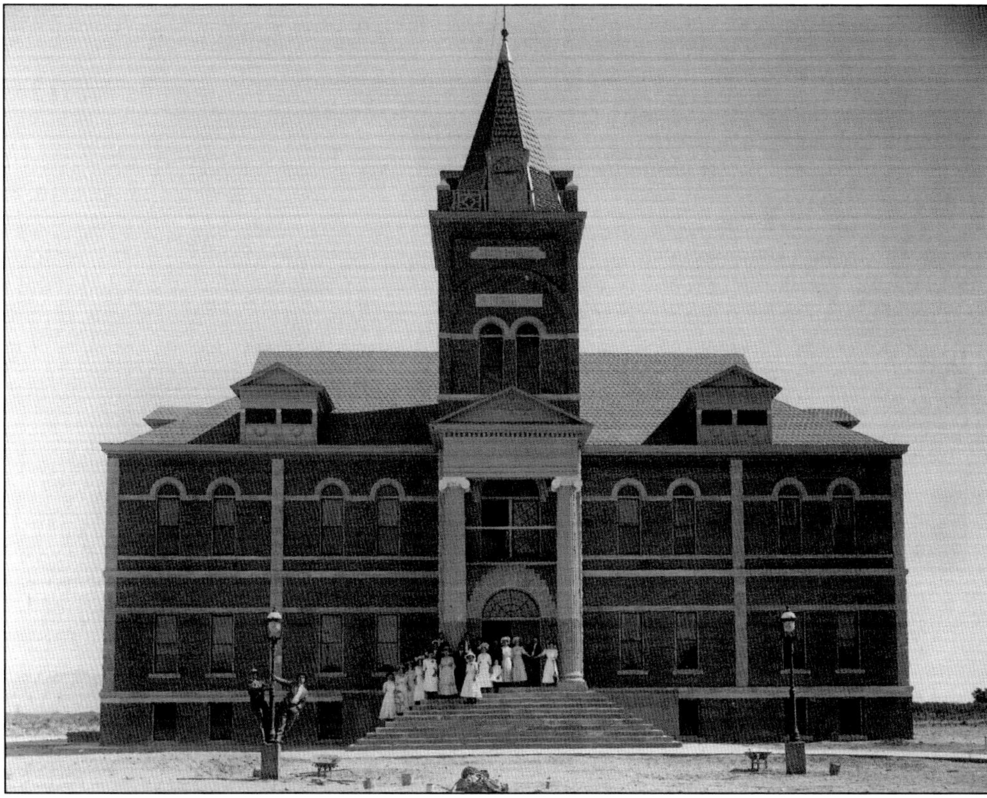

The Luna County Courthouse (above), on Silver Avenue, was erected in 1901 after being designed by W.B. Corwin. This photograph was taken shortly after construction of the building was completed. A wheelbarrow remains in the front of the building at 2:45 p.m., as indicated by the clock on the front of the building. The clock was built by the Seth Thomas Clock Company. The bell was forged by the McShane Bell Foundry in Baltimore, Maryland. The Deming Ladies' Hospital, once located at 410 Copper Street, was built in 1909 and was the only hospital in town for years (below).

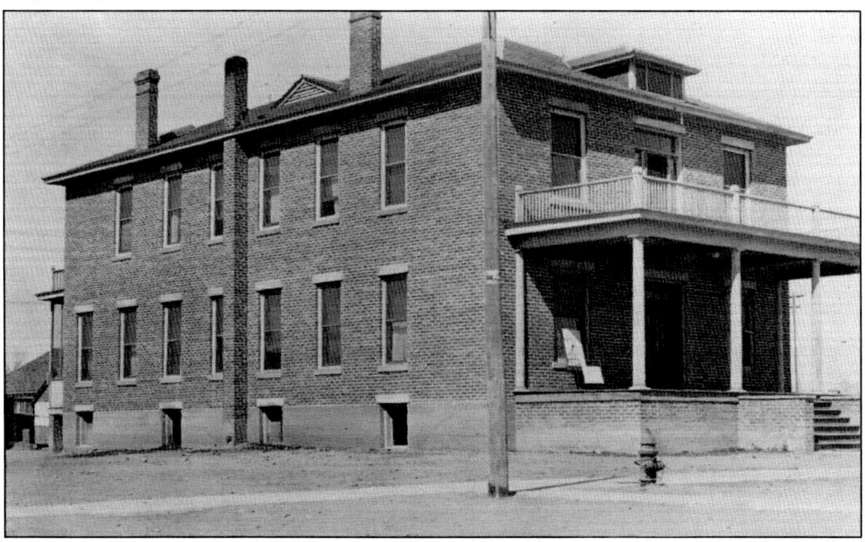

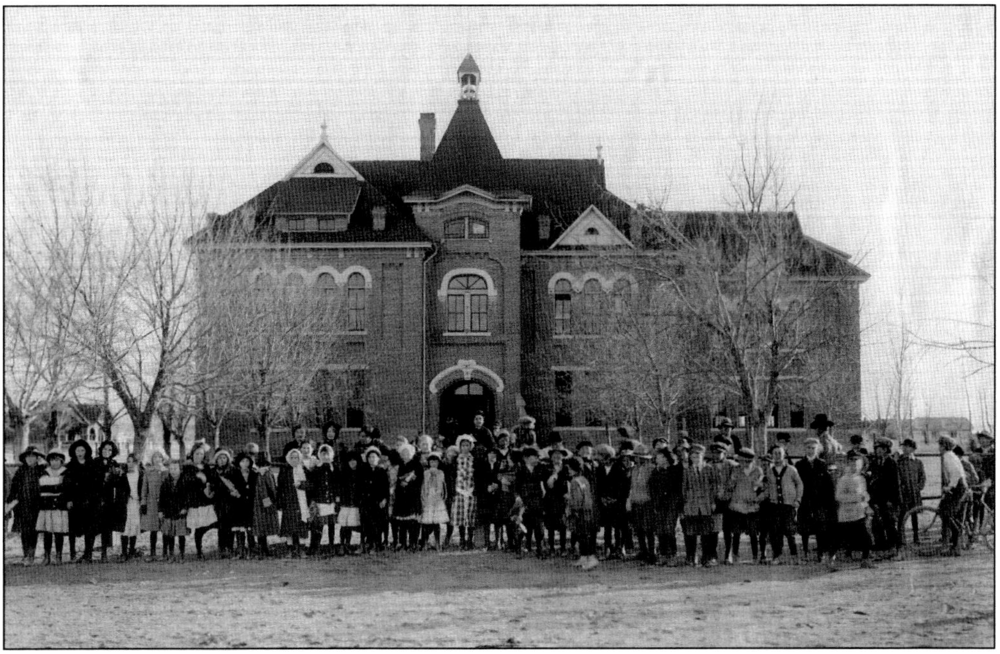

Central School (above) was constructed in 1891 and used until 1928. It was located at Iron and Elm Streets and cost $12,500. Deming High School (below) was built in 1911 and was used until 1961. Six teachers were employed during the 1900–1901 school year. There were 273 pupils enrolled in school, with a daily attendance of about 176 pupils. Six senior high school students graduated that year. Schoolteachers were paid $4,495 yearly. The expenditures for the schools, such as lighting and heating, were $1,465.88. The school property, including the two large buildings, was valued at $25,000 in 1901.

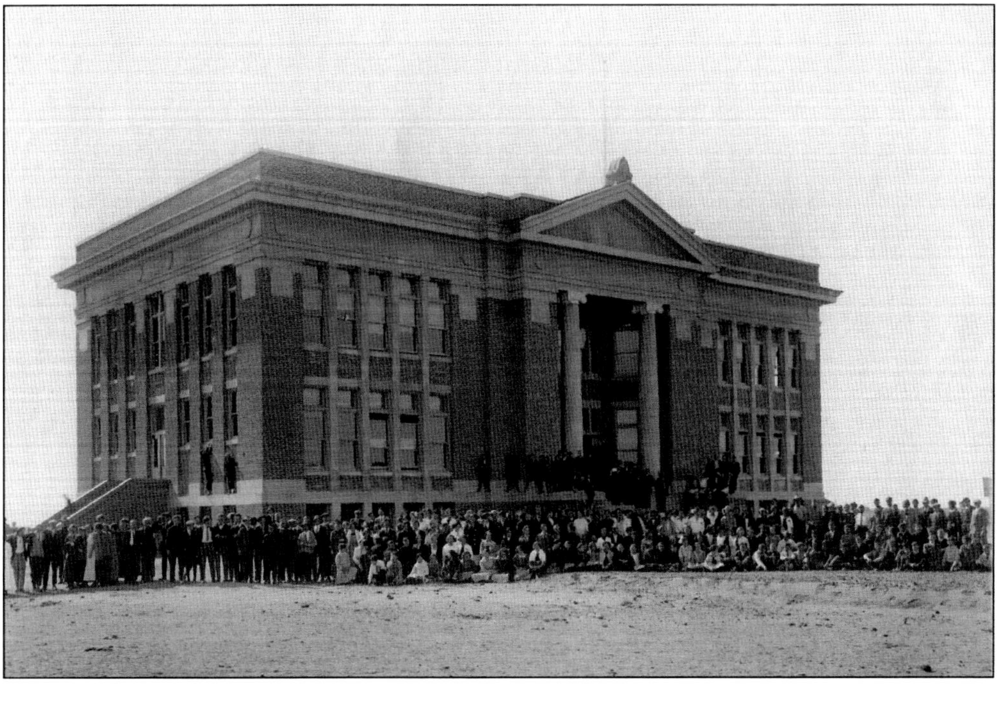

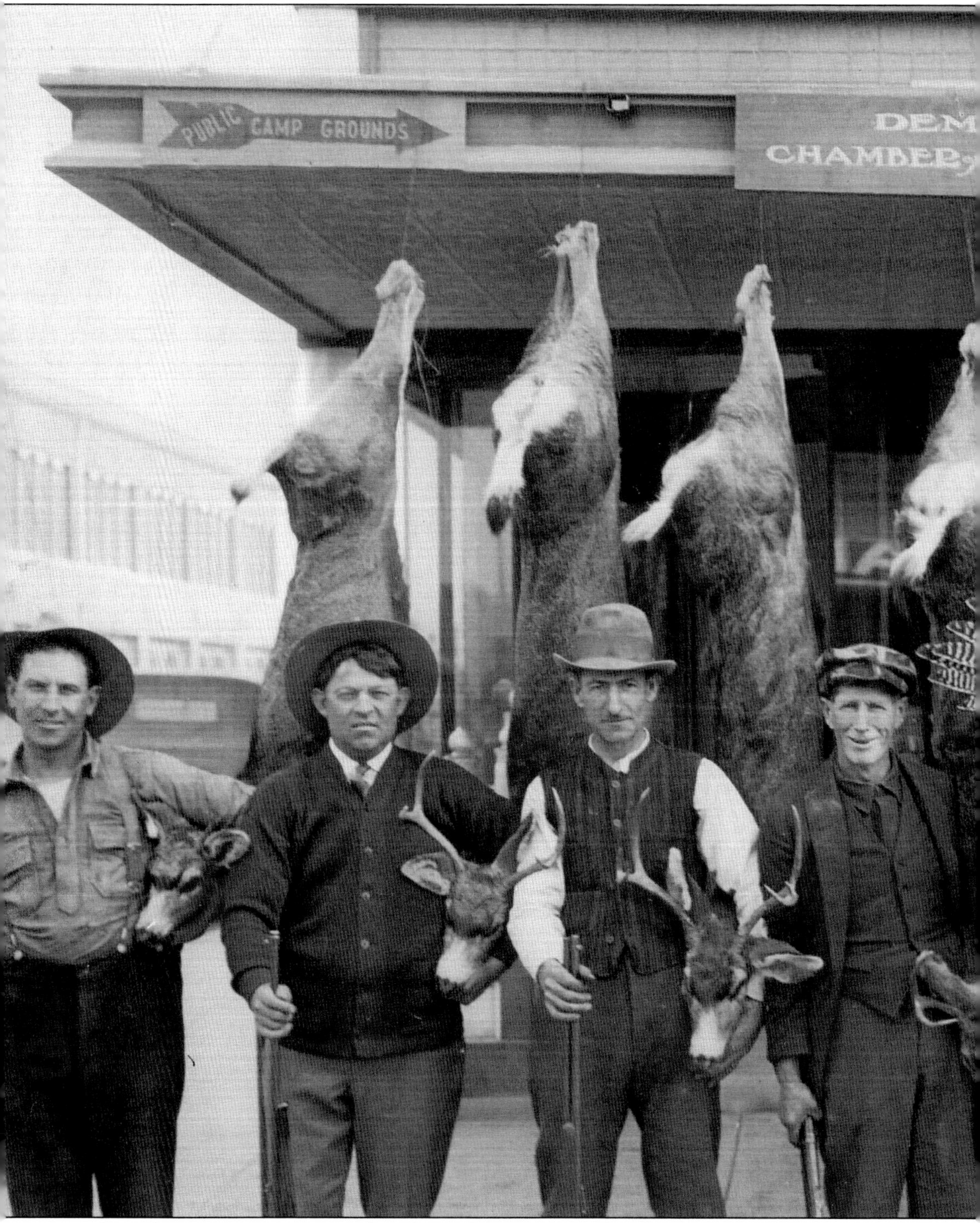

The welcoming committee stands in front of the Deming Chamber of Commerce on South Gold Avenue. They are, from left to right, Joseph Deckert, Henry Raithel, Irving Raithel, Henry Foster, D.F. Weatherred, Arthur J. Huxtable, an unidentified man, and an unidentified trapper. All were businessmen in Deming. The Deming Chamber of Commerce was established in March 1910,

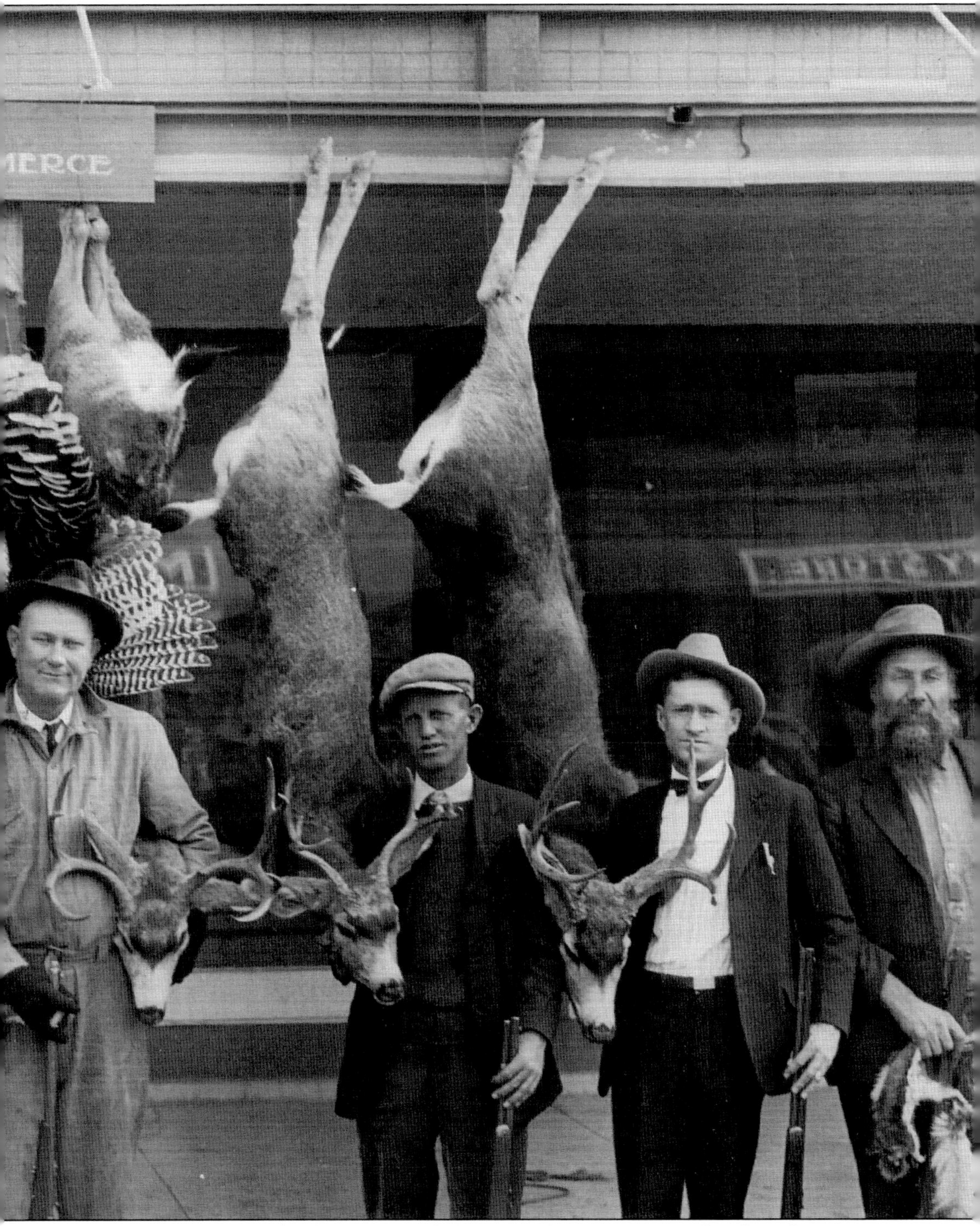

two years before statehood. The first recorded minutes from a Deming Chamber of Commerce meeting, in which a previous meeting was mentioned, date back to March 16, 1910. The first directors of the Deming Chamber of Commerce were John Corbett, G.M. Saddler, Dr. Pickney M. Steed, and Anthony J. Clark.

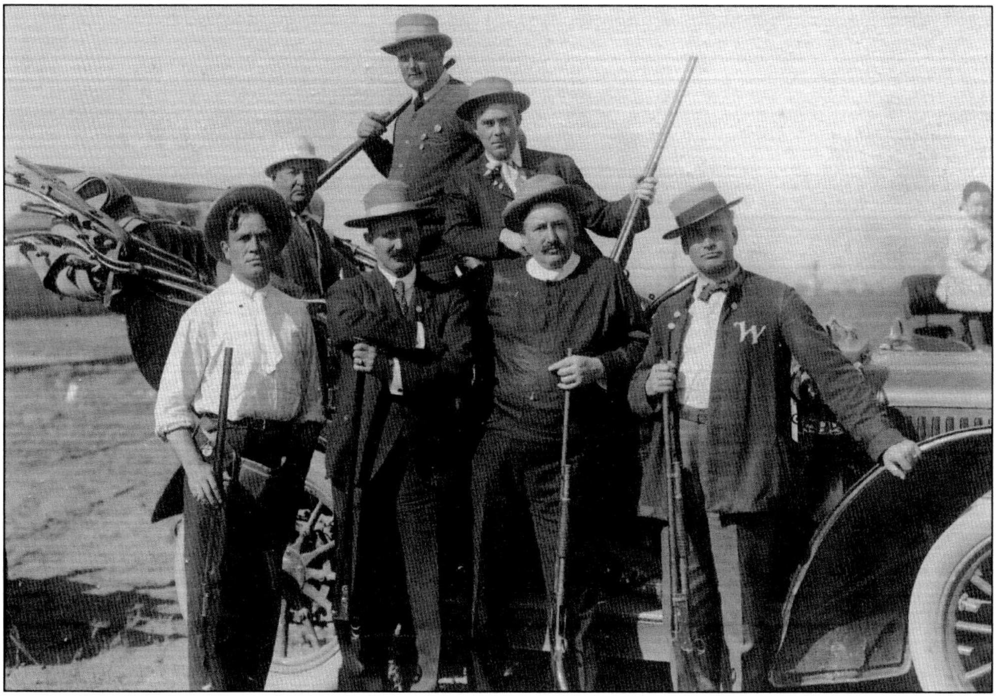

The Deming Skeet Club stands in front of an automobile in 1908 (above). Club members (below), from left to right, are Henry Meyer, Chris Raithel, ? Cobb, ? Young; they are posing with their shotguns. Meyer was the owner of a large meat market. Raithel was the Luna County treasurer from 1909 to 1917.

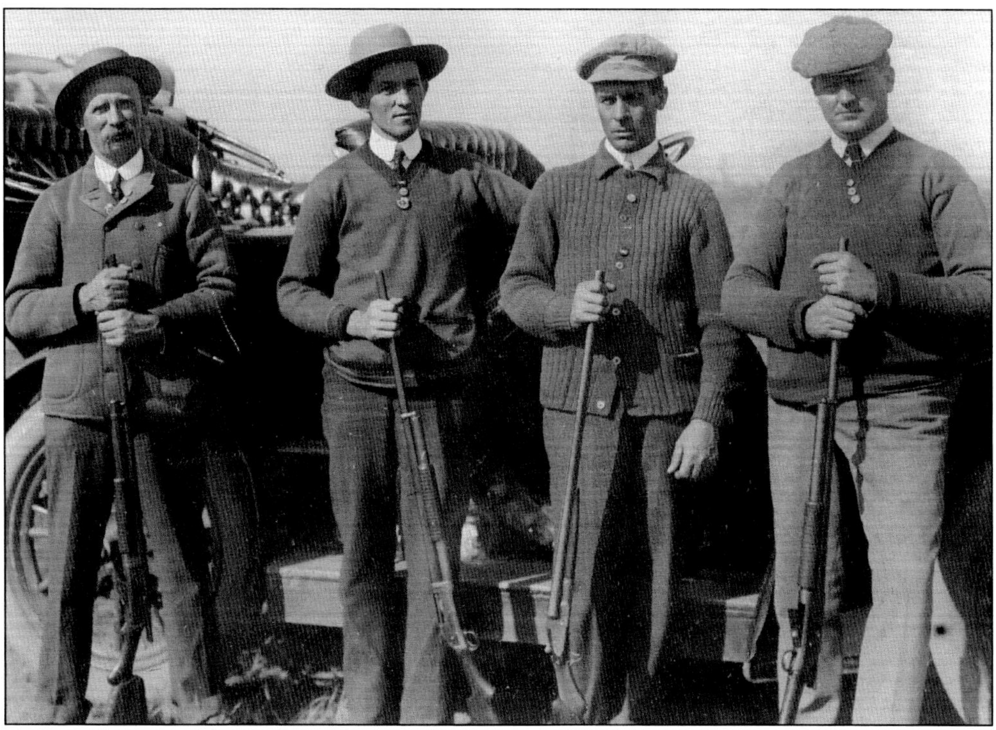

Four

Early Economy of Business and Agriculture

Deming's early economy was centered on agriculture and small business ownership. Small towns, including Iola and Hondale, were created around Luna County where agriculture developed. These towns would rely on Deming.

Many area businesses began as partnerships, since all parties involved would assume the risk of the business. Some of these partnerships dissolved, and the separate parties began their own sole proprietorships, many of which were very successful. The business district of Deming was located on what was a Wyandotte Script Location. The federal government issued land warrants as the result of treaties with the Wyandotte Indians on March 17, 1842, and January 31, 1855. Wyandotte Script was good for land that was held in the public domain. E. Germain and Company opened the first store in Deming, which used old boxcars for storerooms. In 1882, it advertised crockery, glassware, beer, tobacco, and hardware.

Deming had a Methodist Episcopal church, a public school, two brickyards, smelting works, a brewery, one hotel, the First National Bank of Deming, several special and general stores, blacksmith shops, and two newspapers, the *Deming Headlight* and *Deming Tribune*, by 1884. Three years later, in 1887, Deming had one public school and a private school, two churches, and four hotels.

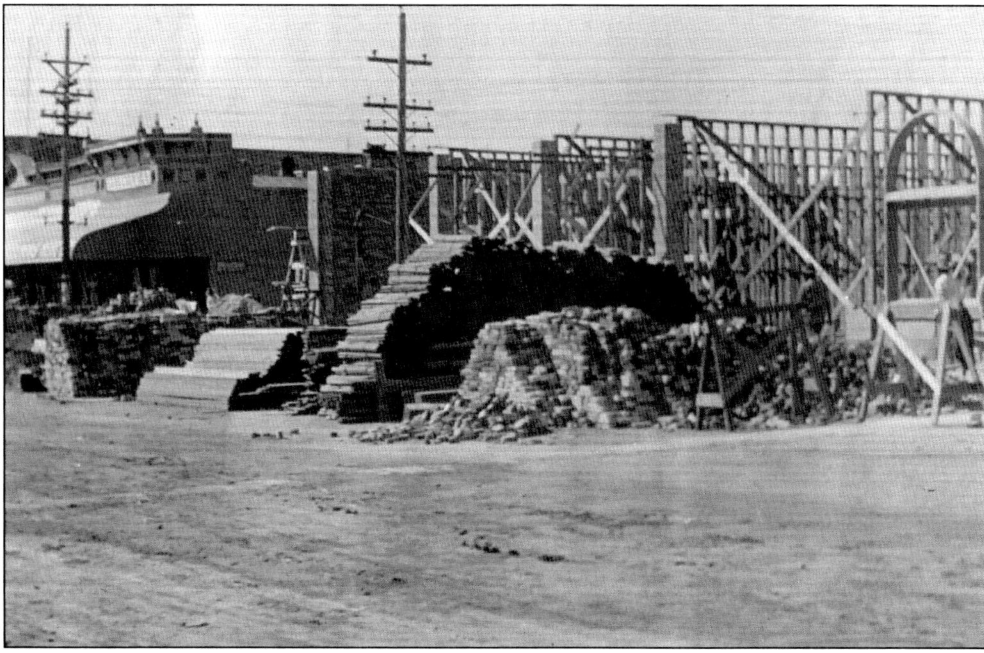

The Clark Buildings are being erected in this 1883 photograph. Anthony J. Clark, a prominent Deming dry goods businessman, was the owner. This building is located on the corner of Pine Street and Gold Avenue in Deming. Over the years, many different businesses have been located in these structures.

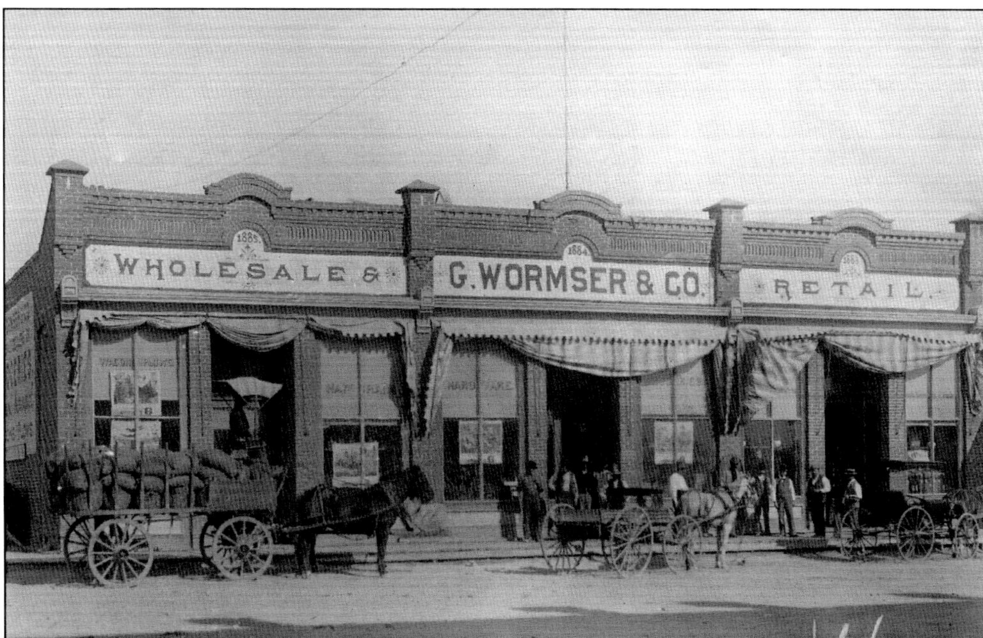

Gustav Wormser was born in Aldingen, Ludwigsburg, Germany, and moved to Deming in 1888. He opened the G. Wormser & Company Store. Wormser eventually moved back to his wife's home of San Francisco. In 1896, he and two other men founded S&W, the home of whole-egg real mayonnaise, which can still be bought today.

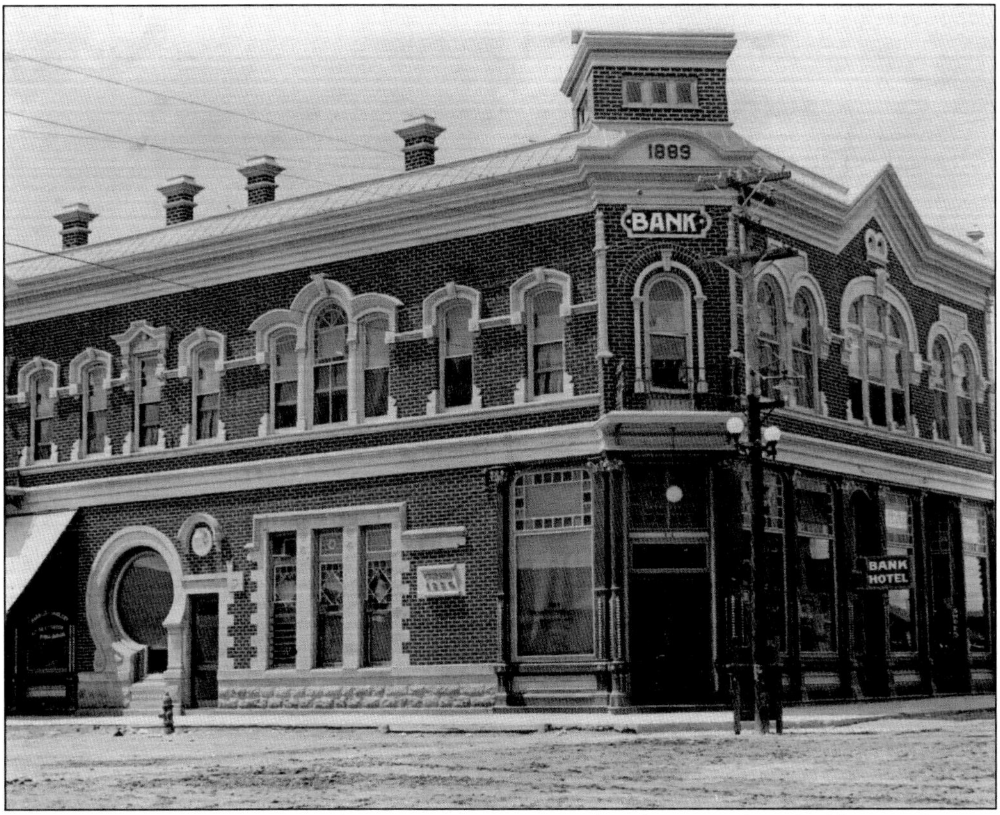

The Bank of Deming was established on June 10, 1889, and paid in capital stock of $30,000 by 1910 with a surplus and undivided profits of $15,540.72. By January 1, 1909, the bank had $280,000 on deposit. In 1910, bank officials were as follows: John Corbett, president; Joseph A. Mahoney, vice president; Arthur Raithel, cashier; H.C. Brown, assistant cashier; and A.C. Brown, director.

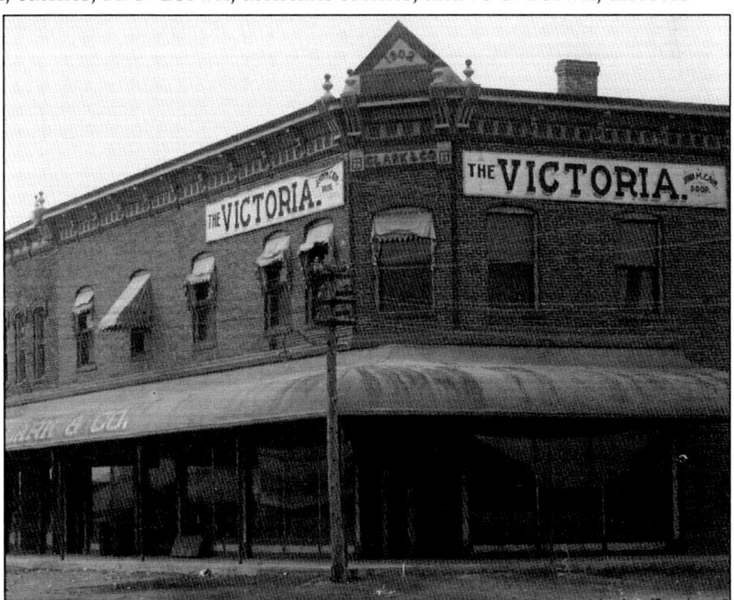

John M. Cain was the proprietor of the Victoria Hotel when it opened in 1902. It welcomed out-of-town visitors for 12 years before a tragic fire engulfed the entire block. Steve Nixon was the proprietor of the lodging at the time of the fire. He felt that the hotel suffered a loss of $2,500.

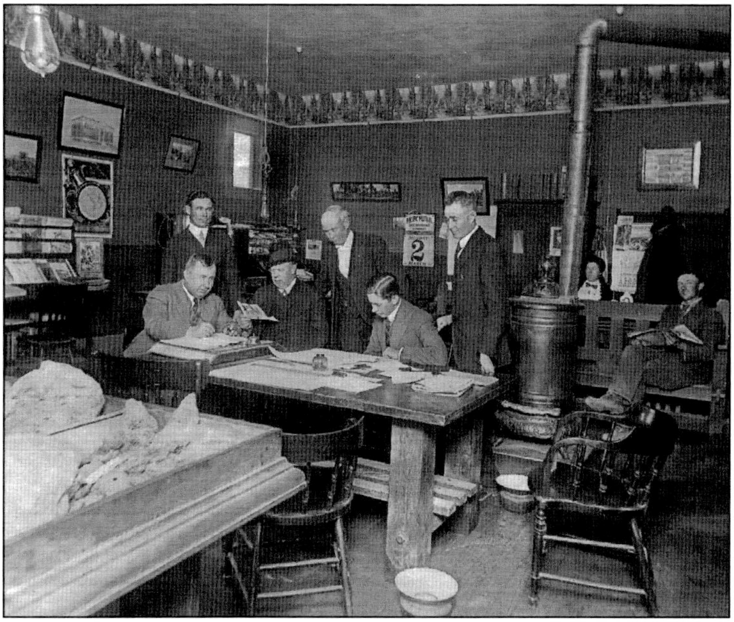

The *Deming Headlight* was established in July 1881 by James E. Curren. Curren was known as a pioneer editor in New Mexico and was considered a Johnny Appleseed who "planted" newspapers. A few weeks after the paper was established, Curren's son, Arthur, was born. He was believed to be the first white child born in Deming. The *Deming Headlight* is the longest-running newspaper in the state of New Mexico.

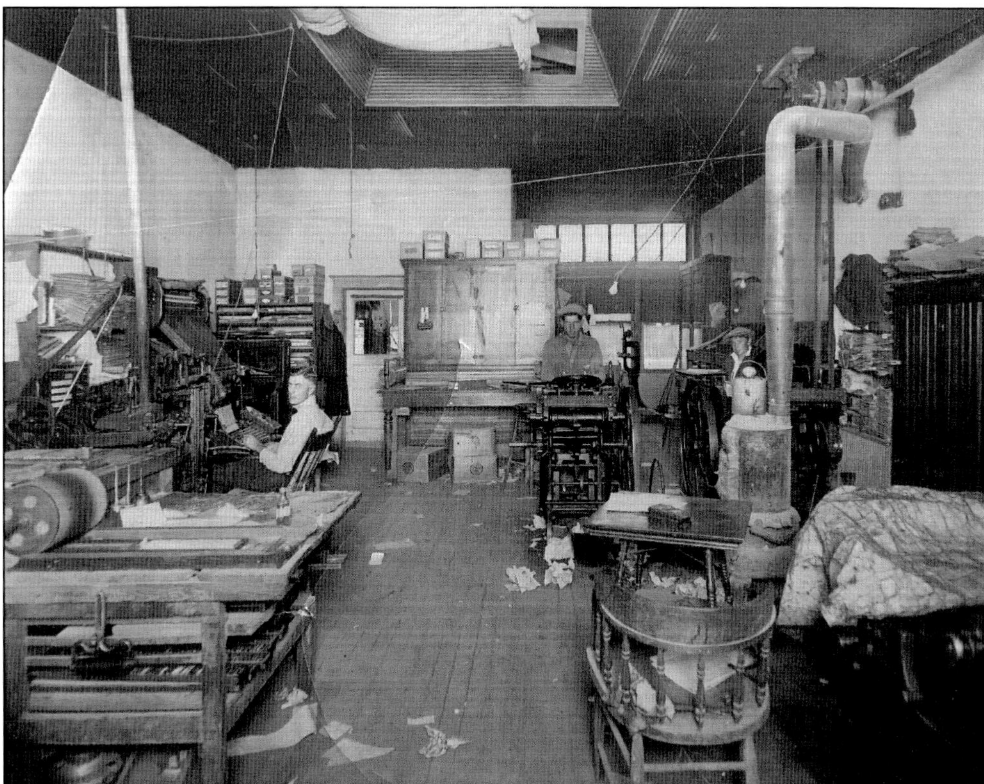

The *Deming Graphic* office is shown with Henry D. Stutts (center) working. The *Deming Graphic* operated in town from 1903 to 1948. The *Graphic* and *Headlight* consolidated under single ownership in 1949. One issue ran on Tuesday, while the other was published on Friday. The two newspapers returned to separate titles in 1956, and the *Deming Graphic* was published until 1979.

The Aquarium Bar was owned by James W. Hannigan, who also operated the Harvey House. Fritz Ritcher (left), the bartender, and Henry Rosencrans were photographed in front of the business in 1907. Pints of beer cost 20¢ and quarts of beer cost 35¢ at that time. In the photograph, someone is peering out of the door's left window, and the photographer's image appears in the right door's window.

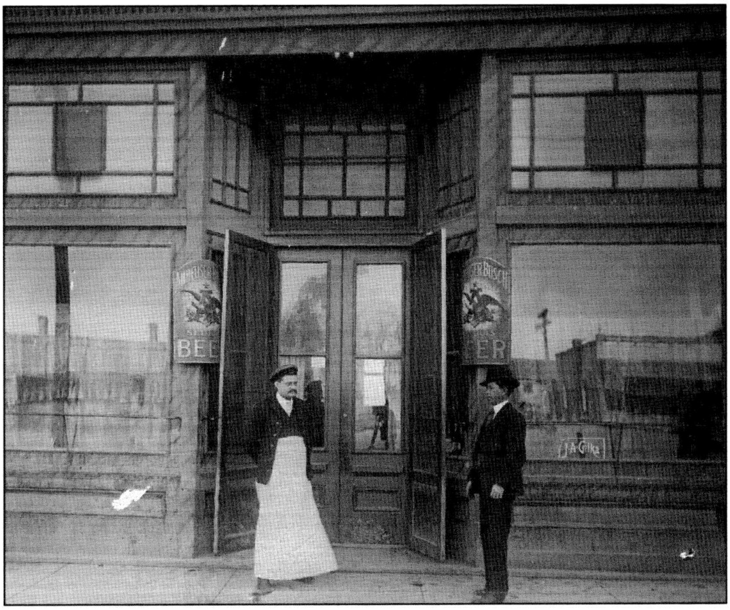

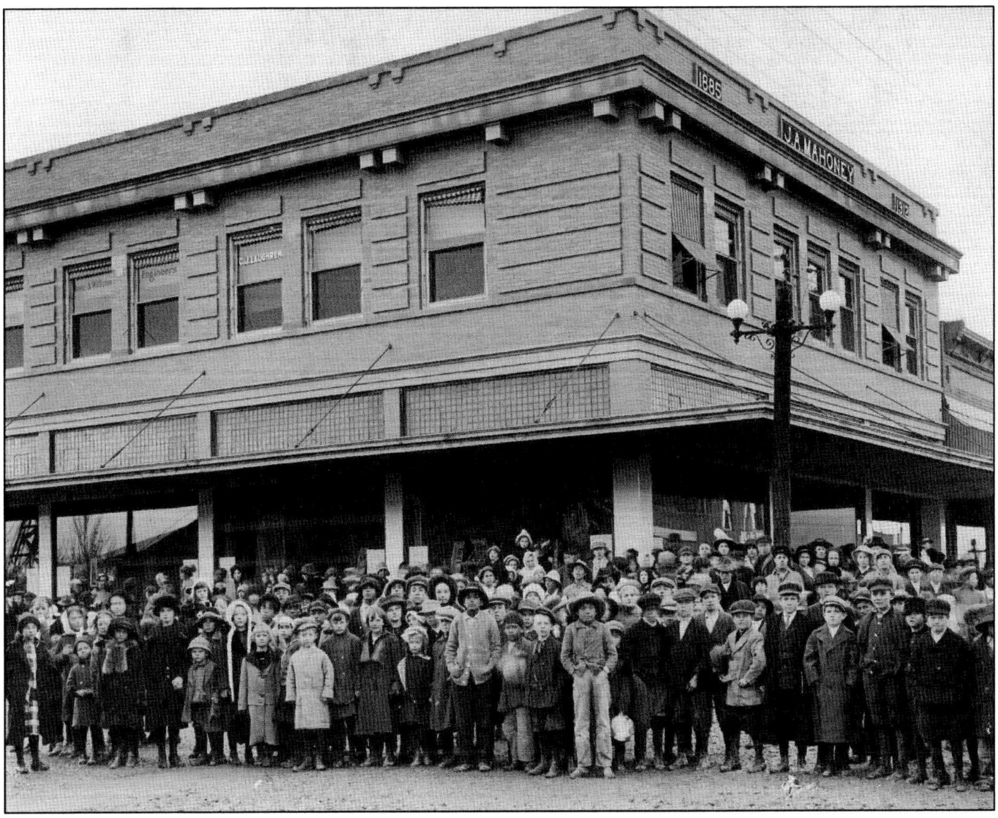

Joseph A. Mahoney welcomed many school-age children during the Christmas season of 1912 or 1913 at his store on the corner of Gold Avenue and Spruce Street. Waiting for Santa Claus, numerous children line Spruce Street for a photograph. The store windows are filled with Christmas displays reminding customers of the gift-giving season.

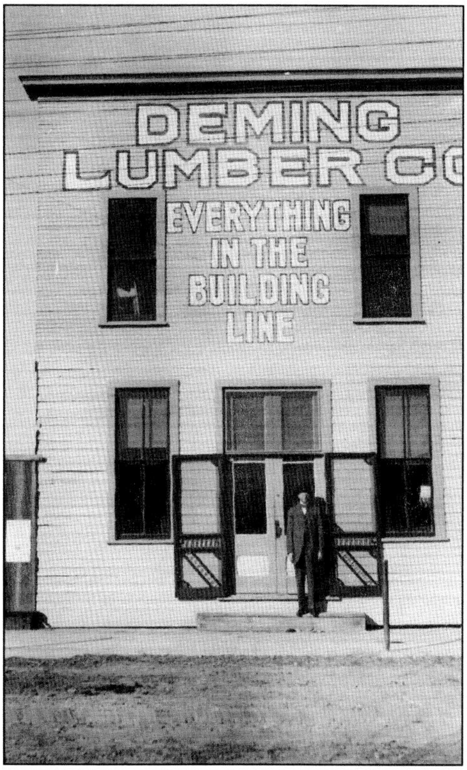

Deming Lumber Company has a long history of business in Deming. Opened prior to World War I, the firm secured lumber for many businesses and for the military camp that was established in Deming. In 1918, the company was transferred to Foxworth Galbraith Lumber Company.

Foxworth Galbraith Lumber Company, located at the corner of Copper Street and Cedar Avenue, was worth over $1 million during World War I. After it bought Deming Lumber Company in 1918, it acquired Gibson-Hines and Southwestern Lumber Companies in 1919. Foxworth Galbraith Lumber Company is still doing business in Deming today.

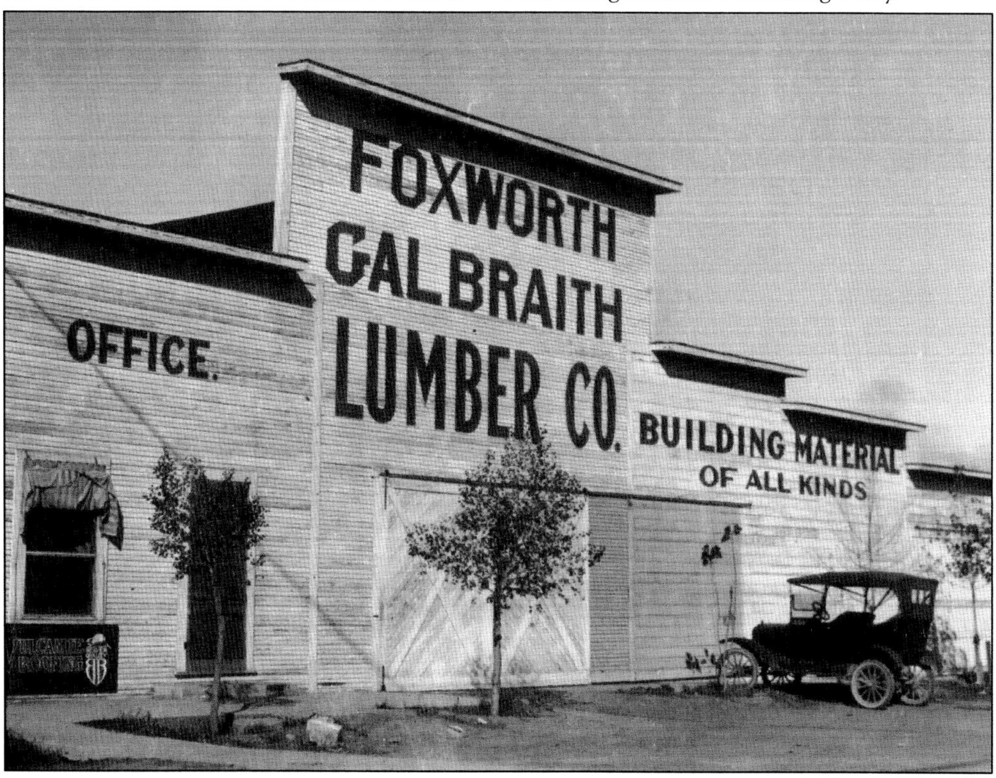

Deming Roller Mills was established in August 1917 and operated by John W. Clark. With a staff of five, Deming Roller Mills had a warehouse containing two million pounds of first-class wheat waiting to be milled and 75,000 pounds of sacked flour. It was selling sacked flour for $3.25 for a 48-pound sack and $1.65 for a 24-pound sack in 1917.

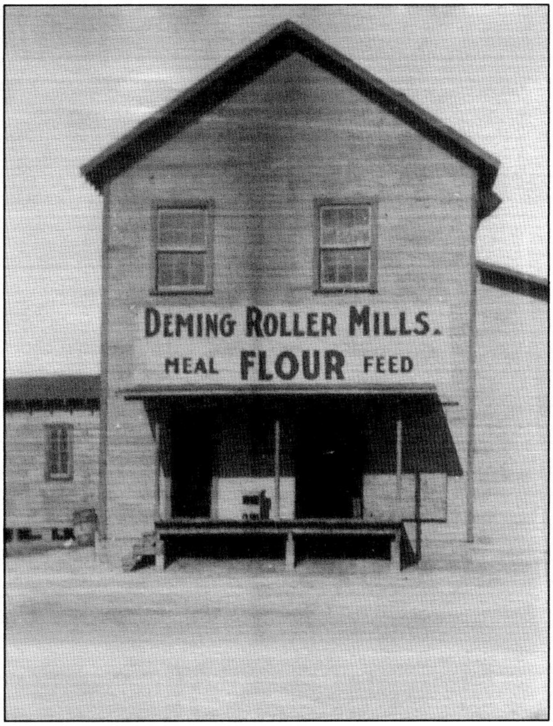

Henry Meyer's Meat Market was at 200 South Gold Avenue. Meyer moved to Deming in 1888, and Sigmund Lindauer helped him get a job with Henry Holgate, a butcher. Lindauer also helped him buy the property for his own market. Meyer sold at least one million pounds of T-bone steaks at three pounds for $1 at the market. The market closed in 1932, as many people owed debts.

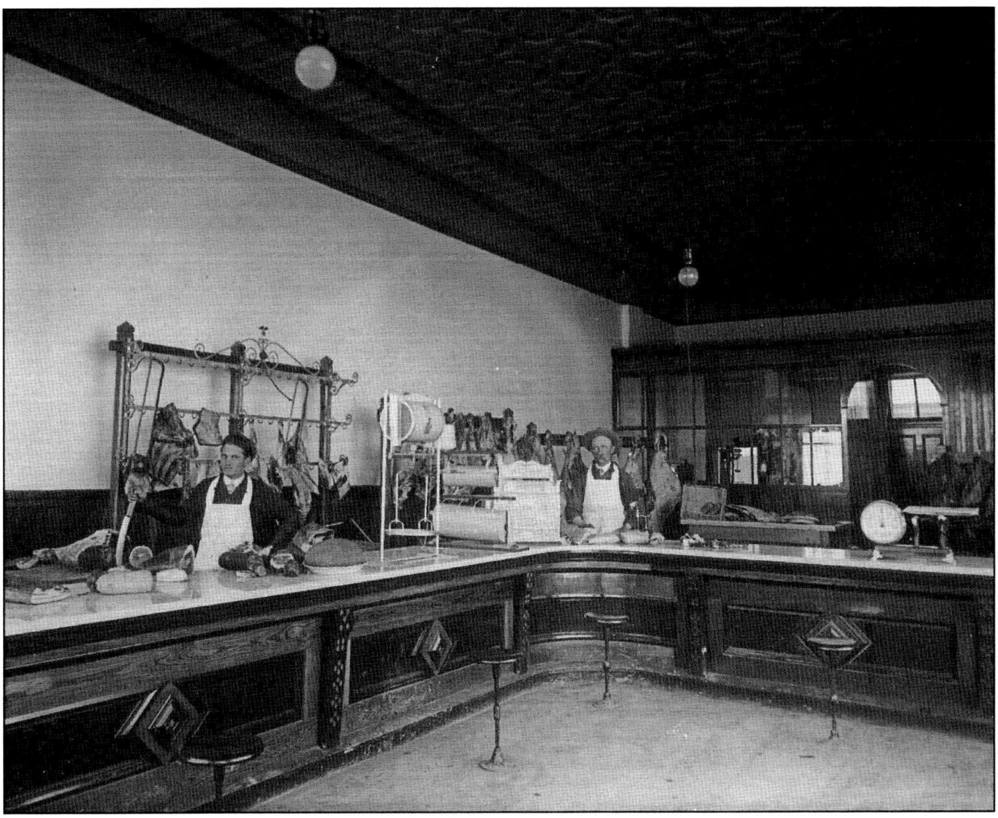

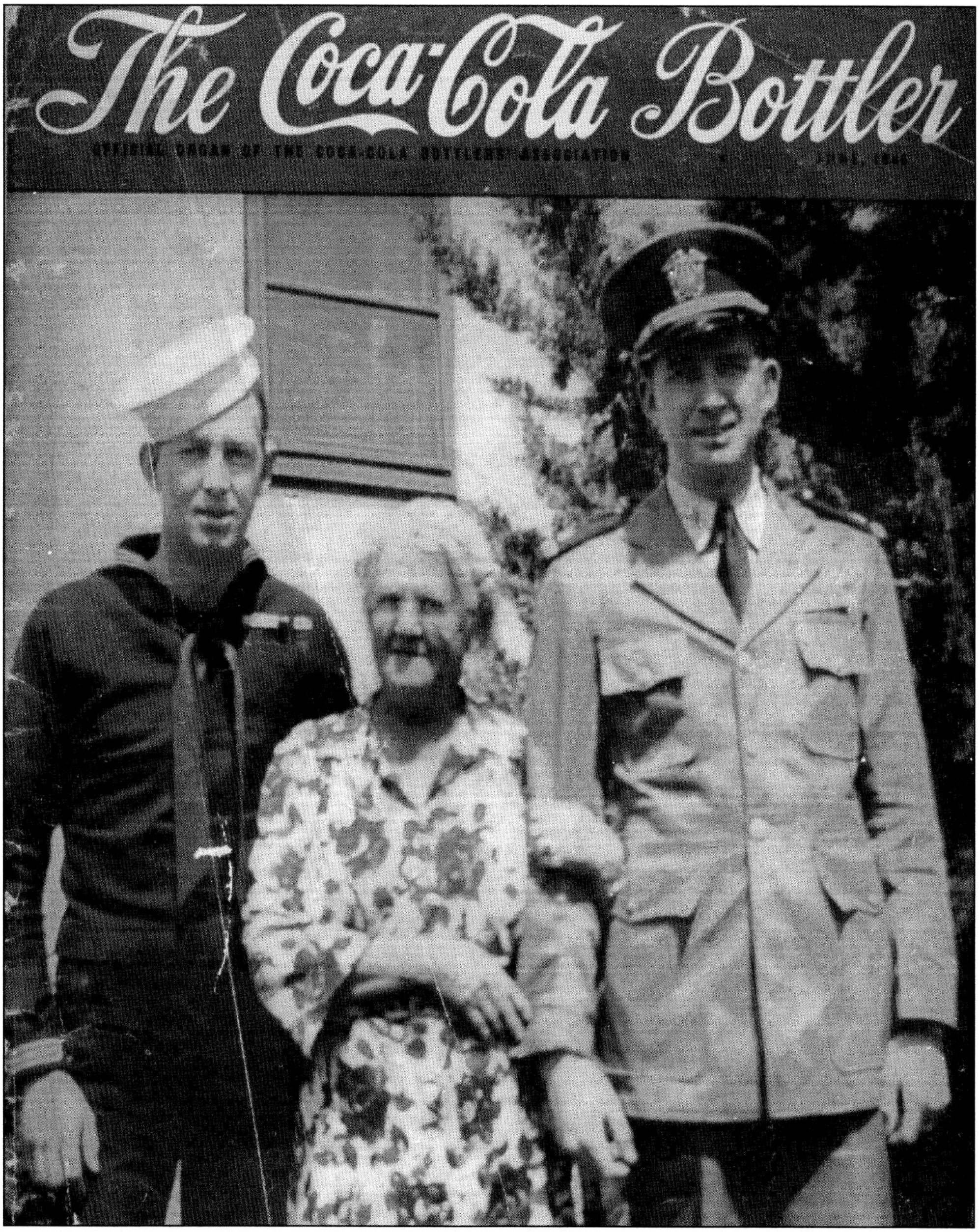

Lucy E. Link, owner of the Deming Coca-Cola Bottling Company, welcomes home her two sons, Paul Jr. (left) and Sam (right), from World War II in 1946. After the boys returned from war, they managed the business with their mother until she retired. Mrs. Link had taken over the company after her husband's passing in 1937. Prior to that, they owned bottling plants in Abbeville, South Carolina; San Bernardino, California; and Pampa, Texas, before moving to Deming for Paul Sr.'s health. The Deming Coca-Cola Bottling Company has been in the family for five generations. (Courtesy of the Link and Schultz families.)

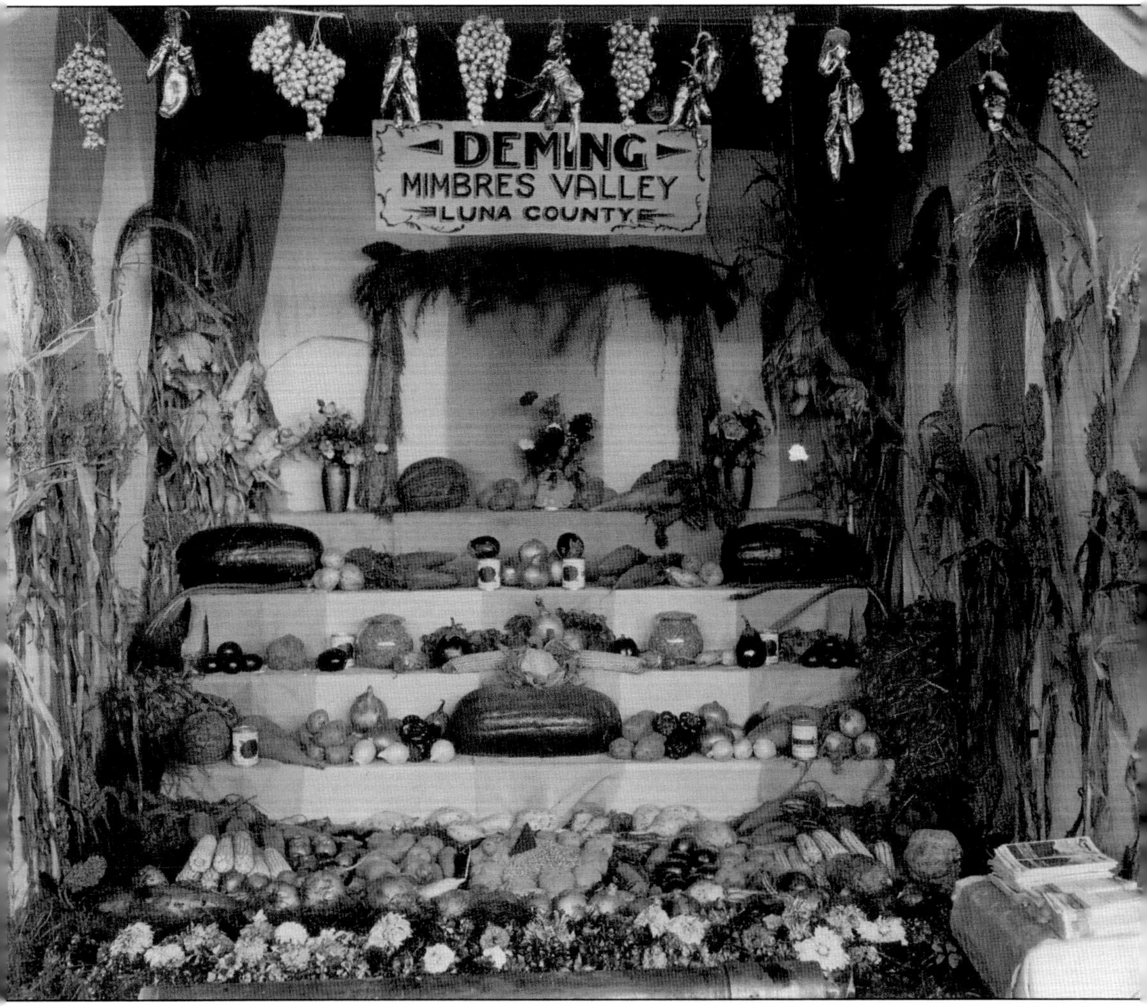

A colorful booth advertises the numerous products grown in the Mimbres Valley. Those just passing through the town may not notice the expansive fields that are in the area. Vegetable farming was the first agriculture in the area. Wheat, eggplants, very large carrots, potatoes, tomatoes, watermelon, corn, cauliflower, celery, onions, bell peppers, and beans are just some of the products that have been grown in the Mimbres Valley. Continuing to the present, the Mimbres Valley offers rich water and soil for local farmers. Chilies, pumpkins, onions, pecans, watermelon, cantaloupe, grapes, and several other crops are harvested today.

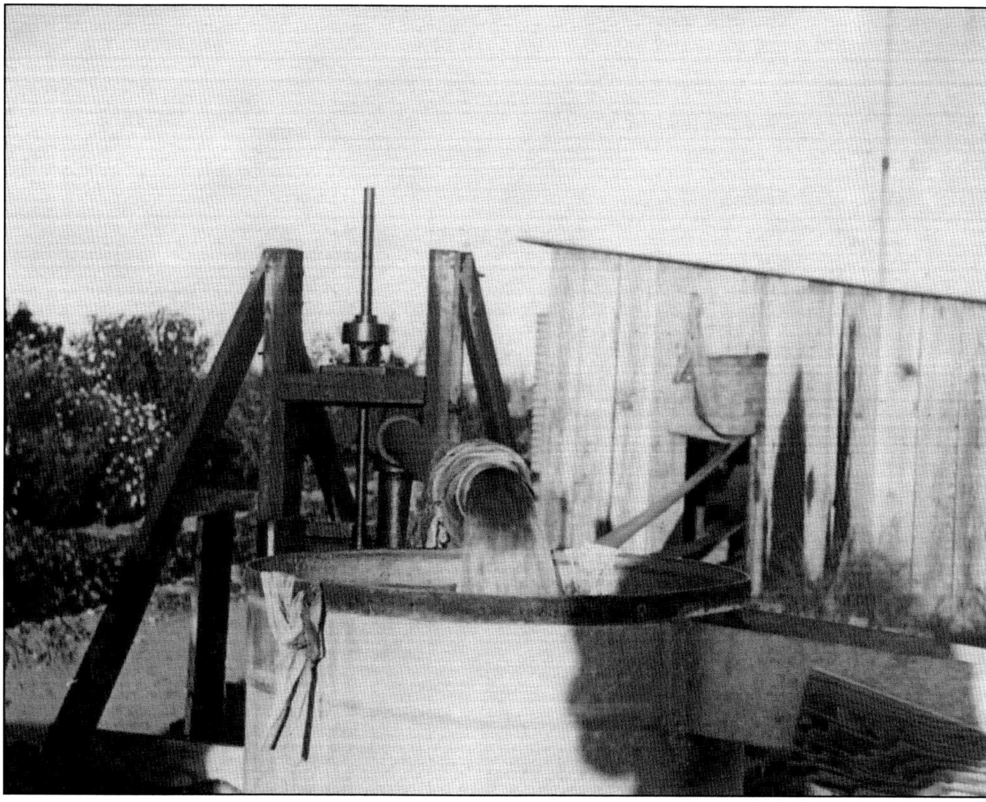

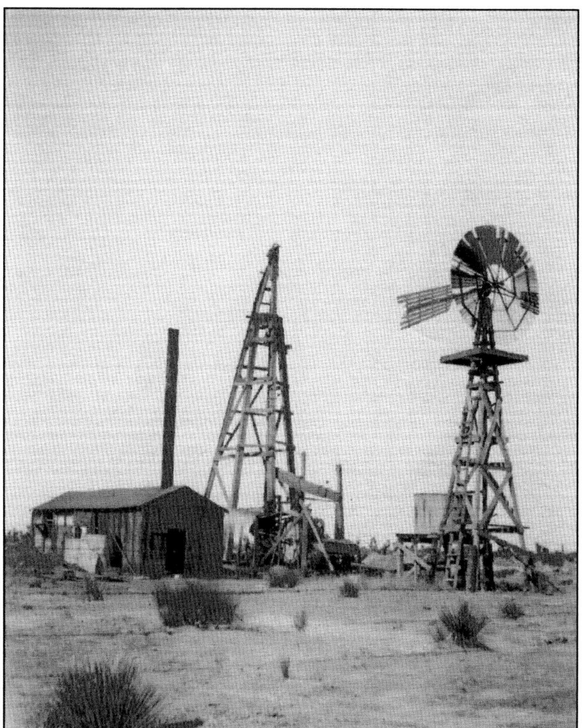

Water was the biggest asset to farming and ranching in the Mimbres Valley. There were many wells that contained large volumes of water around the county. Most water could be reached within 150 feet from the surface, according to the *1914 Hydrology Report* compiled by the US Geological Survey. The wells yielded 800 to 1,200 gallons of water per minute at that time. The water in Deming is 99.9-percent pure coming out of the ground. Many people moved to Deming just for that reason, and the purity was a key in the city's advertising.

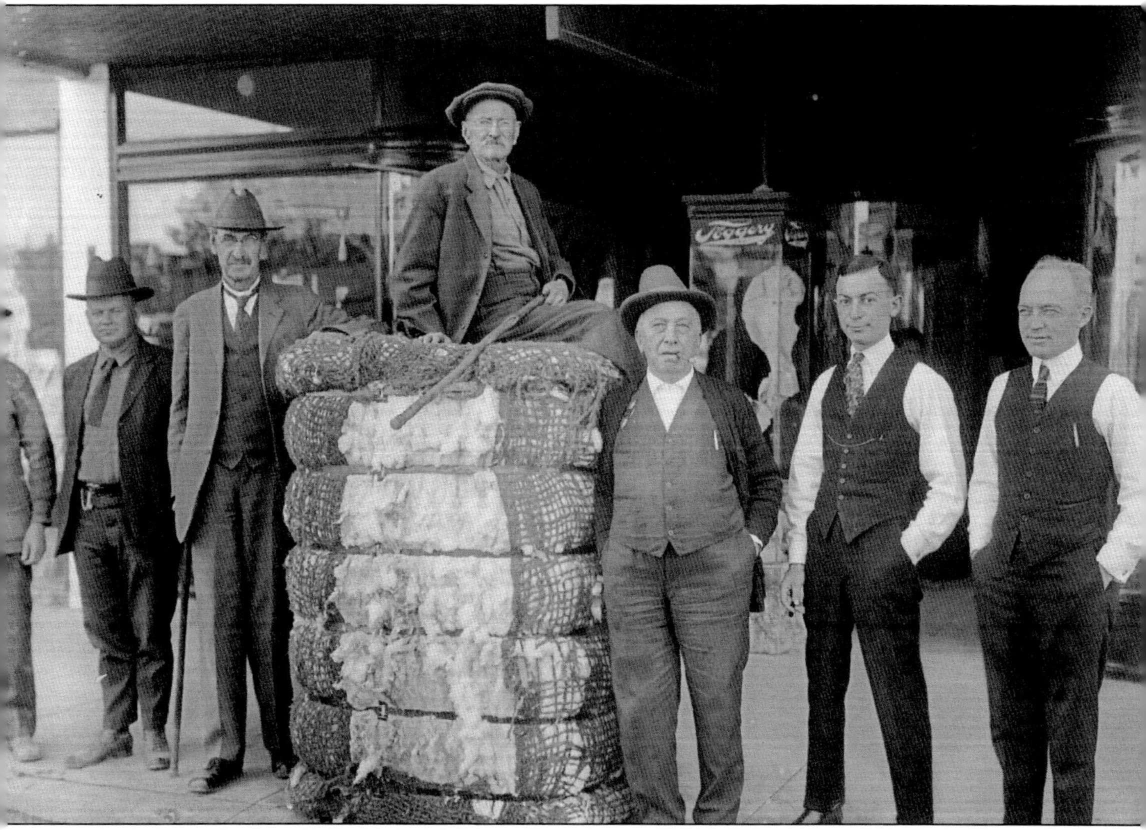

The first bale of cotton harvested and ginned in Luna County is displayed in front of the Toggery on Pine Street in October 1920. From left to right, two unidentified, Jim Tracy, unidentified, Sigmund Lindauer, Herman Lindauer, and Andrew J. Tidmore stand in front of the 500-pound bale. Tidmore and Herman Lindauer owned the Toggery and offered $250 in gold for the first bale of cotton raised and ginned in Luna County. The cotton used to create this bale was planted on May 3, 1920, and picked on September 23, 1920.

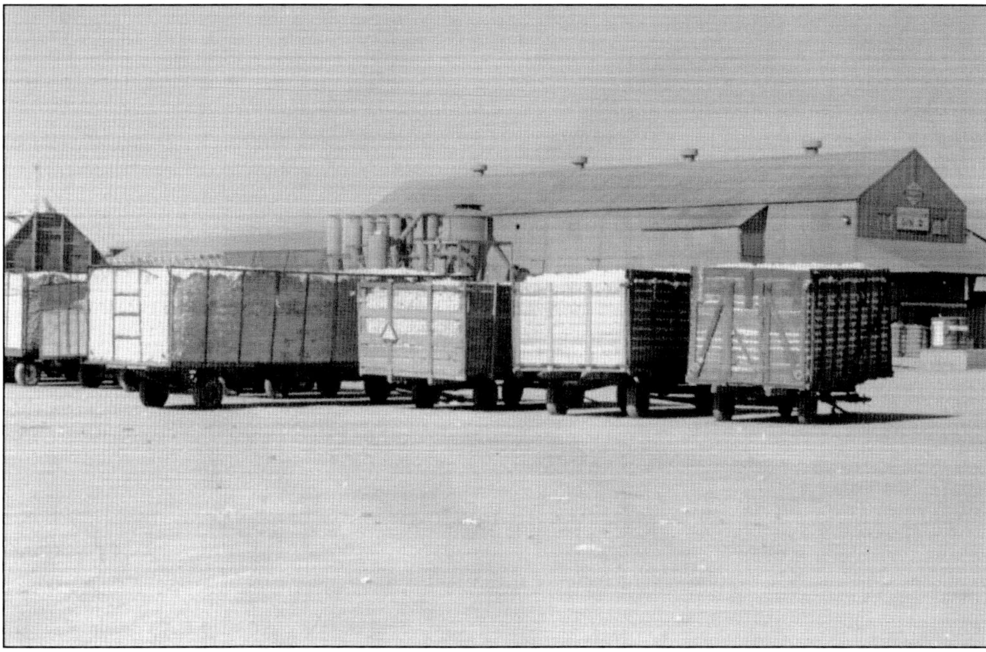

J.N. Williams, originally of Mesa, Arizona, moved to Deming once his cotton interests were bought up in Mesa. He began planting farms and, when finished, had about 3,000 acres of cotton, with the hope of harvesting one bale from each acre. Once he planted the field, he built a $20,000 cotton gin that was used until the 1990s. It was disassembled in 2011.

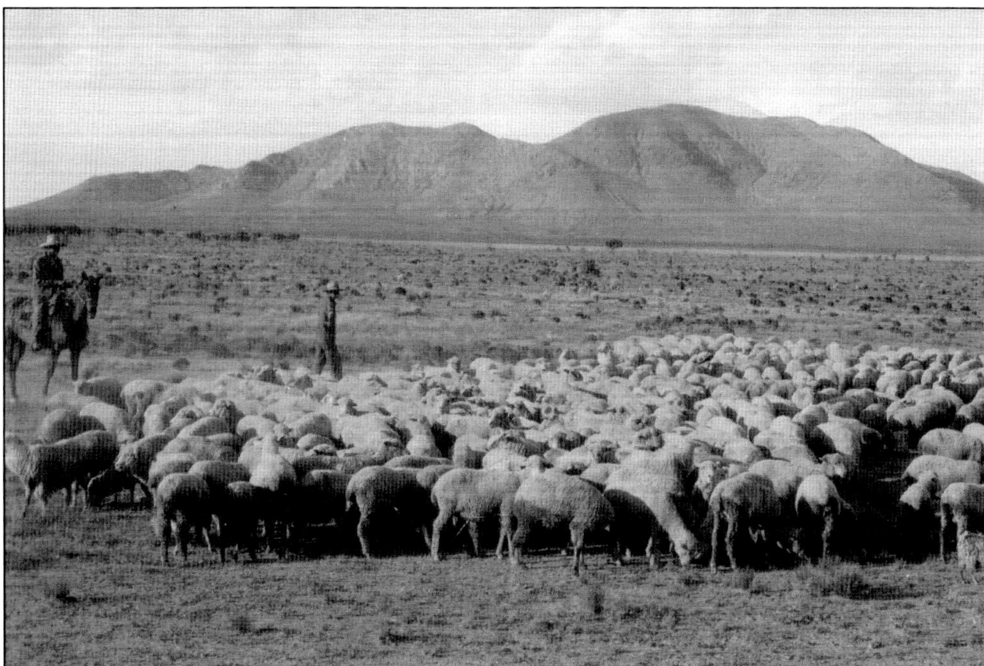

Dozens of sheep were raised on this farm outside of Deming. One man on a horse herds the sheep, while the other man on the ground assists. Sheep were popular livestock in early Deming, and ranchers raised large groups. Today, there are very few sheep raised in the county.

The First Annual Southwestern Irrigation Convention was held in Deming on November 7–8, 1893. This handmade banner welcomed guests from New Mexico, Arizona, West Texas, and Chihuahua as they discussed plans for promoting and extending the cultivation of lands through irrigation, how to protect the water supply from unlawful diversion, and methods for saving and utilizing surplus water.

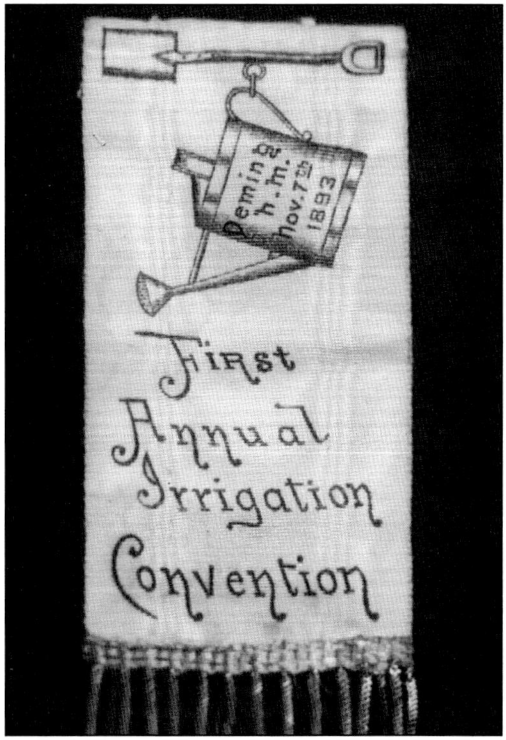

This is an experimental potato farm located outside of Deming. The unidentified man photographed holds up some potatoes to show their larger size. The Irish potatoes planted and harvested were considered to be of superior quality. A maximum yield of 400 bushels per acre was secured in the Mimbres Valley in the early 1900s.

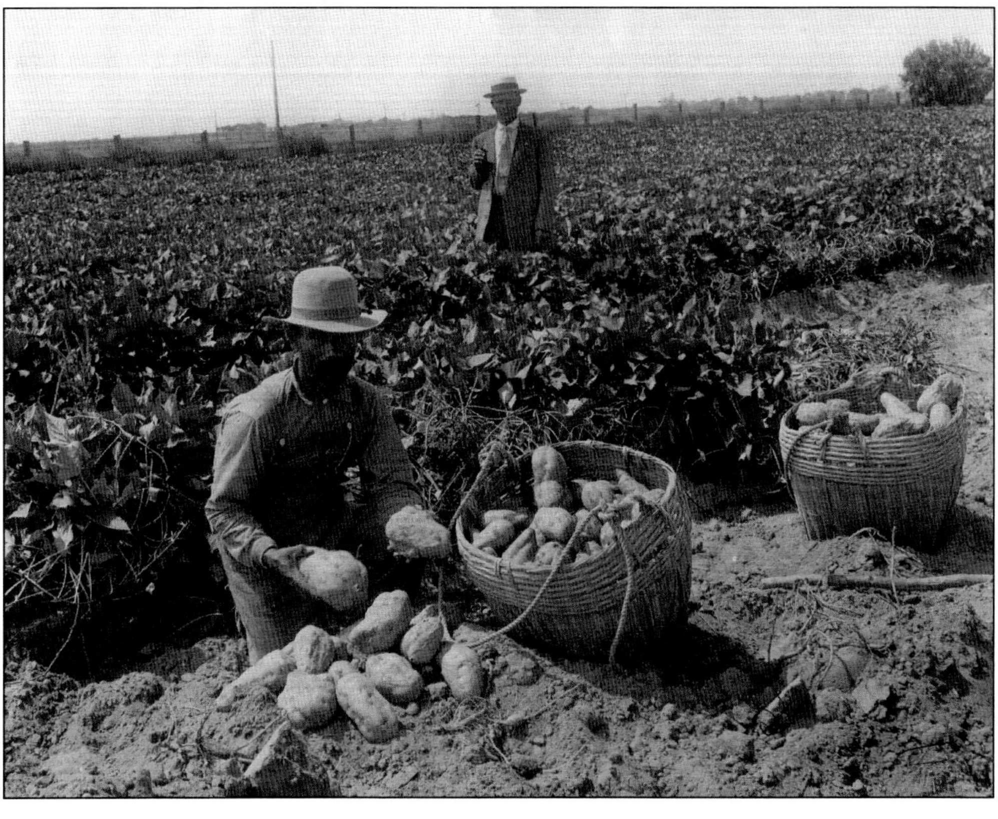

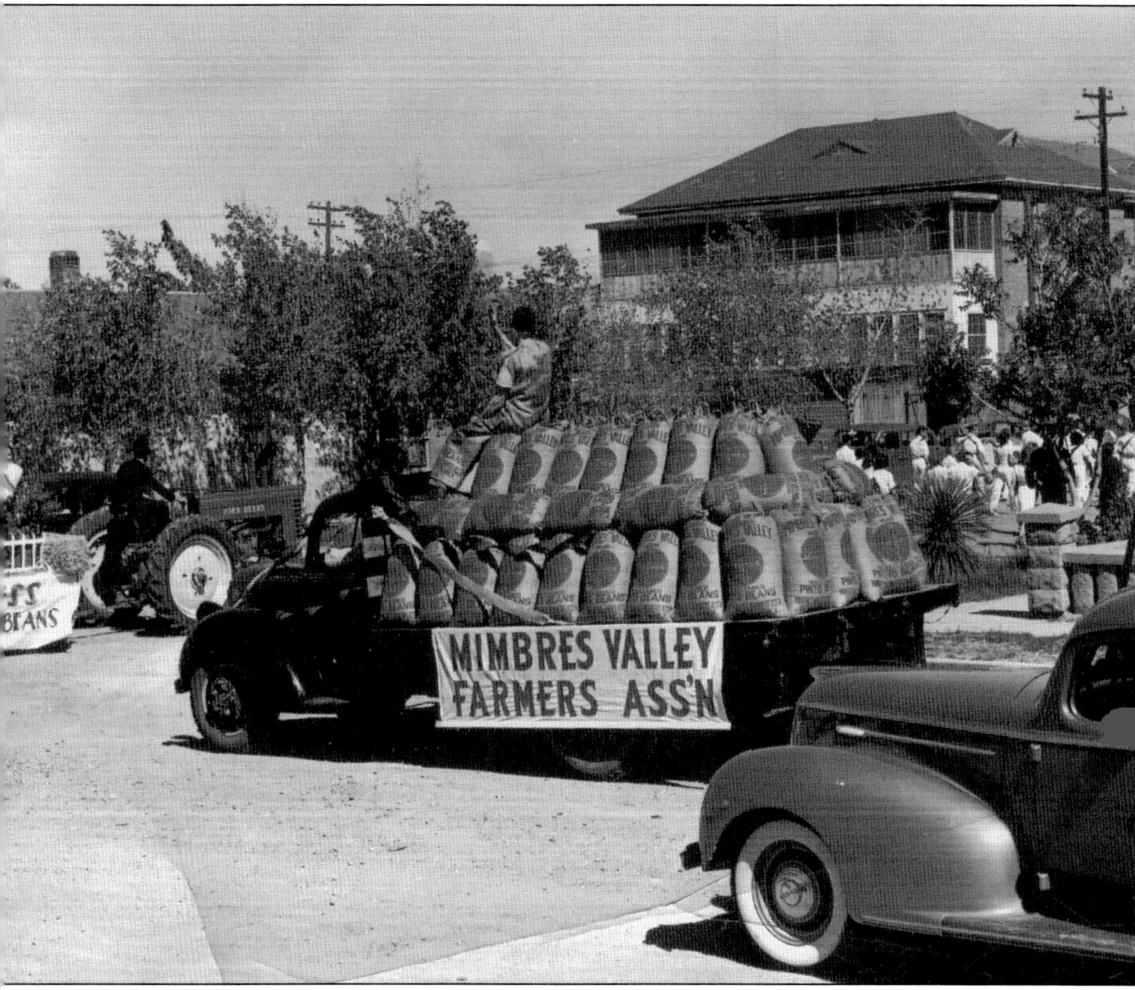

Bean crops were very successful in 1939. Over 50,000 sacks of pinto beans were raised in the Deming area and sold at about 5¢ per pound. These large bags of beans were grown as a part of the Mimbres Valley Farmers Association based in Luna County. The association began handling its first commodity, fuel oil, in the 1910s and drastically branched out over the years. The man waving at the top of the bean stack has an outfit made out of the same material as the 100-pound bean sacks featured on this float for a local parade.

C.W. Bud Lewis holds five tomatoes grown in the Mimbres Valley. He is standing inside a large packing shed for the processing and sale of tomatoes at the Mimbres Valley Cannery. A group of farmers organized the Mimbres Valley Cannery Association in 1955. Members would grow the tomatoes themselves and then process them at the cannery.

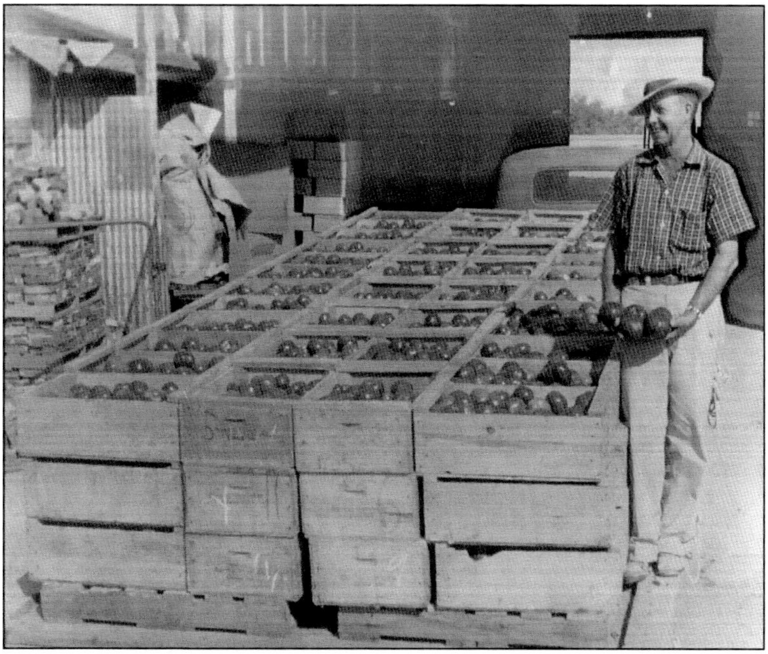

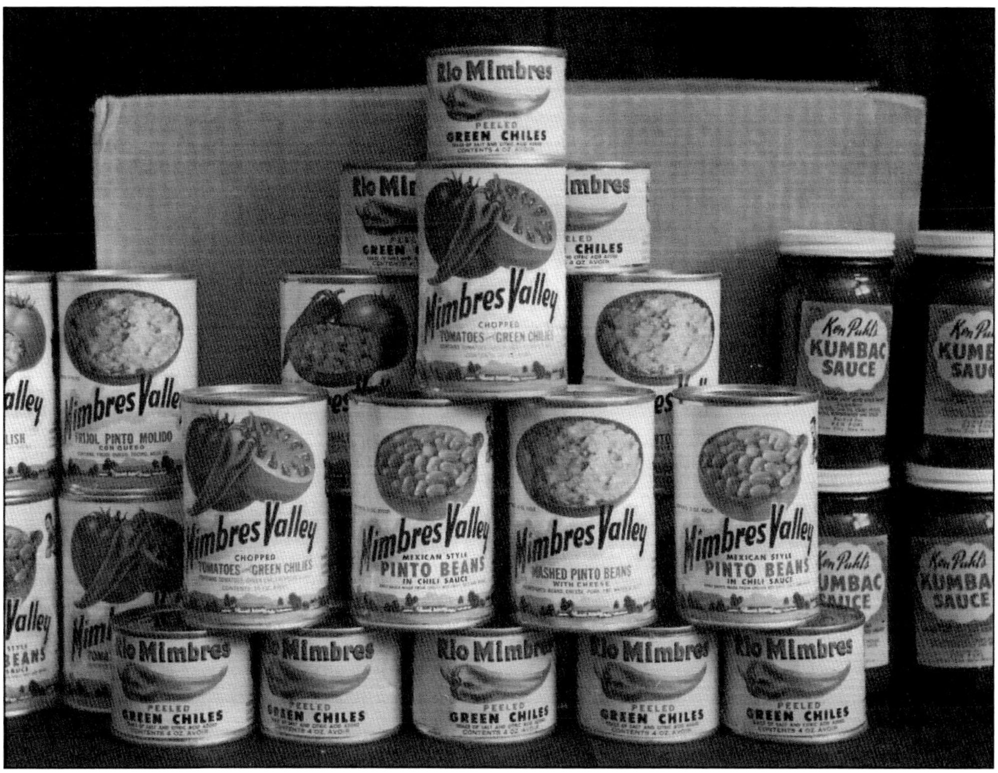

Deming and Silver City products compose a large display. Mimbres Valley and Rio Mimbres were both Deming brands, while Ken Puhl's Kumbac Sauce was packed by Ken Puhl in Silver City, New Mexico. Tomatoes, onions, celery, chilies, pickles, lemons, horseradish, and spices make up the eight fluid ounces contained in one jar.

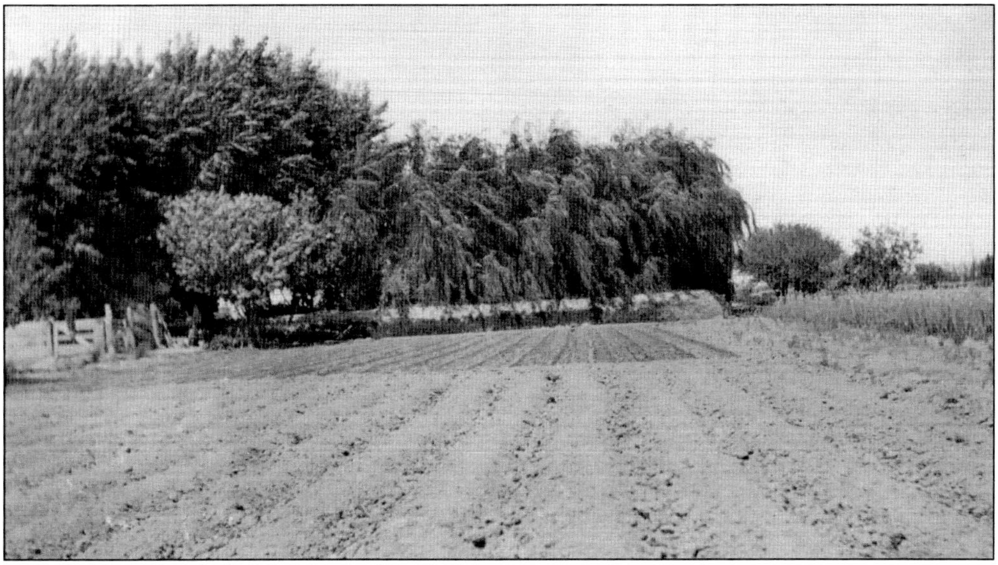

The Chinese Gardens, northeast of Deming, were operated by the Wah family (above). The Wah brothers farmed 22 acres in 1911 and made about $6,000 from their crops. At that time, they were growing asparagus, celery, cabbage, cauliflower, dry onions, sweet potatoes, Irish potatoes, peaches, pears, plums, apricots, grapes, watermelon, and nectarines. Most of the produce was marketed in Deming, Lordsburg, and Silver City, New Mexico, and in Morenci and Clifton, Arizona. Friends gather at Chinese Gardens to eat watermelon (below). From left to right are Leah Barracks, Bill Collins, Eula Holstein, Paul Major, Ruth Measday, Dollie Layne, and Arthur J. Huxtable.

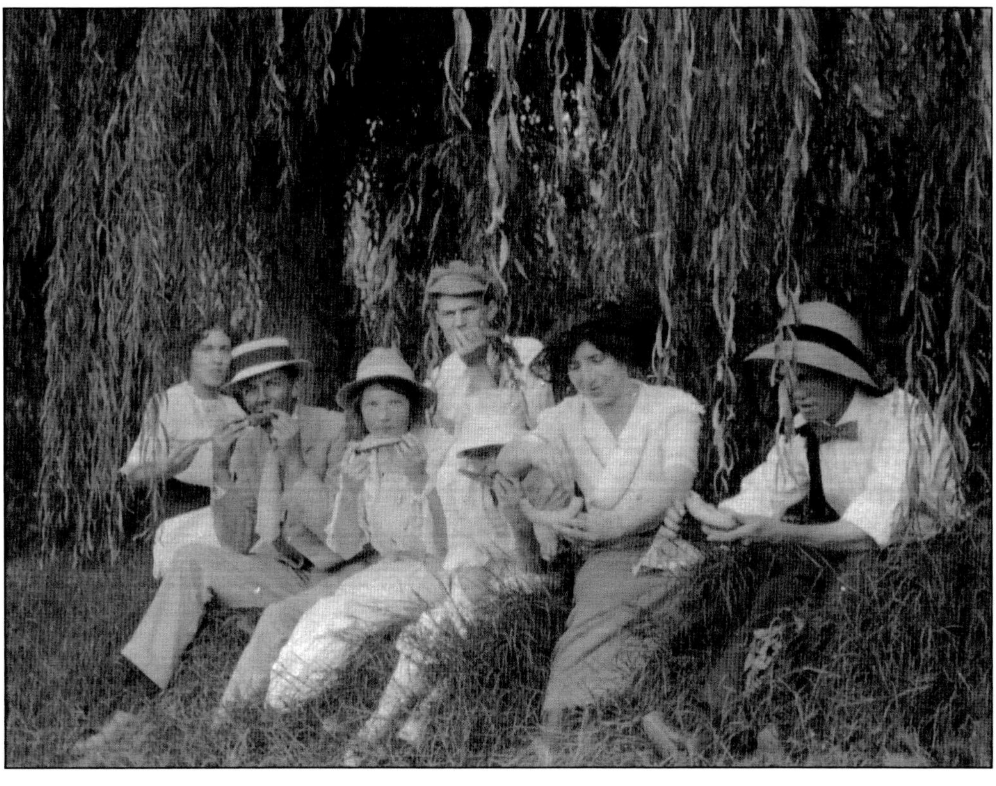

Five

Early Churches in Deming

Deming's establishment in the American West was much like that of any other town. First, lawlessness—including gun shooting, excessive alcohol consumption, and prostitution—was in order. For many men getting off the train at Deming, their first task was to buy a gun—or at least the locals told new arrivals to do such. Many of the men had never shot a gun before, but they had one, just in case.

After an initial period of disorder, foundational businesses and establishments were created. The first church building was erected in 1883, and many other churches followed. At first, there were not many choices as far as denomination. World War I helped out the church community in this way. Since Deming was bombarded with a large number of soldiers, many of the churches were overcrowded and held services at the Luna County Courthouse, gyms, and parks. Other churches built larger buildings to hold the attendees.

It is common to see church fundraisers throughout the community at various times; they help pay for mission trips and campaigns for the needy, along with other expenses. One of the largest church fundraisers is that of Holy Family Catholic Church. The church needed to pay the priest's salary, property maintenance, and fuel bills, among other things. Since the church had a large population of Czechoslovakians, organizers thought that having a festival would raise the funds needed to support the church. The first Klobase Festival, as it has been known for many years, was held in 1929.

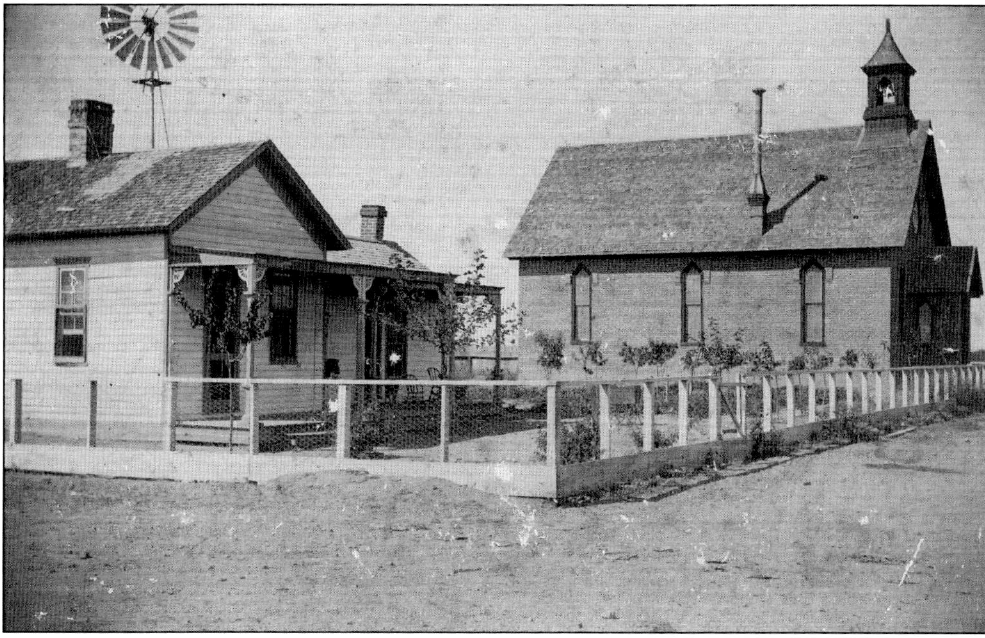

The first brick building in Deming, the Methodist Episcopal church (right) was located on the corner of Iron and Hemlock Streets (above). The church was built in 1883, mostly by Rev. P.L. Stanton, the first preacher in Deming, and money was raised by the board of extension. The congregation met in the schoolhouse until the church was constructed. Reverend Stanton put a baking powder can under the floor of the church with a note that read: "Isaac Sollers and Rev. P.L. Stanton finished laying this floor October 11, 1883." There were 15 church members the first year. The Methodist Episcopal church maintained a Spanish mission that had 20 members in 1903 (below).

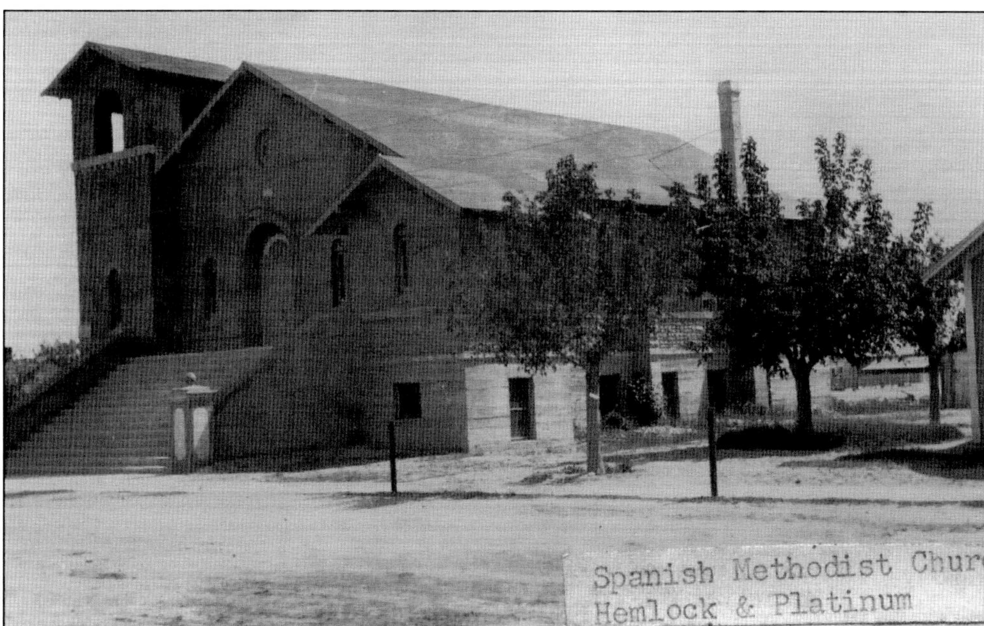

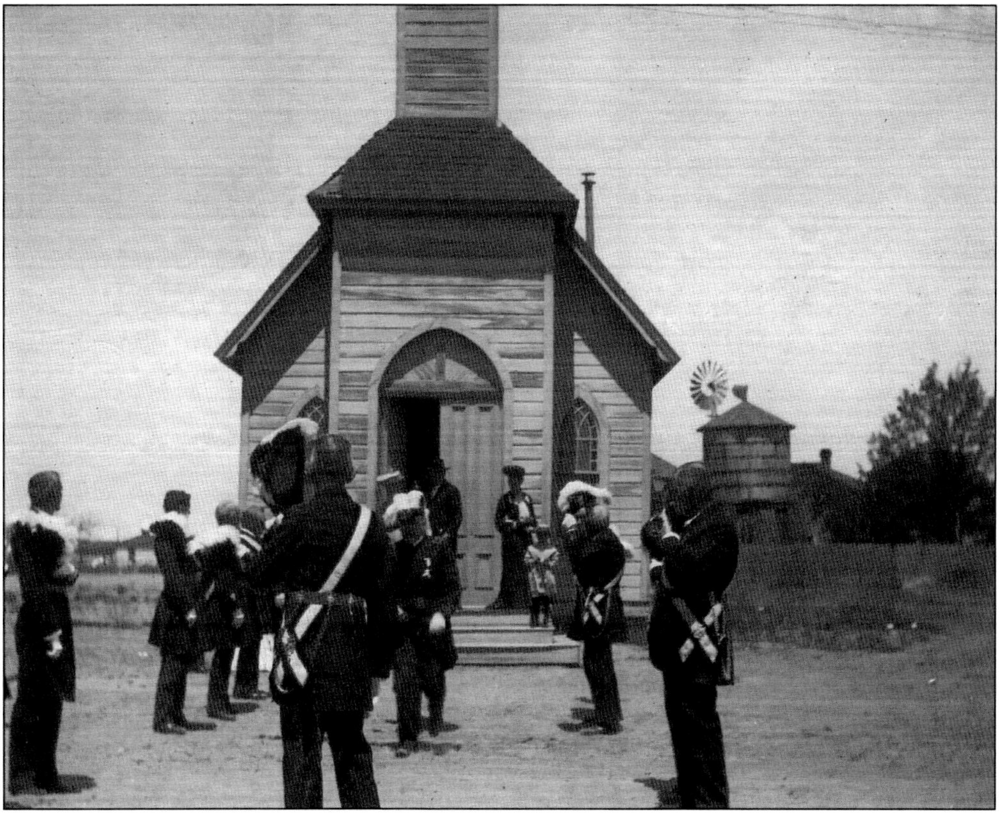

The Episcopal church, known today as St. Luke's, was erected in the summer of 1890 on the corner of Spruce and Tin Streets and was consecrated by Bishop Kendrick on December 20, 1890. The lots were given as a donation by the Atchison, Topeka & Santa Fe Railway under the condition that they be used for a church. Services were held regularly from 1884 to 1886 in a mission. This photograph was taken of St. Luke's during the time Camp Cody was established in 1917 (above). It is believed that Charlotte Thurmond, a former Texas gambler, made or donated an altar for the church. Some even think she might have held a poker game to pay for the altar (below).

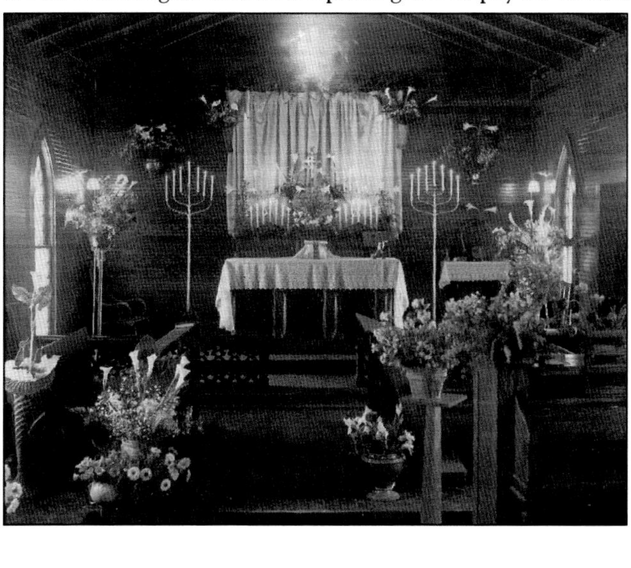

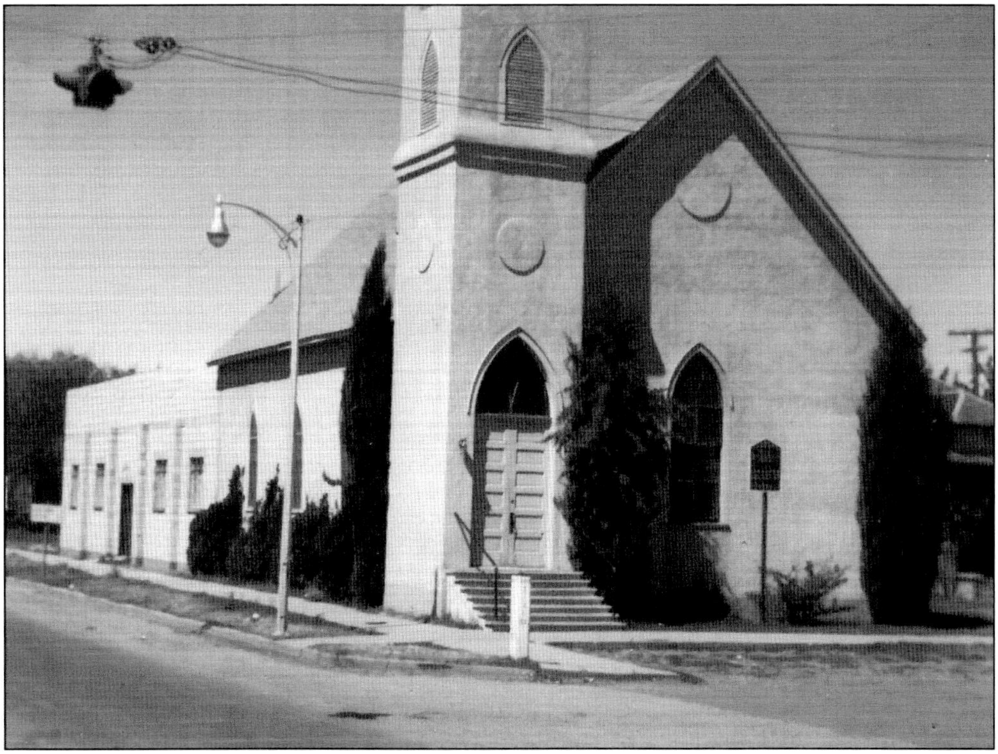

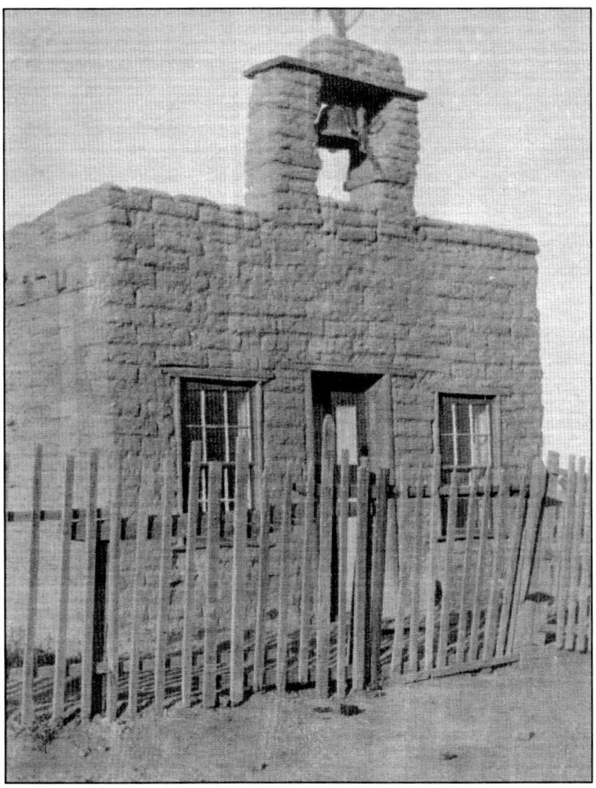

The First Presbyterian Church was organized in 1898 with 27 members. The original church building was constructed in 1900 on the corner of Spruce and Zinc Streets. Many times throughout the latter decades, the church contemplated erecting a new building. Finally, in 1949, this church building was erected, and it is still in use today.

Santo de Nino was a small adobe building located north of the railroad tracks in Deming. It served as the first Catholic church in Deming. Bonifacio Gonzales owned the structure that was built in 1900. It was known to many at the time and was labeled on old postcards as the "Mexican Church."

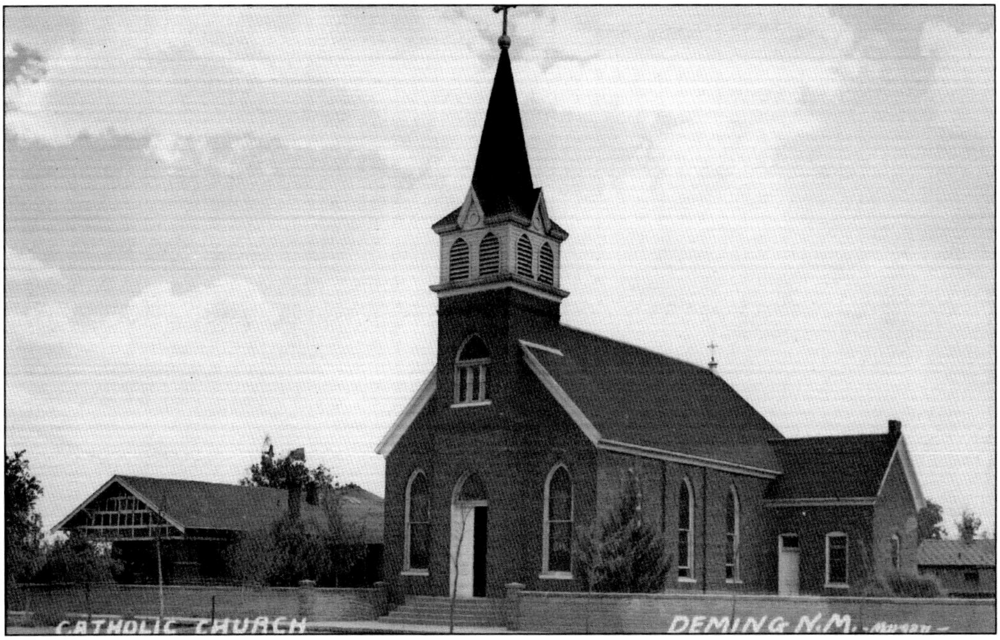

Holy Family Catholic Church was built in 1905 at 600 South Copper Street, but the tradition of mass was said for many years prior. The first mass held in Deming was in the home of Anthony J. Clark with Rev. Peter Bourgade of Silver City, New Mexico, presiding. Subscriptions to raise money for a church building began in 1901 and resulted in the church being constructed in 1905 for $7,000.

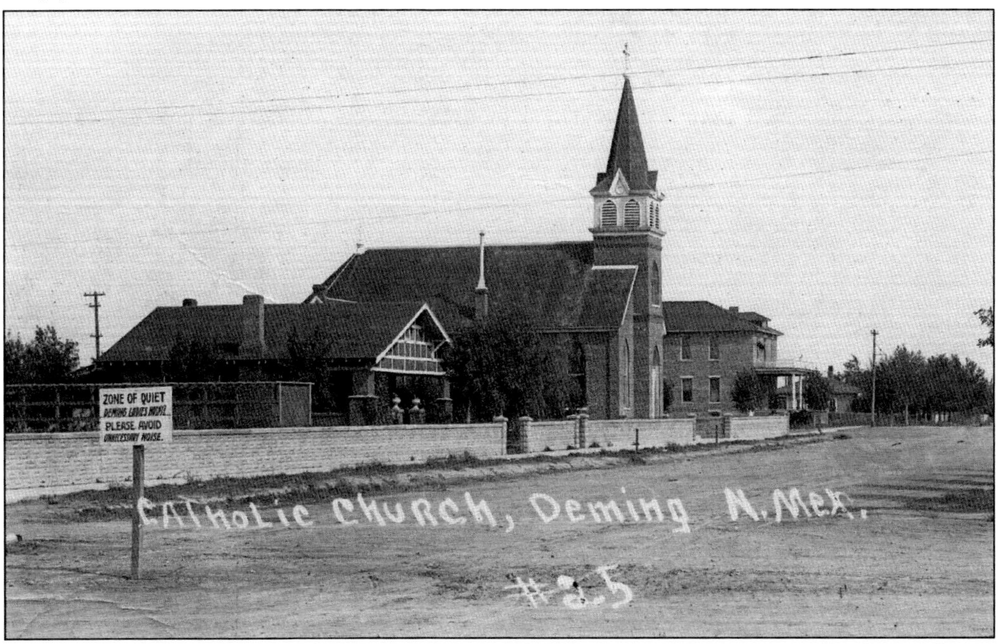

The Holy Family Catholic Church's rectory was built in 1914. The contract for the work was awarded to Edward F. Moran for $1,887.40. During the creation of the building, at least 34 wagons of sand were hauled from the Mimbres River north of Deming. Over 40 men volunteered their time to build the church "gratis pro Deo."

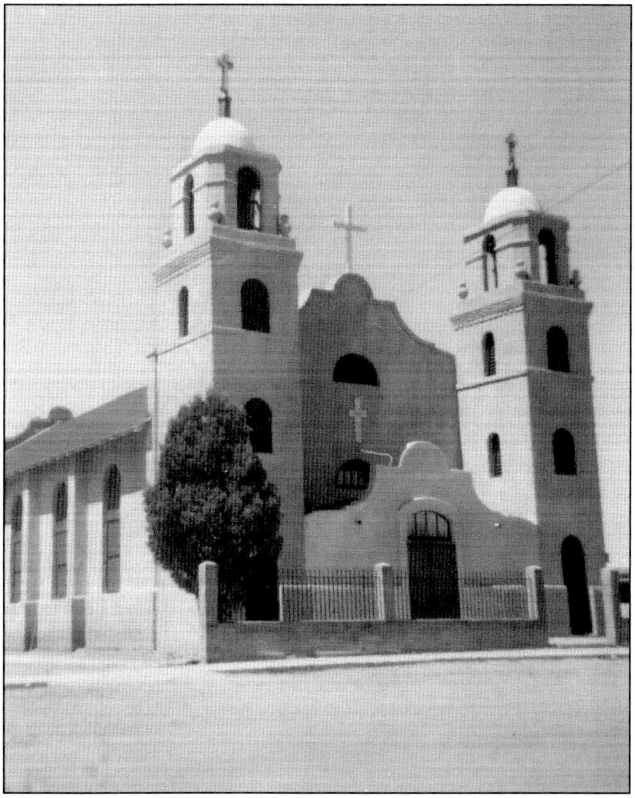

St. Ann Catholic Church was dedicated on Thanksgiving Day, November 28, 1918. Rev. Joseph Carnet of Holy Family Catholic Church felt that there was a need to build a church on the east side of Deming that would cater to the Spanish-speaking population and relieve the overcrowding at Holy Family. The structure cost $15,000, and the lots for the church were purchased for $900.

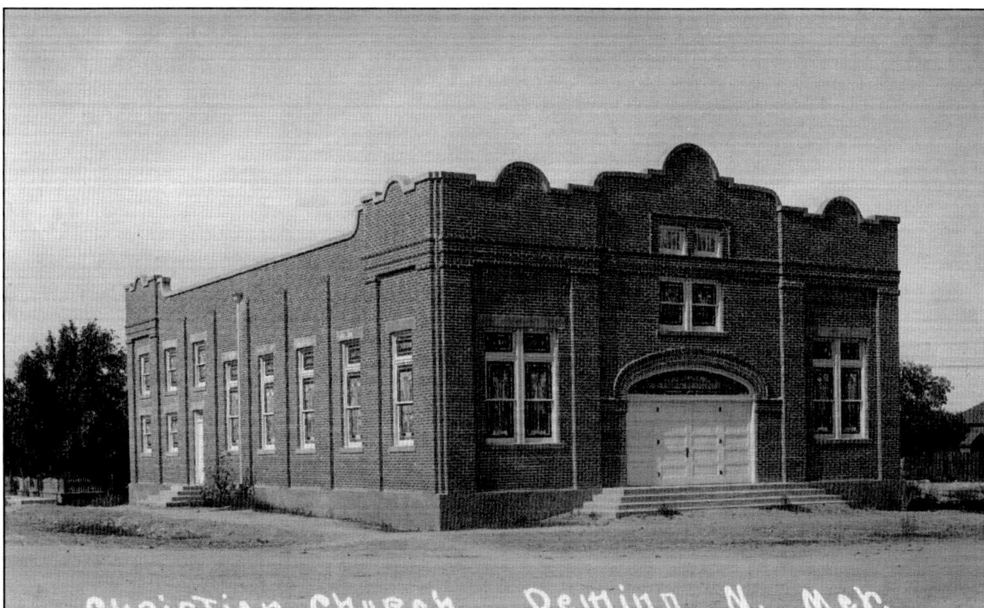

The Maple Street Church of Christ was located at 119 West Maple Street from 1921 to 1923. The building was erected in 1918 and was home to the Christian church. Ten years prior, the church met in the old city hall building and then in a basement at Platinum and Hemlock Streets. Today, the First Christian Church occupies this building.

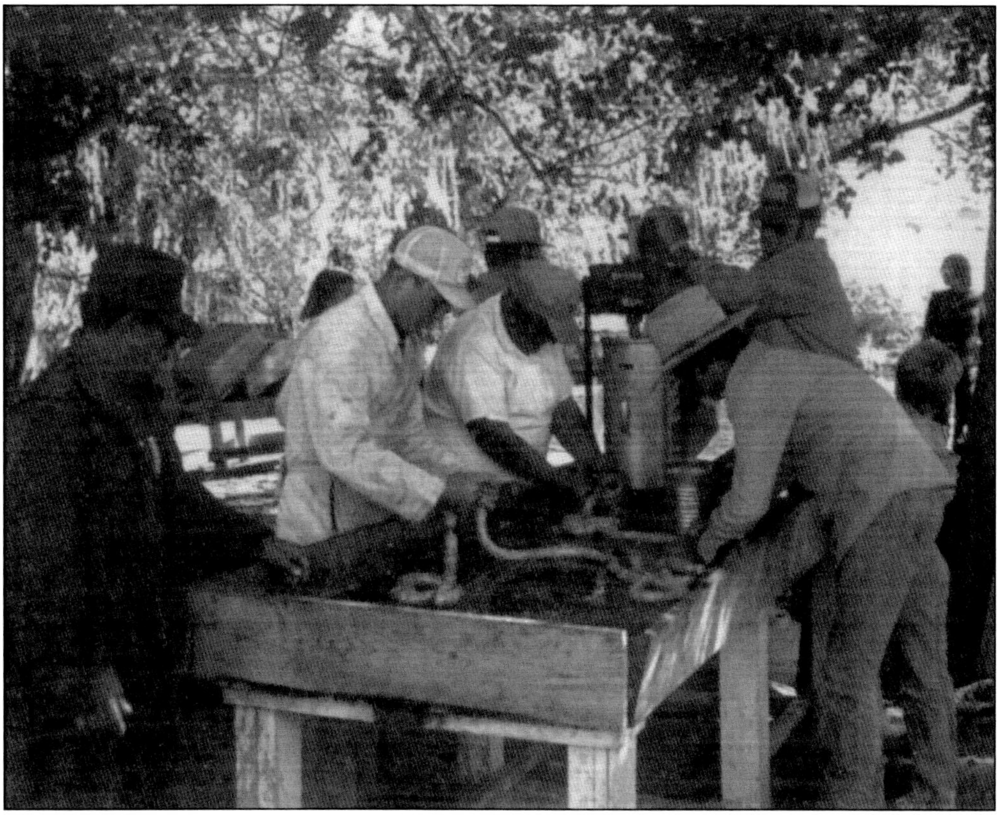

Men from Holy Family Catholic Church cut the meat for the *klobase* sausages on the third Saturday of October. The Holy Family Catholic Church members as well as other volunteers prepare a large meal for their annual fundraiser. The Klobase Festival has assisted the parish in building the new church, rectory, chapel, classrooms, and meeting hall. (Courtesy of Holy Family Church.)

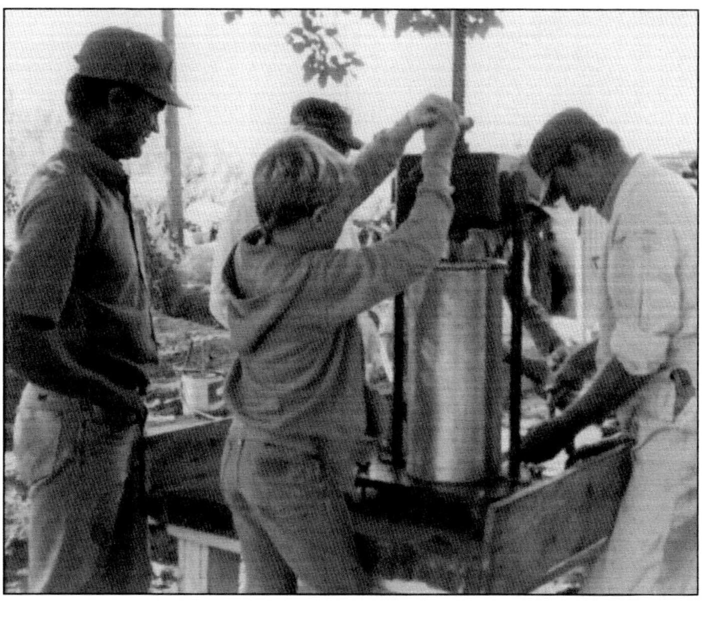

Frank Hervol (left) watches his son (center) crank the sausage press making the klobase sausages as Edward Remondini Jr. fills the casings with meat. Thousands of authentic Czechoslovakian sausages are prepared yearly for the festival to the delight of the Deming crowd. Some Czechoslovakian families in Deming have family reunions that coincide with the festival, inviting many out-of-town guests. (Courtesy of Holy Family Church.)

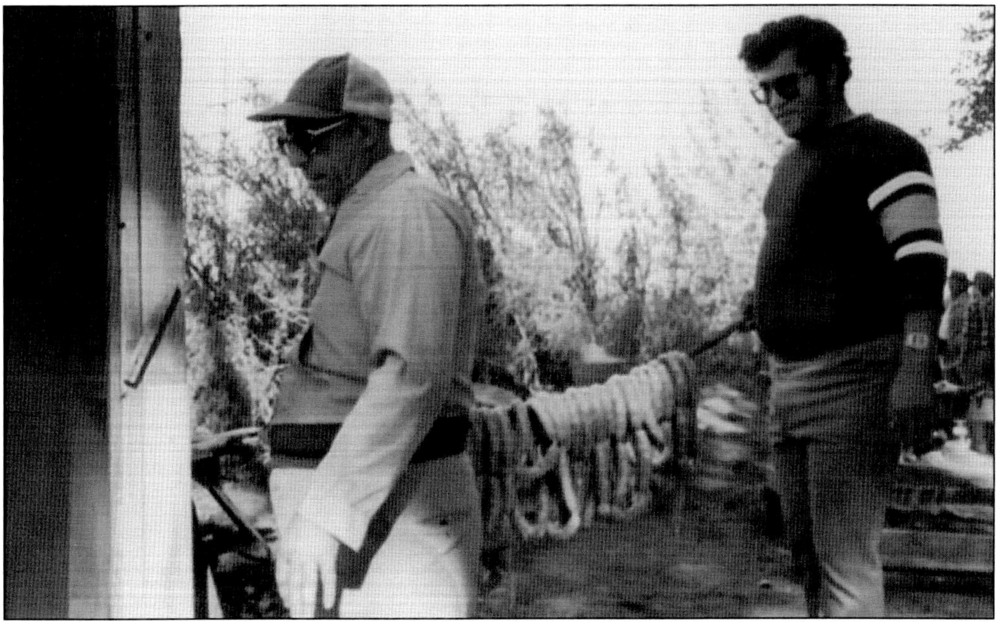

Men carry traditional klobase sausages into the smoking shed on the third Saturday in October for overnight cooking in anticipation of the Sunday festival. The sausages are smoked using mesquite wood. The men keep the fire going all night. The beef was originally cooked in a pit overnight and basted every hour. Today, the beef is barbecued in steel cookers. (Courtesy of Holy Family Church.)

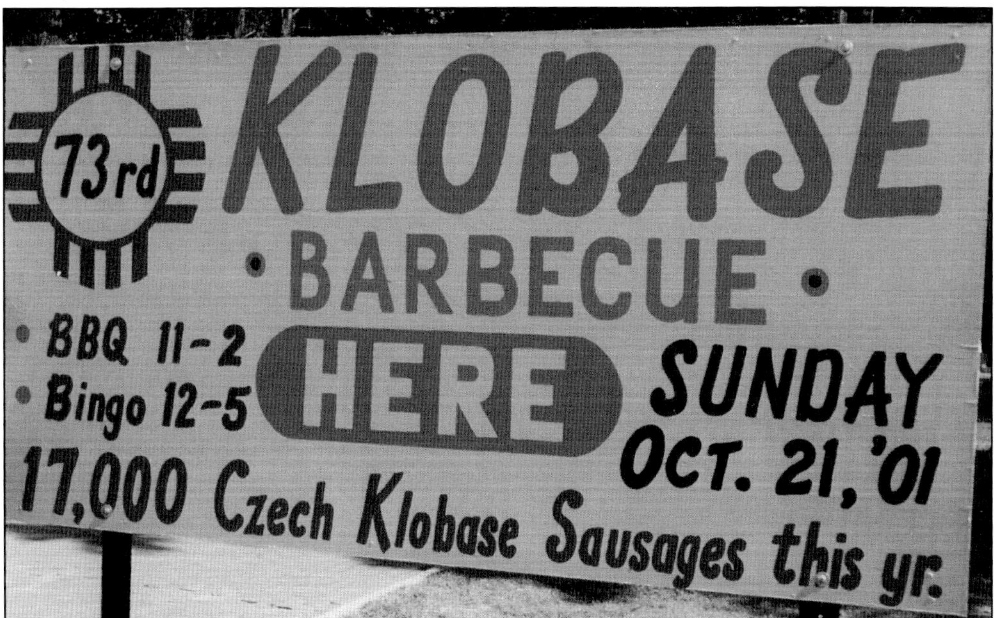

The large fundraiser for Holy Family Catholic Church sells over 2,500 plates of food annually on the third Sunday in October. The Klobase plate features two traditional sausages, slices of tender beef, creamy potato salad, homemade coleslaw, and local pinto beans. The plate is garnished with sliced tomatoes, sliced raw onions, barbecue sauce, and salsa.

Six

Mexican Revolution and World War I

The rise of the Mexican Revolution created problems not just for Mexico but also for the United States. Many Mexican leaders were rising in power, and the United States became concerned with a looming threat that the Army would need to intervene in Mexico. Eventually, the United States' fear became a reality when Francisco Pancho Villa ordered an attack on Columbus, New Mexico, 25 miles south of Deming. Villa had nearly 500 villistas, or Villa followers, including the *soldaderas*, or women warriors. Many of the "followers" were forced.

While a large part of the town was destroyed by fire, 17 Americans were shot and killed by the villistas. Pres. Woodrow Wilson ordered Gen. John J. Pershing to lead an expedition into Mexico in search of Villa. Men from across the country enlisted and were called upon to do border service. Deming played a vital role in hosting a camp for the soldiers. Camp Deming housed 500 men in 1916. As the hunt for Villa faded, a larger problem was being contemplated by the US government: entry into the Great War in Europe.

The United States declared war on Germany on April 6, 1917, and only had about 200,000 trained men. The War Department made an immediate decision to construct training camps throughout the United States to increase American forces. Within a few months, 16 National Army cantonments and 16 National Guard encampments were built throughout the United States.

Deming was shocked on June 15, 1917, when word was received that it would soon be home to a National Guard training camp that cost $2.5 million. Twenty-eight thousand soldiers were trained at Camp Cody, which occupied the same land as the previous camp. Deming's population was a little over 3,000 people prior to the announcement of the camp. Within a few months, the population soared to over 35,000 people, including the soldiers. This made Deming the largest city in the state of New Mexico at the time.

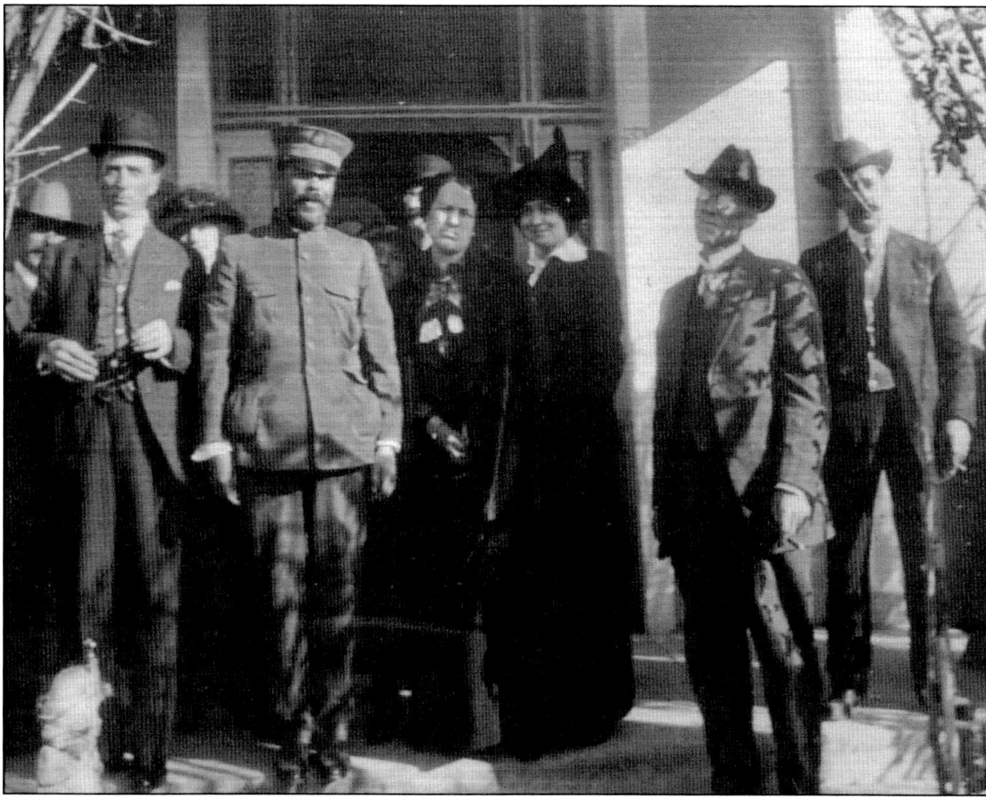

Francisco Pancho Villa poses with his wife. Willard E. Holt, editor and publisher of the *Deming Graphic*, is shown with glasses (right). During the time of this photograph, Villa was rising in power in Mexico. Villa and Venustiano Carranza were both offered support by the United States to become copresidents of Mexico, but the US only recognized Carranza in the end.

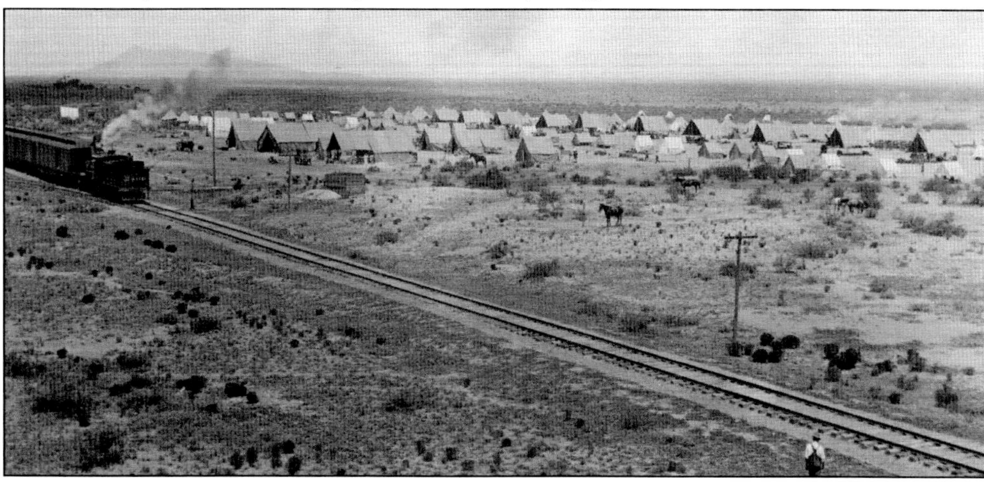

Camp Brookes was established in Deming, New Mexico, from July 11 to 21, 1914, in the event an armed intervention needed to occur in Mexico against Pancho Villa. It was a joint maneuver between the New Mexico National Guard and the US Army from Fort Bliss at El Paso, Texas. The National Guard normally held its summer camp in Las Vegas, New Mexico, but changed the location due to the threat.

This scaffolding was located at the old jail on Platinum Avenue and Spruce Street. This would be used to hang men involved in the Villa Raid. Out of the 17 men captured, six men in total were hanged in Deming. Rev. Joseph Carnet of Holy Family Catholic Church offered spiritual support for the men, who admitted to him they were willing to die for Villa.

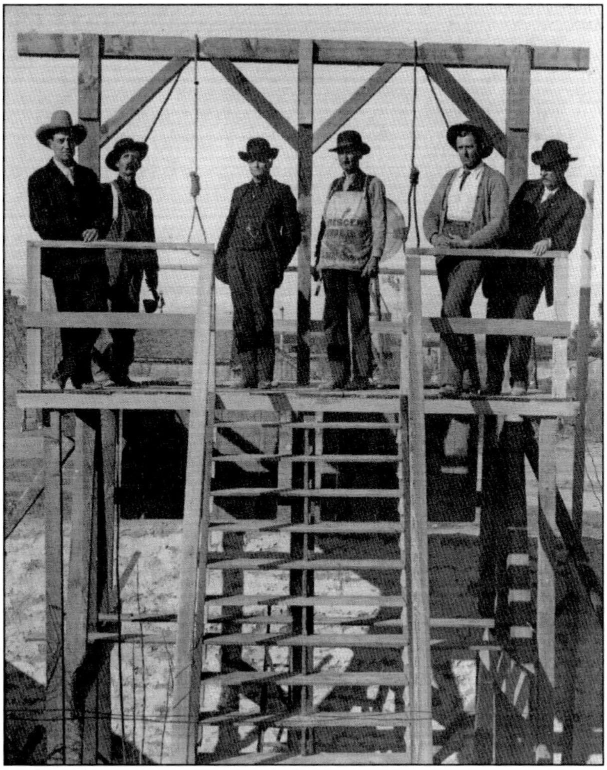

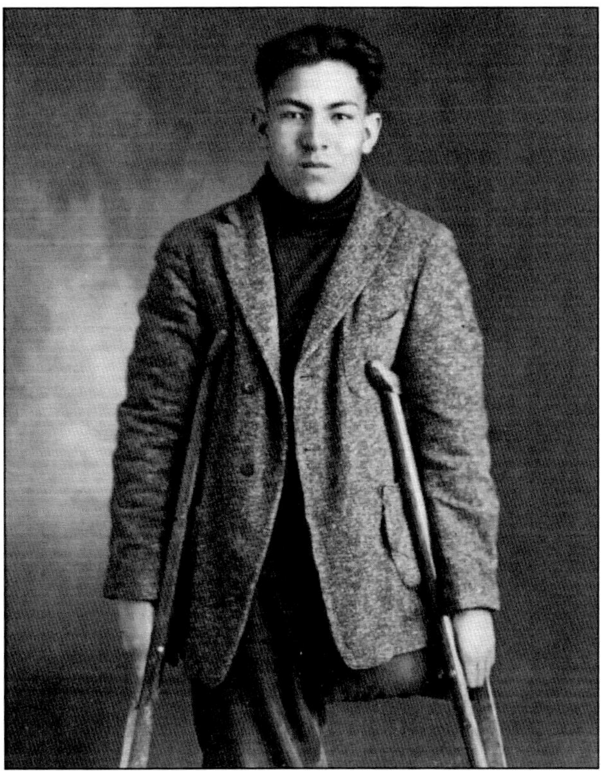

Jesus Paez was a 12-year-old boy captured during the Columbus Raid. He suffered a gunshot wound to the leg, which had to be amputated. He was held in Deming, New Mexico, at the Deming Ladies' Hospital, where he received treatment. He was sentenced to hanging in Luna County but was saved by Henry Meyer's wife.

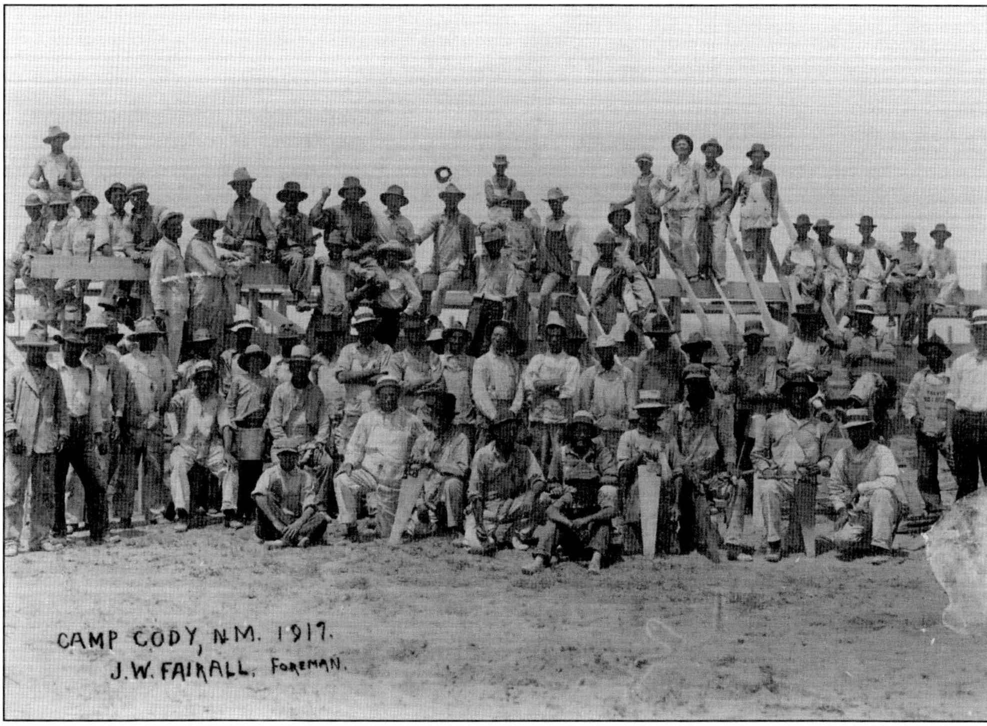

Many construction workers erected the camp (above) in less than one month in July 1917. First, they built structures in which they slept since there was not enough housing in Deming for all of them (below). The majority of the workers came from El Paso, Texas, since hiring the few dozen workers who resided in Deming expended the labor force. Work went quickly as the troops began coming in August. The enlisted soldiers primarily came from Minnesota, Iowa, North Dakota, South Dakota, and Nebraska. They came in sleeper cars by rail. This was the first time many of the young recruits left their home states.

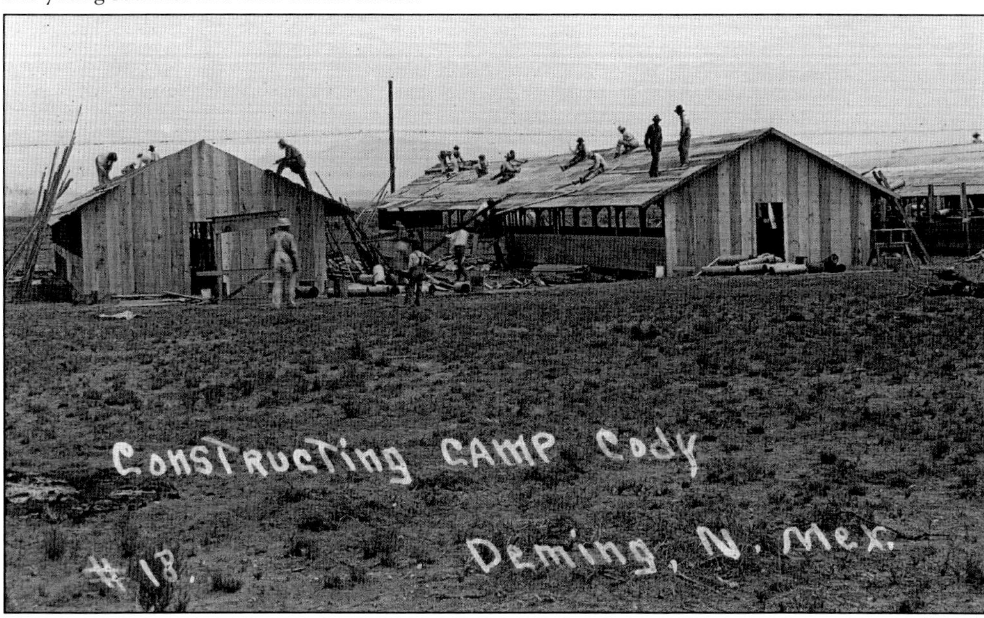

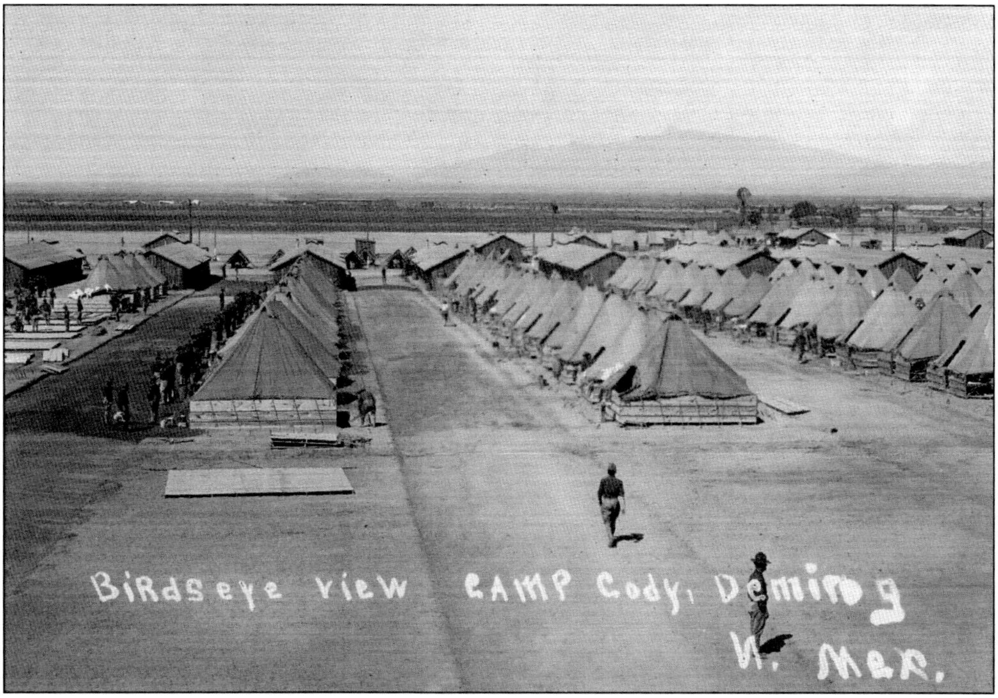

Enlisted men at Camp Cody slept eight to a tent. All of the training camps in the War Department's Southern Department had men sleeping in tents because of the milder climate. Over 1,200 wooden buildings were erected, as seen in the photographs. In both views, the wooden structures can be seen near the top of the photographs. The lumber needed for the camp was tremendous. By the time the camp was announced, the government had secured all of the lumber in Deming and the surrounding area. Camp Furlong, a military camp near Columbus, New Mexico, 25 miles south of Deming, provided 364,372 board feet of lumber. Fort Bliss, at El Paso, Texas, provided 1,827,750 board feet of lumber. About 16 million board feet of lumber was needed to complete the camp.

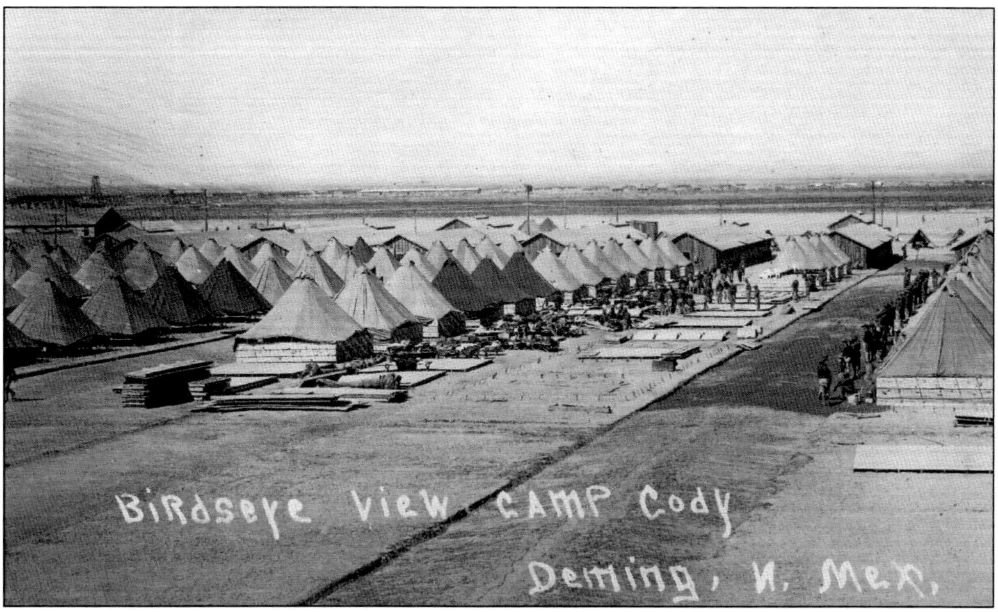

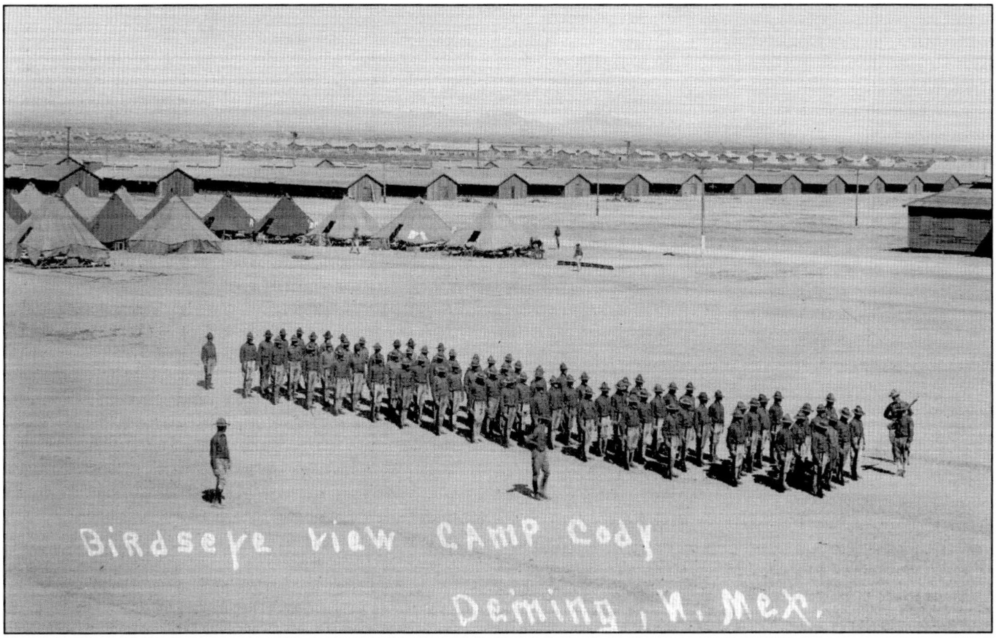

Troops also marched in formation at Camp Cody and were often held under inspection by their leaders. They also held inspections when outside visitors, including congressmen, went to the camp. There was great concern from many of these political leaders about weather conditions at the camp, including tremendous sandstorms and any cold weather, since the soldiers slept in tents.

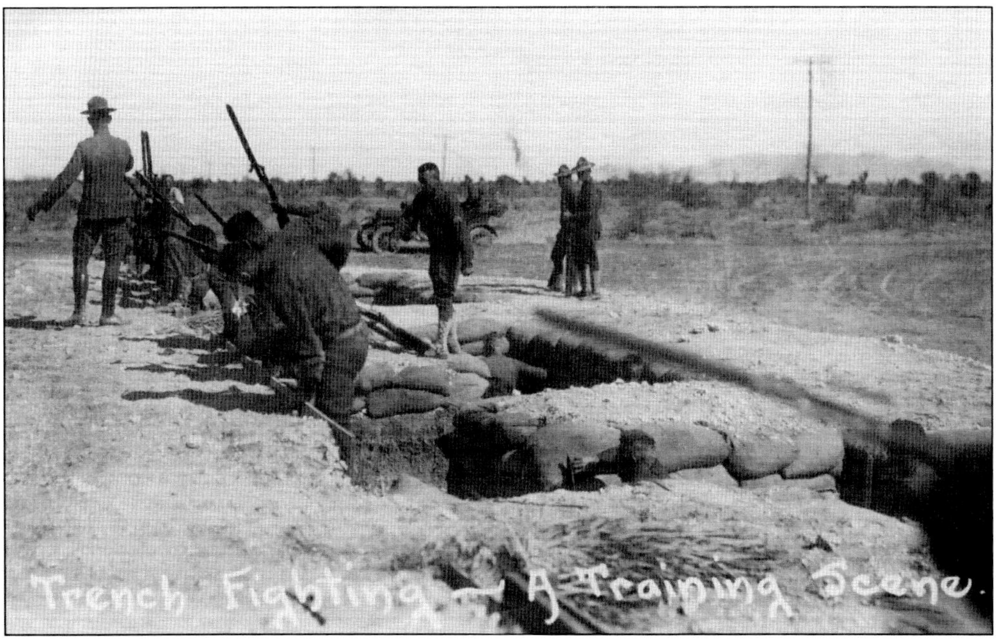

Troops trained in trenches in preparation for the Great War. Trenches were created so that soldiers opposed each other along a front. The trenches were protected from assault by barbed wire. The area between the opposing trench lines was fully exposed to fire from both sides. The troops at Camp Cody regularly practiced maneuvers.

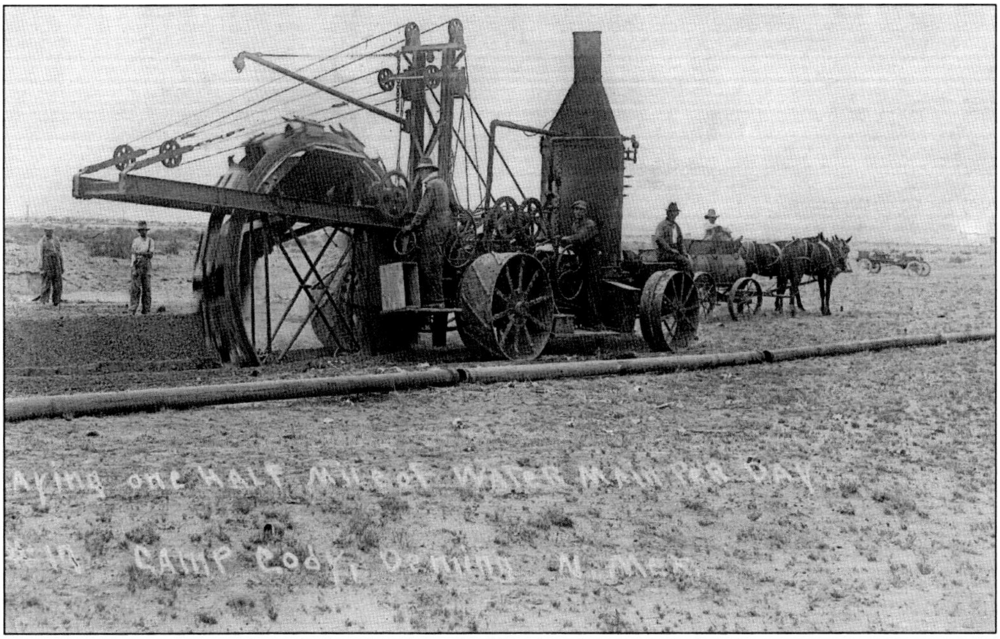

This large ditching machine helped lay one-half mile of pipe each day for the water to be carried throughout the vast camp. There was at least eight miles of water main throughout the camp at its establishment. An additional water main was laid in 1918 when the sewer system was replaced.

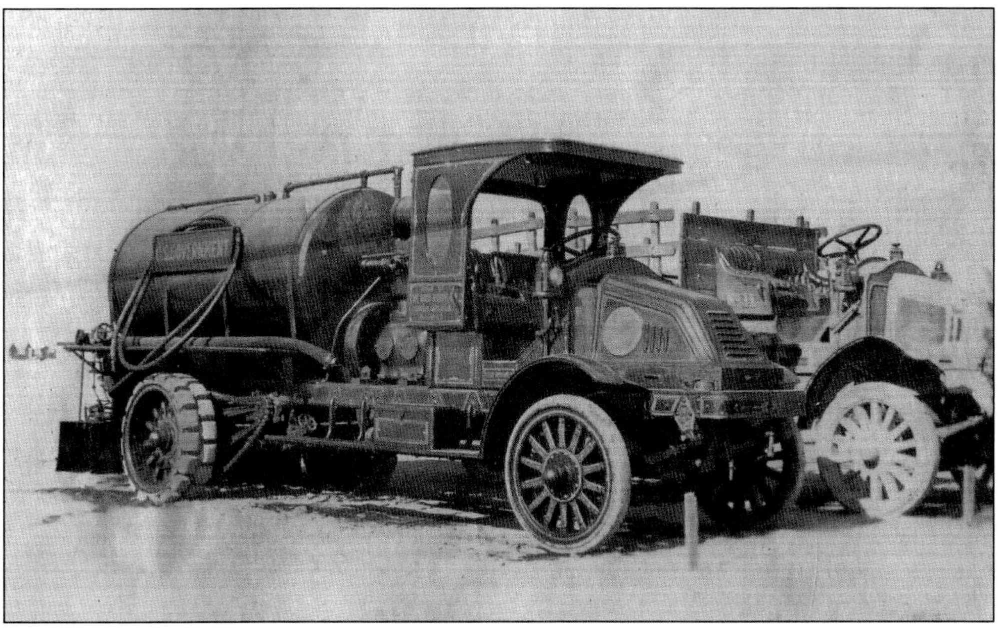

US government water trucks at Camp Cody were used to suppress the constant sandstorms that troubled the enlisted men from the Midwest. This water truck was manufactured by the Good Roads Company of Kansas City. The sandstorms were so unbearable that the American Red Cross collected money from the Midwestern states and purchased goggles for the men to wear during the dust.

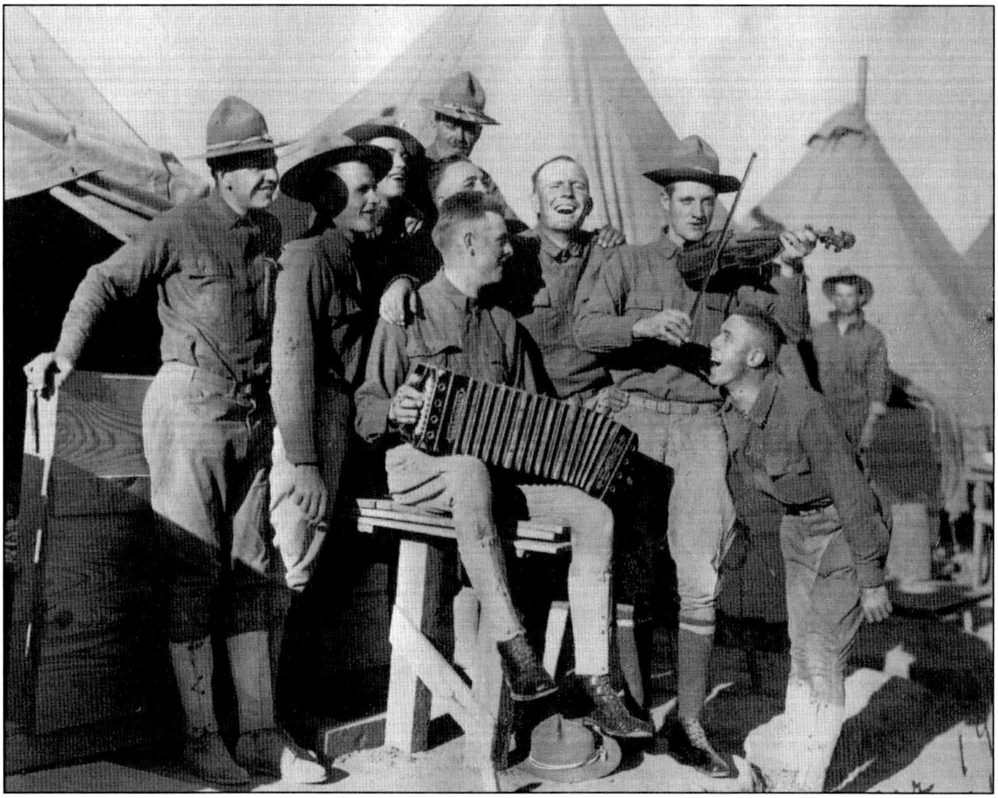

Nine men gather and one looks on as an accordion and violin player entertain the others at Camp Cody in Deming. Music was a large part of the entertainment at the camp. Soldiers even composed songs about the place. "Camp Cody Blues Fox Trot" was written by Harry Baisden of the 2nd Iowa Infantry Band. Willard Robison composed "Dem Deming Blues."

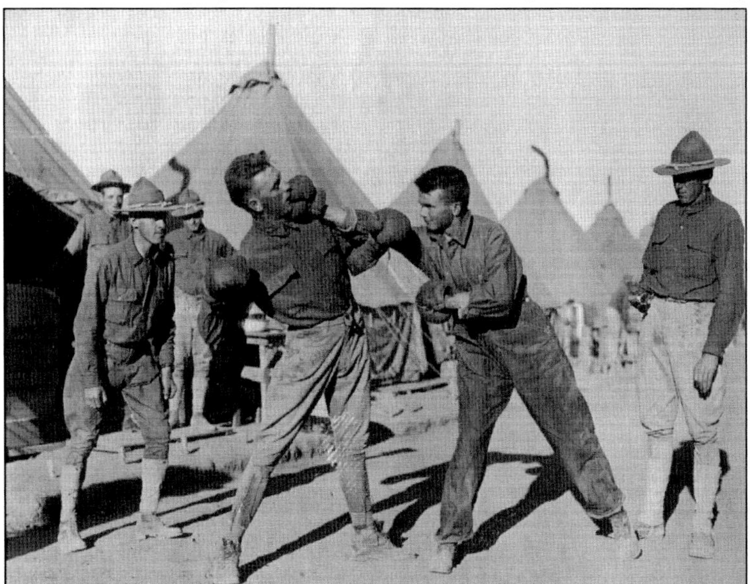

Two enlisted men practice for a boxing match in front of their tent while others watch. Boxing was a widely practiced sport at Camp Cody. Other sporting events that were enjoyed included basketball and baseball. If the soldiers were not involved, they did attend the events to get out of their tents.

Two large water towers rise above the extensive stadium at Camp Cody. Each tower held 100,000 gallons of water. Thousands of eager soldiers gathered at the stadium to witness an event. One soldier stands on the platform (center) while the camp band plays a musical piece (right). The trombones can be seen in playing position.

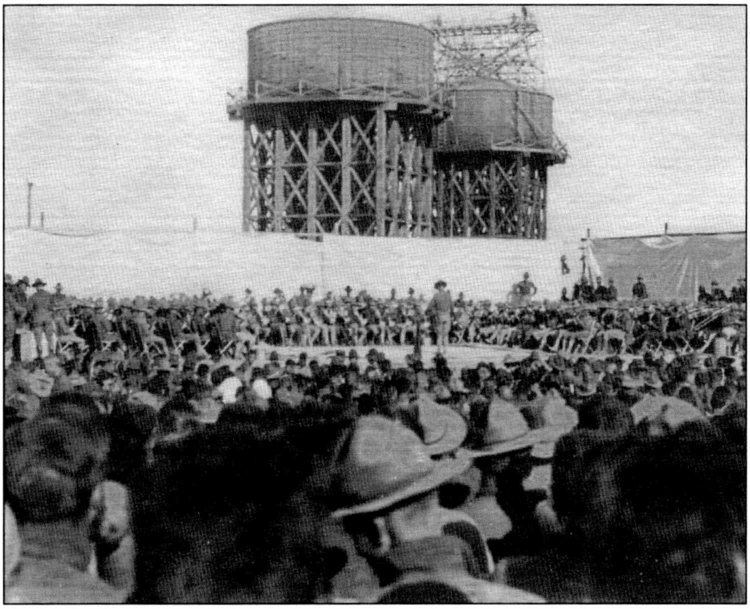

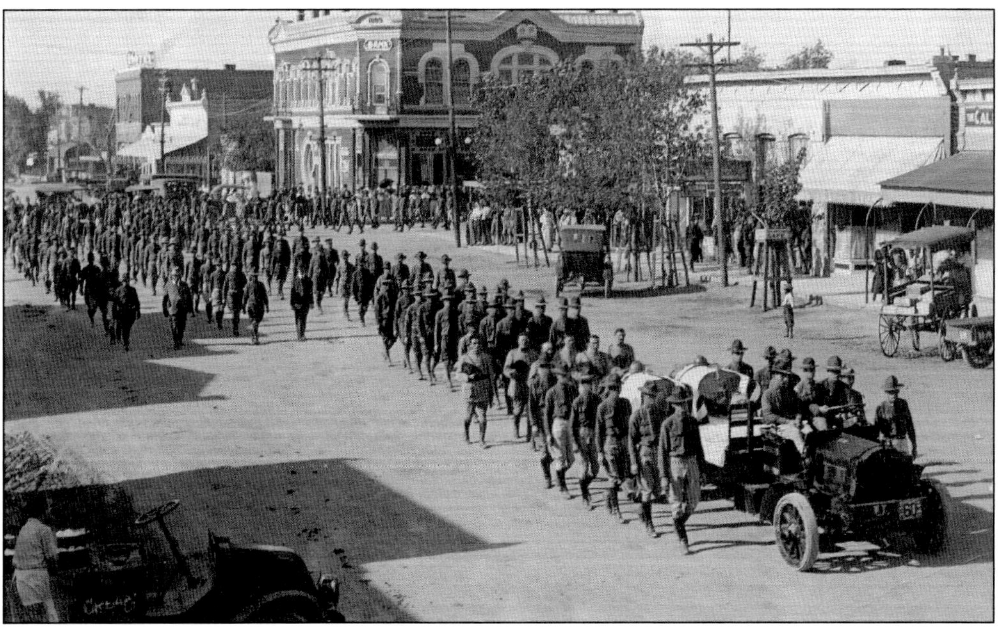

Military processions for funerals were not an uncommon scene in Deming. Many of them were photographed. In this instance, two soldiers' bodies are carried by vehicle along Silver Avenue. Soldiers follow the caskets on Silver Avenue as community members walk behind the procession on Pine Street. There was large support from the Deming community for the Camp Cody soldiers.

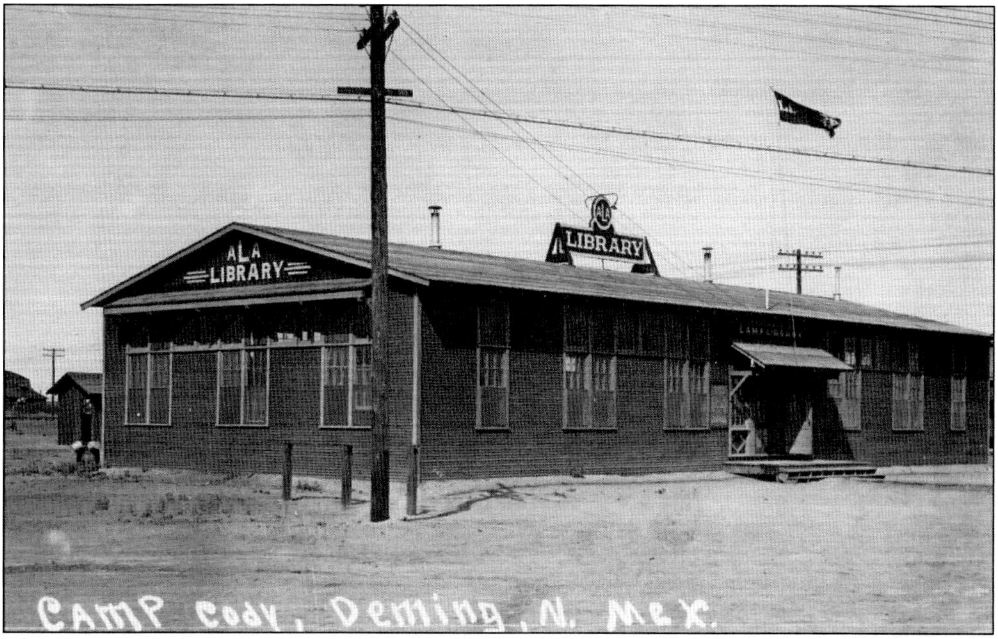

The American Library Association operated a large library at Camp Cody. Books were a popular form of entertainment for the young troops, especially during times of quarantine with measles or Spanish influenza. At these times, the large camp was shut down, and boxes of books were delivered to the men.

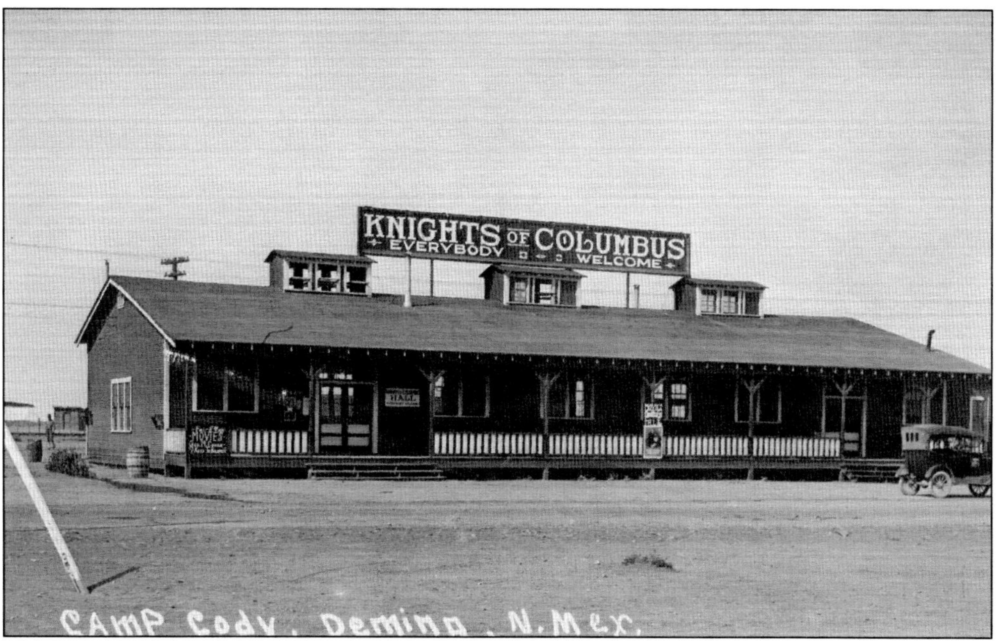

The large Knights of Columbus Building hosted many soldiers. A chaplain was housed in the building so soldiers could talk to him as needed. This was the only Catholic post at the camp. Holy Family Catholic Church in Deming directly supported the Knights of Columbus and the chaplain at Camp Cody.

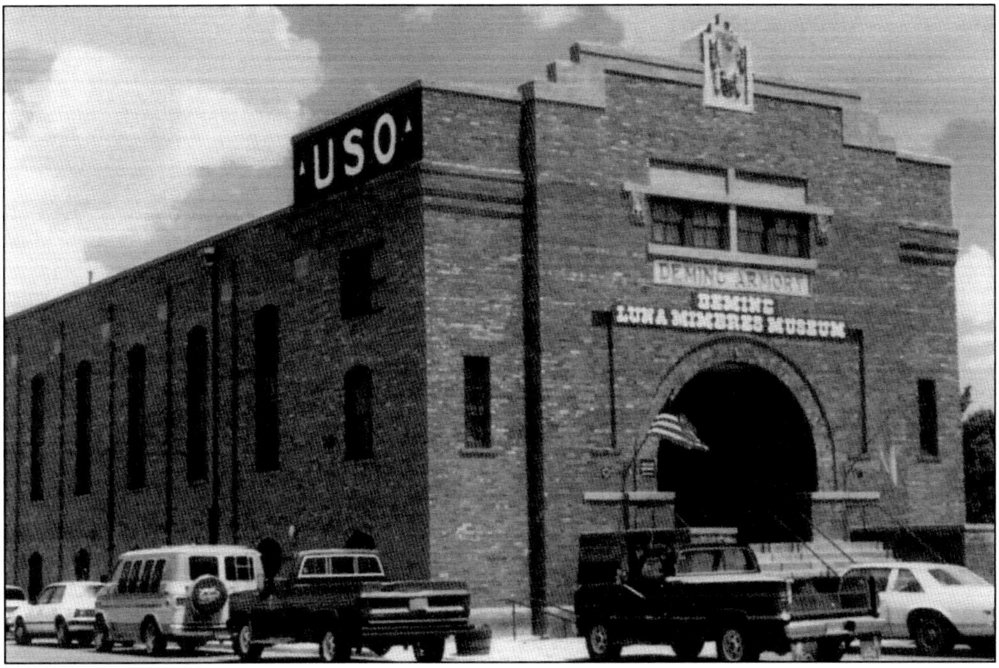

The National Guard Armory was built in 1916. It was the first armory built in New Mexico after it became a state and was used for military purposes and social functions, such as basketball games and dances. During Camp Cody days, the armory was used as the War Camp Community Service building. Today, the old armory, renovated in 2007, houses the Deming Luna Mimbres Museum.

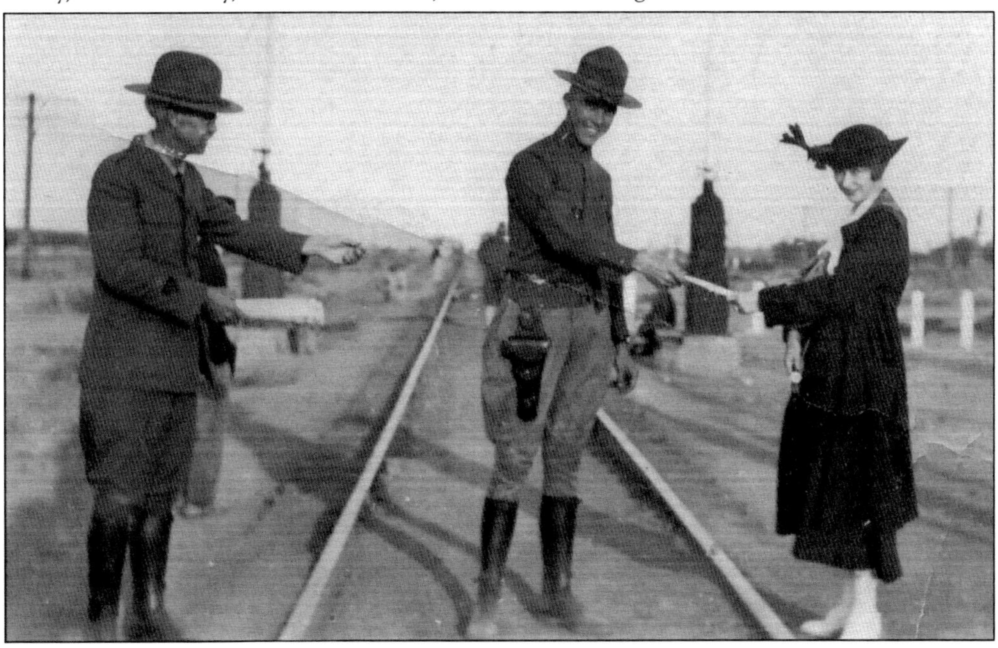

During the Spanish influenza outbreak in the fall of 1918, there was no traffic allowed in the camp. One soldier (center) hands Helen Holt (right) mail for her father, Willard E. Holt, near the entrance to the camp. Holt was editor of the *Trench and Camp*, a Camp Cody newspaper published by the Young Men's Christian Association. Helen Holt was a pianist at the camp.

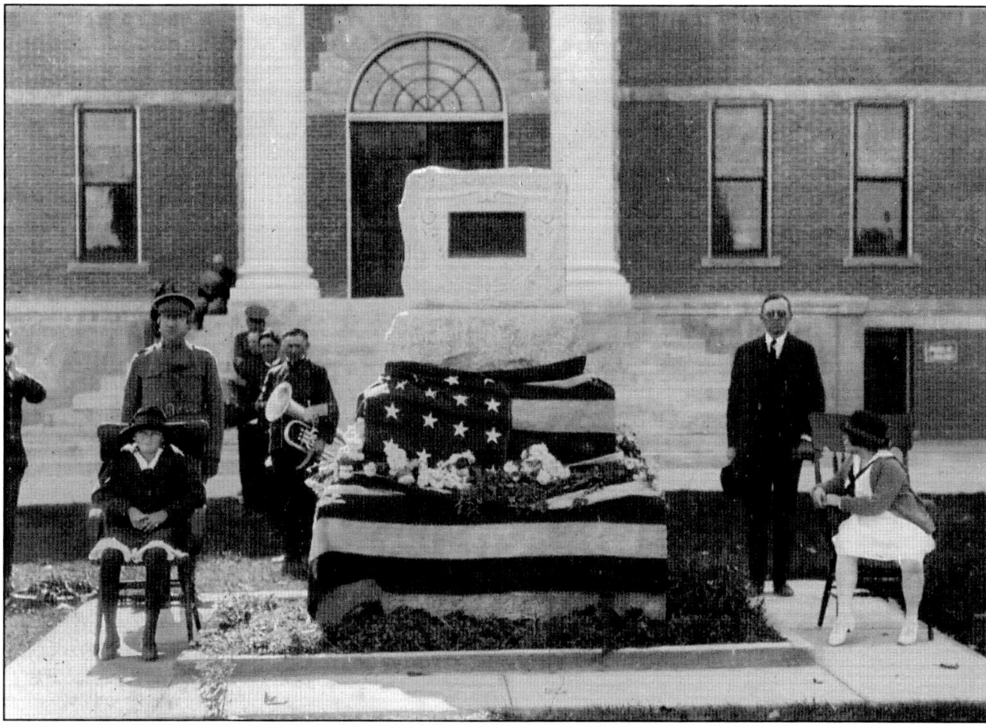

Only one Deming man was a casualty in World War I, Claude Close Howard. He was killed in action on September 24, 1918, in St. Mikiel Sector, France. A large memorial to Howard was erected in front of the Luna County Courthouse. It cost $275, which was raised through public subscription, with a limit of $1 per person. His parents had moved to Deming in 1908 and owned a small motel.

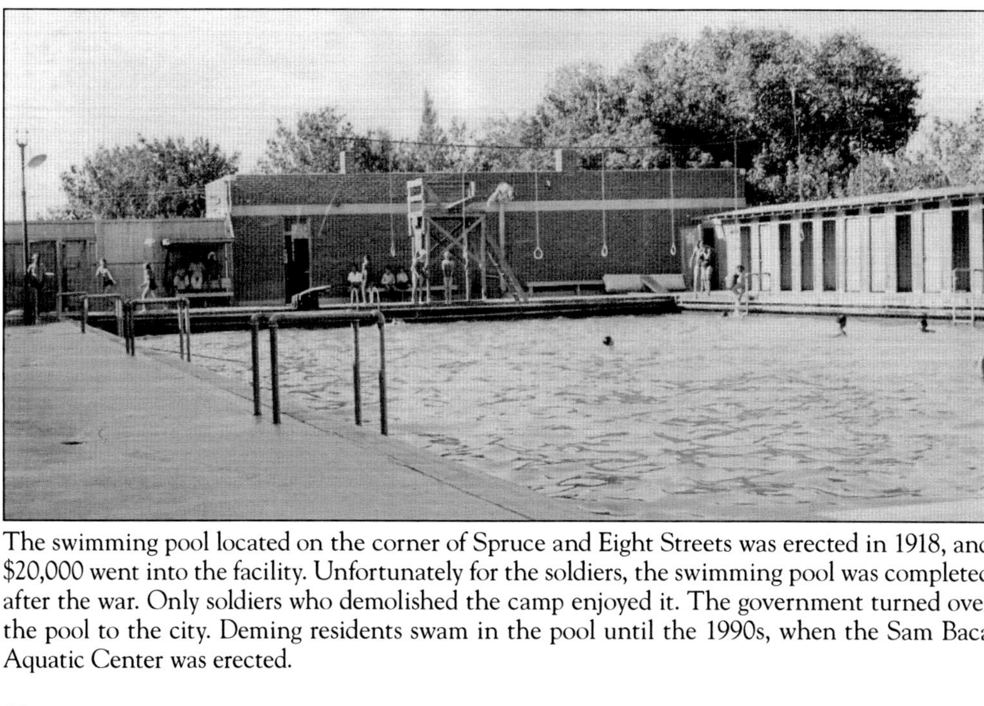

The swimming pool located on the corner of Spruce and Eight Streets was erected in 1918, and $20,000 went into the facility. Unfortunately for the soldiers, the swimming pool was completed after the war. Only soldiers who demolished the camp enjoyed it. The government turned over the pool to the city. Deming residents swam in the pool until the 1990s, when the Sam Baca Aquatic Center was erected.

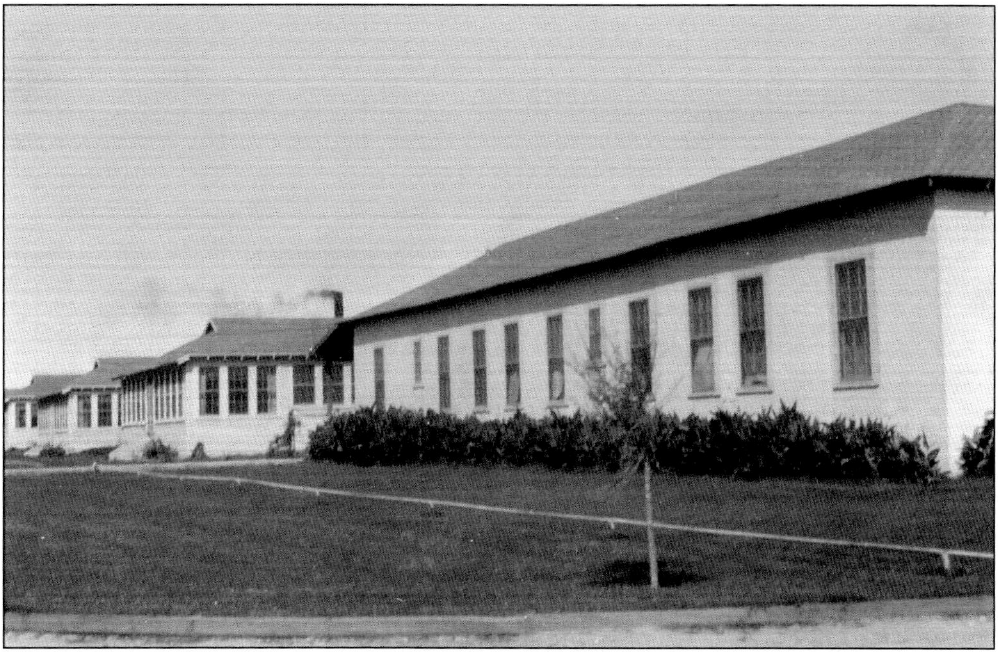

Holy Cross Sanatorium was the nuns' first tuberculosis sanatorium, but they maintained seven general hospitals throughout the United States. In November 1922, the architects, Trost & Trost of El Paso, Texas, completed the plans for the $250,000 sanatorium. Construction was anticipated being completed in January 1923 but ended in May of that year.

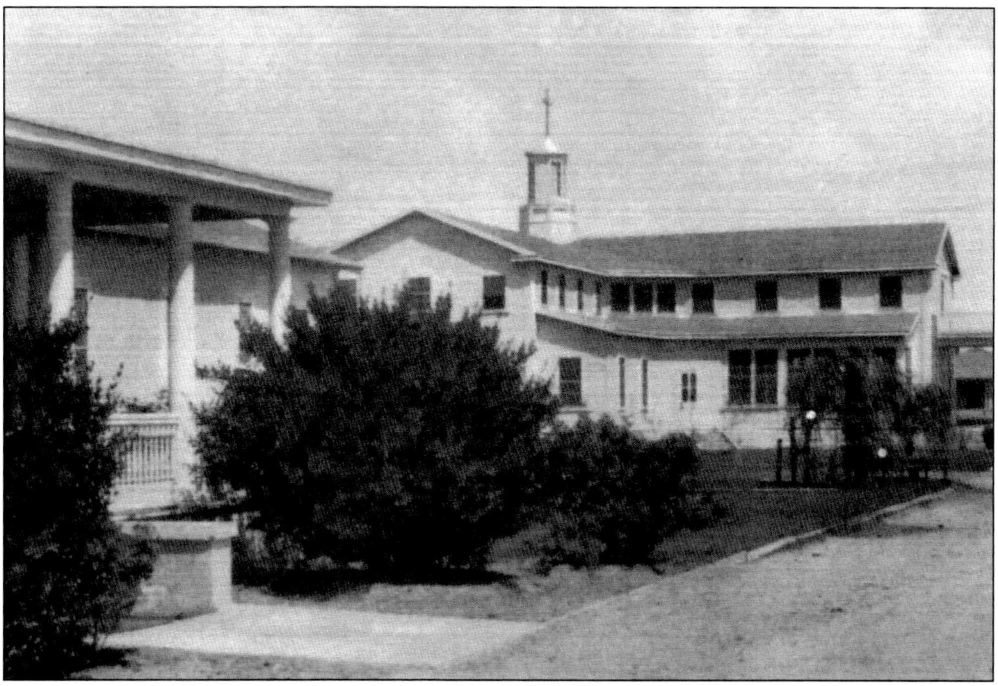

Holy Cross Boulevard is shown to the right and was one of the largest streets in the compound. The rates were $15 to $22.50 per week for tuberculosis patients looking for a retreat. Interested people were encouraged to "come and make a happy cure where the sunshine's always sure."

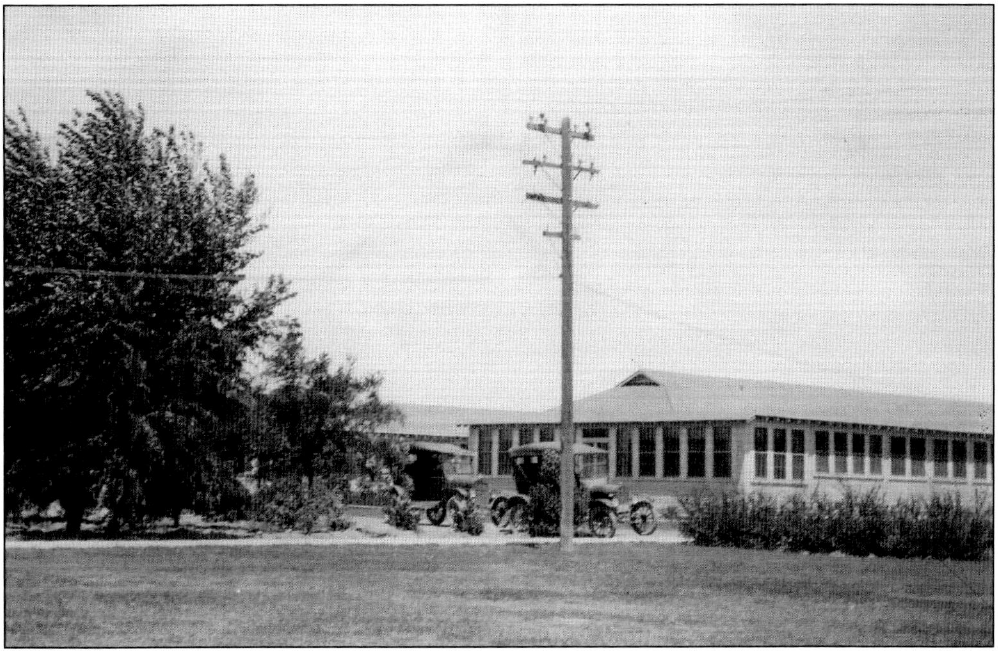

The sanatorium was destroyed by a fire on March 12, 1939. It was reported that there was a lack of water to contain the fire, and this was clarified by one of the nuns present. She stated there were 300,000 gallons of water pumped at 1,000 gallons per minute until the power line burned out, which she felt was the issue. The photograph shows how large the lines were.

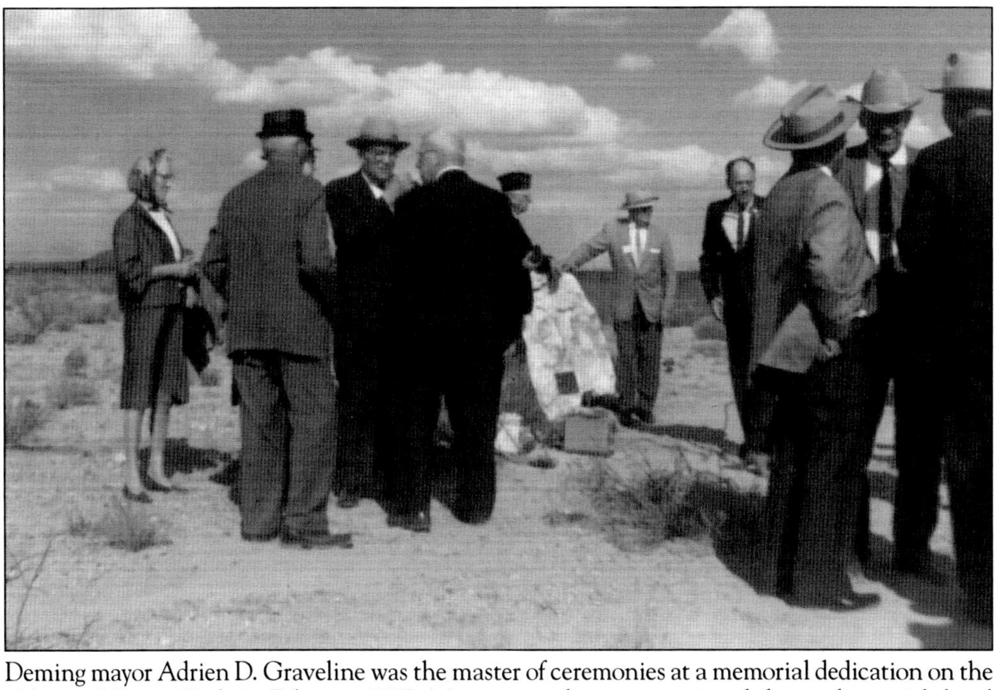

Deming mayor Adrien D. Graveline was the master of ceremonies at a memorial dedication on the old site of Camp Cody in February 1967. Many men who were stationed there, along with local businessmen who were supported by the camp during those days, were present as a plaque was placed on a large rock at the site northeast of Deming. This memorial is no longer at the site.

Seven

New Deal Impacts Deming Greatly

Pres. Franklin D. Roosevelt was known as the "Alphabet Soup" president because of the acronyms of his many programs used to stimulate the nation after the Stock Market Crash of 1929 led to the Great Depression. In his acceptance speech after being nominated for president, he said, "I pledge you, I pledge myself, to a new deal for the American people." The New Deal took shape after the inauguration of President Roosevelt in 1933.

From 1933 to 1942, the Civilian Conservation Corps (CCC) operated an average of 32 camps each year in New Mexico. The idea of the corps was to work simply for the moral and spiritual value of such work. The CCC had a camp erected nine miles northeast of Deming at the railroad station in Mirage. The Works Progress Administration (WPA) built several sidewalks, curbs, and roads in Deming. The trademark WPA stamp with the year of completion can be found at the end of the sidewalks on many streets. Other larger projects were also undertaken. A library (1935), post office (1936), city hall and fire station (1939), and highway department buildings (1940) were all built under the WPA in Deming. All of these structures remain in Deming today except for the highway department buildings; they were demolished and new structures took their place.

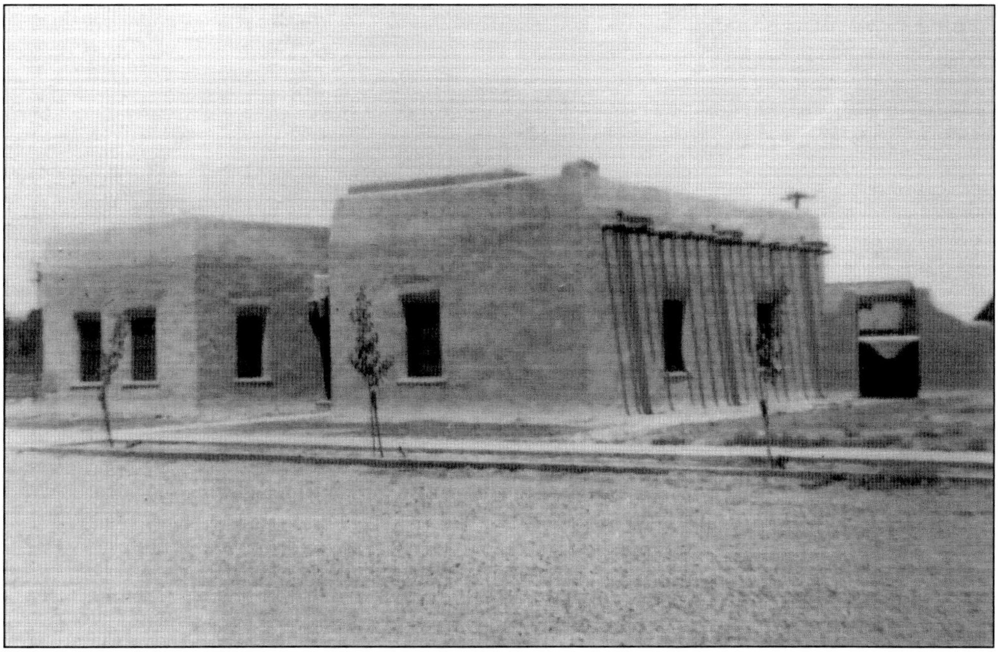

The city library at 301 South Tin Street was constructed with funds provided by the Works Progress Administration. The land was purchased in 1921 for $900 while the library occupied a room at the Luna County Courthouse. The city owned the land for about 14 years before the library was built in 1935.

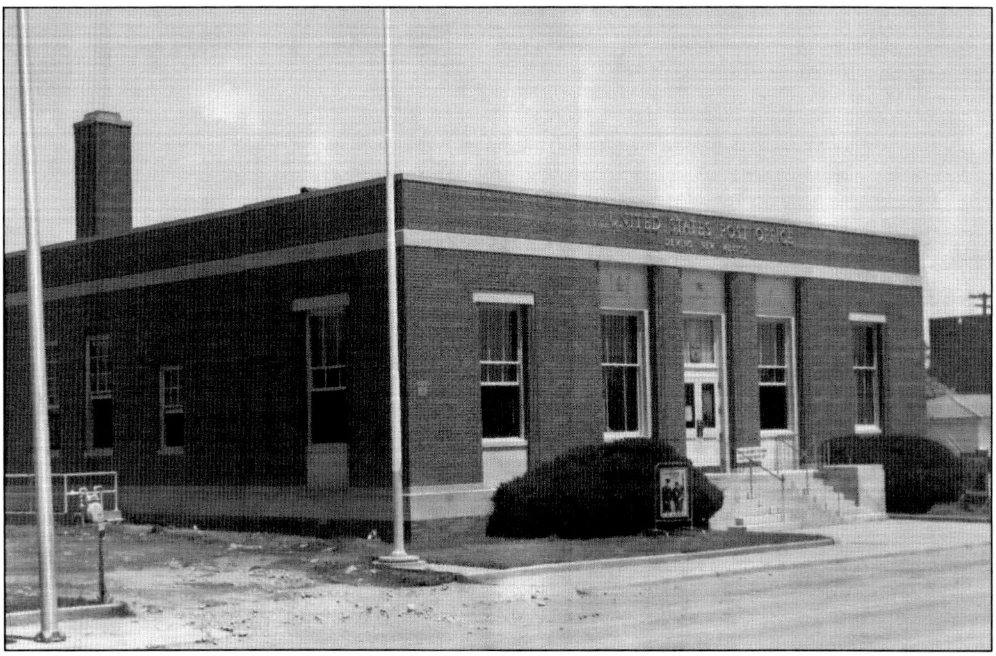

The Deming Main Post Office, located at 201 West Spruce Street, is a redbrick, single-story building with limestone belt courses, lintels, sills, and decorative panels. Inside the lobby of the post office is a WPA mural painted by Kenneth M. Adams entitled *Mountains and Yucca*. This was Adam's last federal art project; he had painted several others.

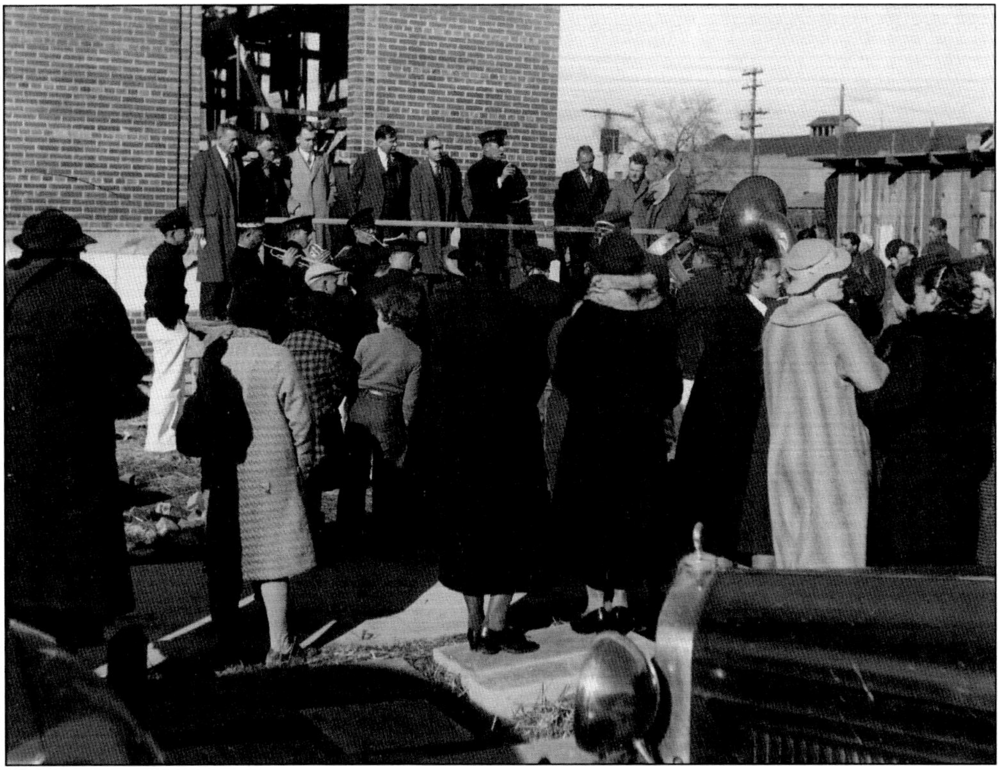

The Deming Main Post Office was dedicated in 1936 in a large ceremony with a band (above). Deming City Hall was erected in 1939 (below). New Mexico governor John E. Miles dedicated the Deming City Hall building at 7:30 p.m. on January 4, 1940. After introducing councilmen, city and chamber of commerce officials, and civic club presidents, a dance was held in the $30,000 building. Not only did the structure house city offices and the fire department, it also was the home to a large 500-seat auditorium. Today, the old city hall is known as Morgan Hall and is at 109 East Pine Street. C.B. Morgan was the city engineer who drew the architectural plans for the structure.

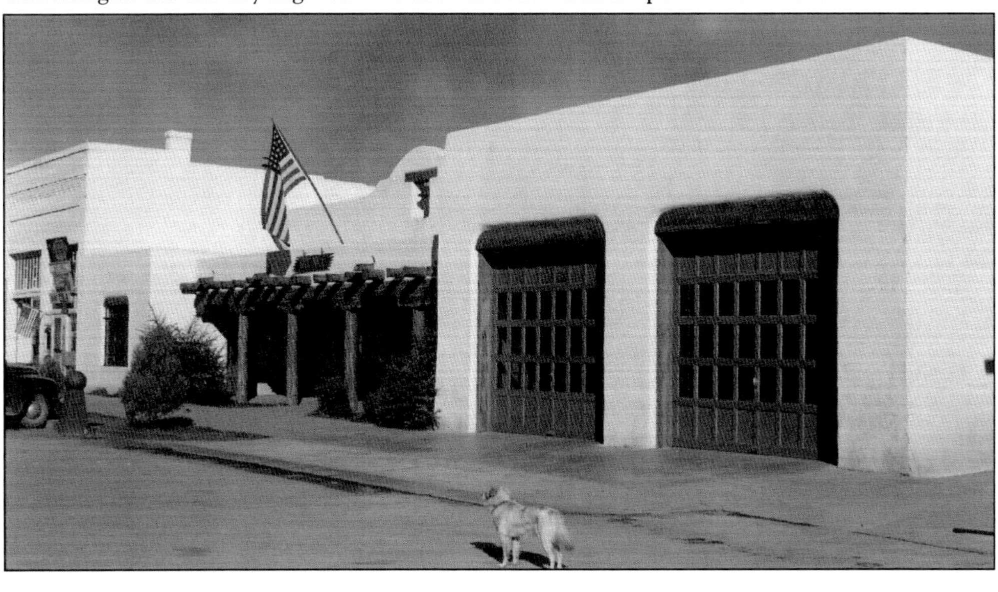

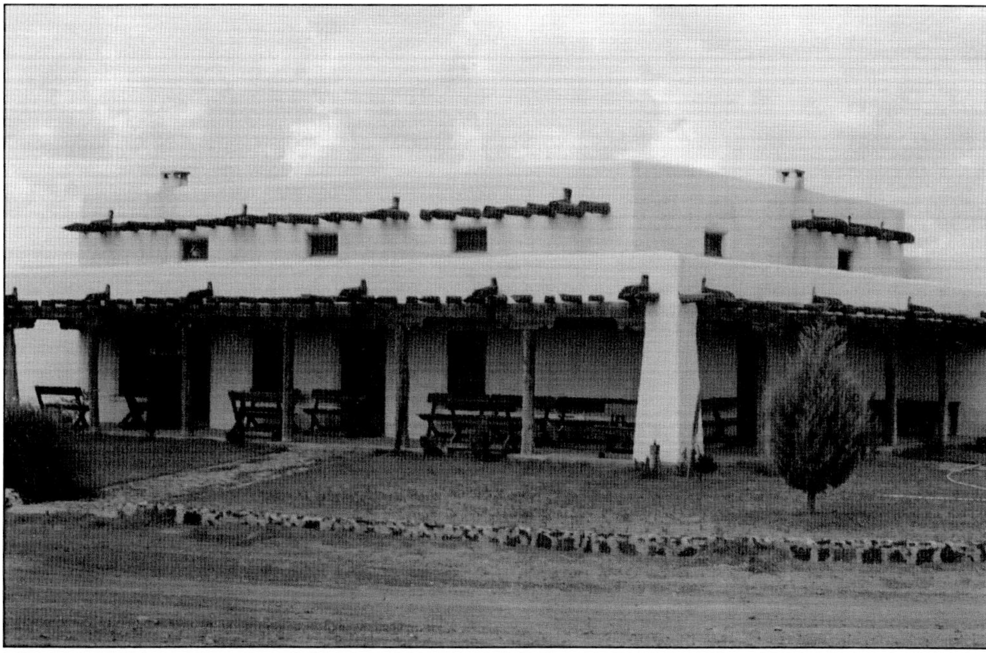

The Rio Mimbres Country Club (above) was opened in Deming in 1938 with 135 charter members. Adjoining the building were a rodeo park, golf course, swimming pool, picnic grounds, tennis courts, and other outdoor amusements. Arthur A. Temke and many others were working at securing funds for the club before the WPA took over the project. Postelle Cooper became the main promoter of the project in the 1930s.

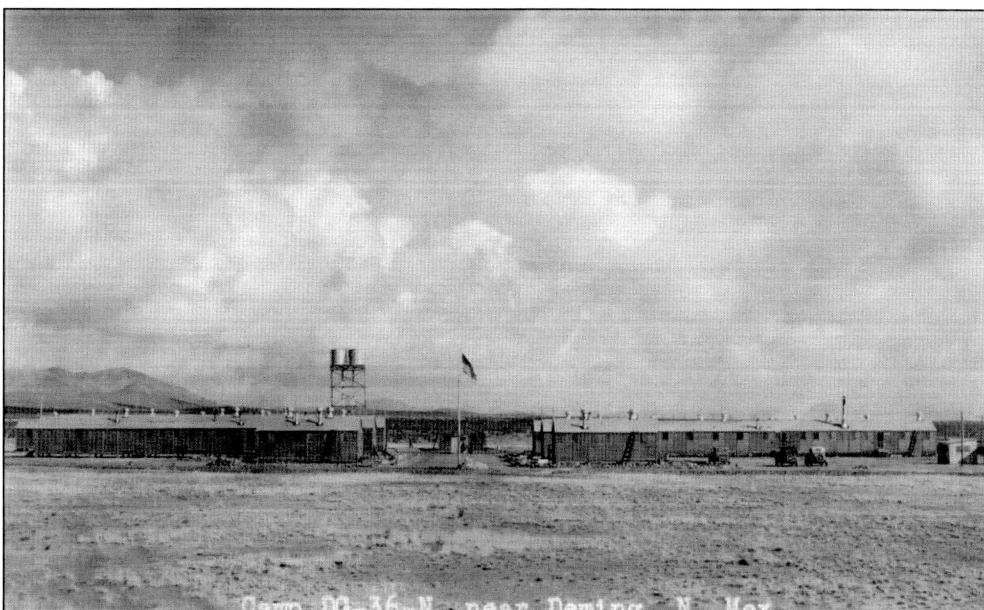

Project DG-36, or Camp Mirage, hosted Company 3838 starting on August 24, 1935. Approximately 175 men worked out of the camp at Mirage. The men were under the Division of Grazing in the Department of the Interior. They were responsible for revegetation and soil erosion, flood, and rodent control.

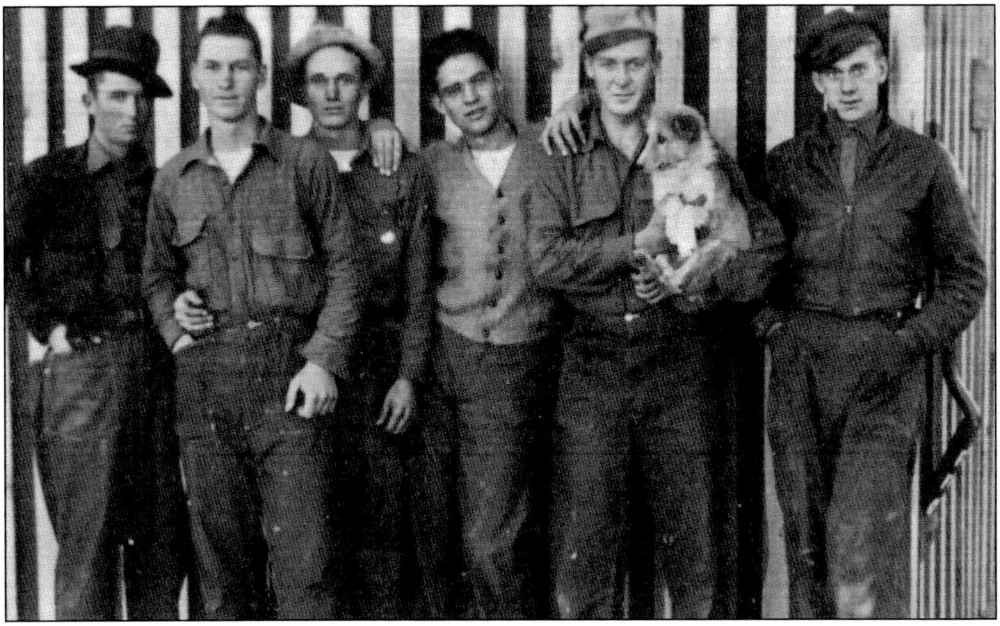

Many of the young men came in a cadre from Texas. The *Deming Headlight* featured an article sponsored by United New Mexico Bank on August 16, 1985, about the men at the camp. The article states: "There were several Deming boys in the CCC, among them Capt. J.L. Nicklas, Ab Bonnie, Wilbur Gaines, Charlie Miller, Fred Almeraz, Foy Riley, Russell Fairres, James Ferguson, 'Tiny' Robinson, and Fred Torres . . . perhaps others, whom we cannot recall." These men may be seen in the photographs on this page. While about 175 men were housed at Mirage, there were a total of 505,782 enrollees in camps across the United States.

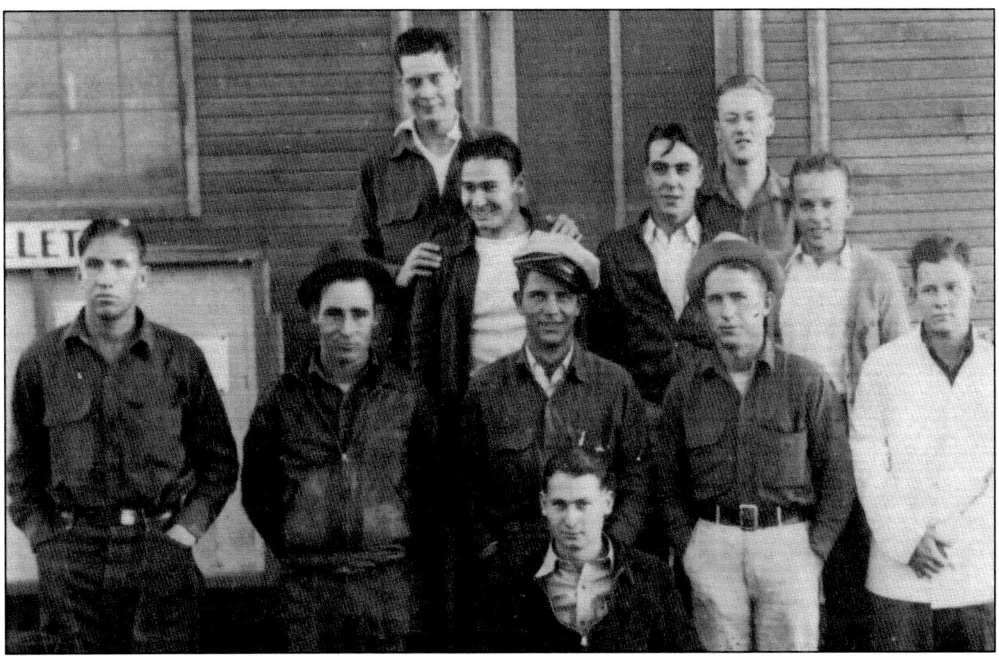

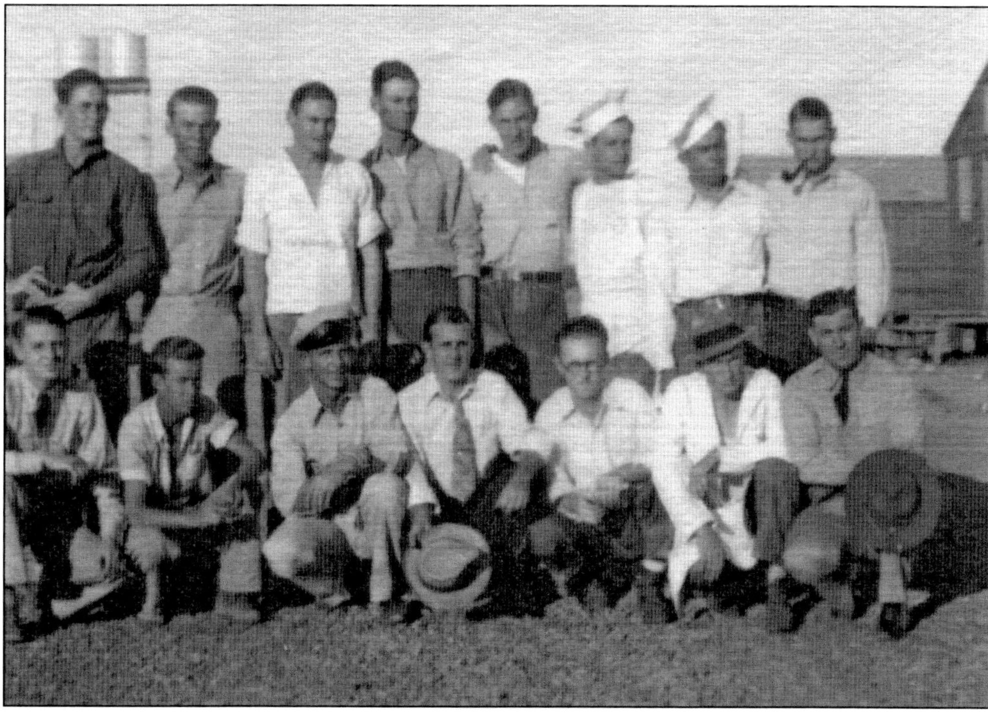

Cooks can be seen in their chef's hats. Two cooks hold cats, but it is unknown what was on the dinner menu that night (below). Thanksgiving Day 1935 was a special day for the men. The chefs stayed up all night preparing a very large feast. Many felt the result was a work of art. The mess hall had never been so full of food, set as a banquet. The men were very thankful for the cooks putting forth all of their efforts. Many of the men became very close, since they spent their time in close quarters (above). After a hard day at work, the young men could play softball, volleyball, basketball, and ping-pong at the camp in the recreation hall.

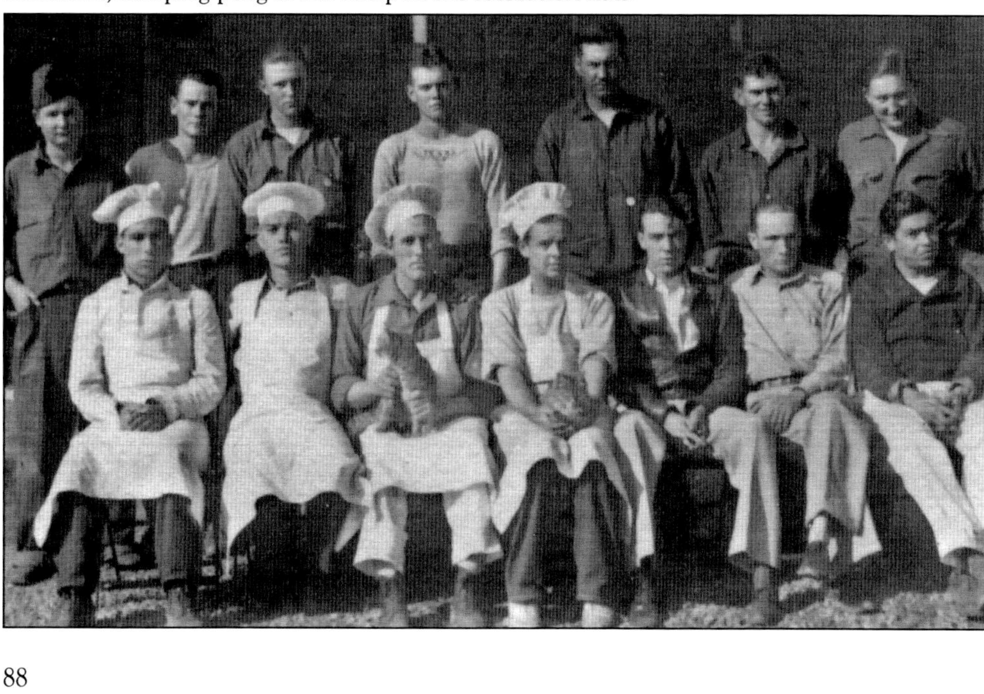

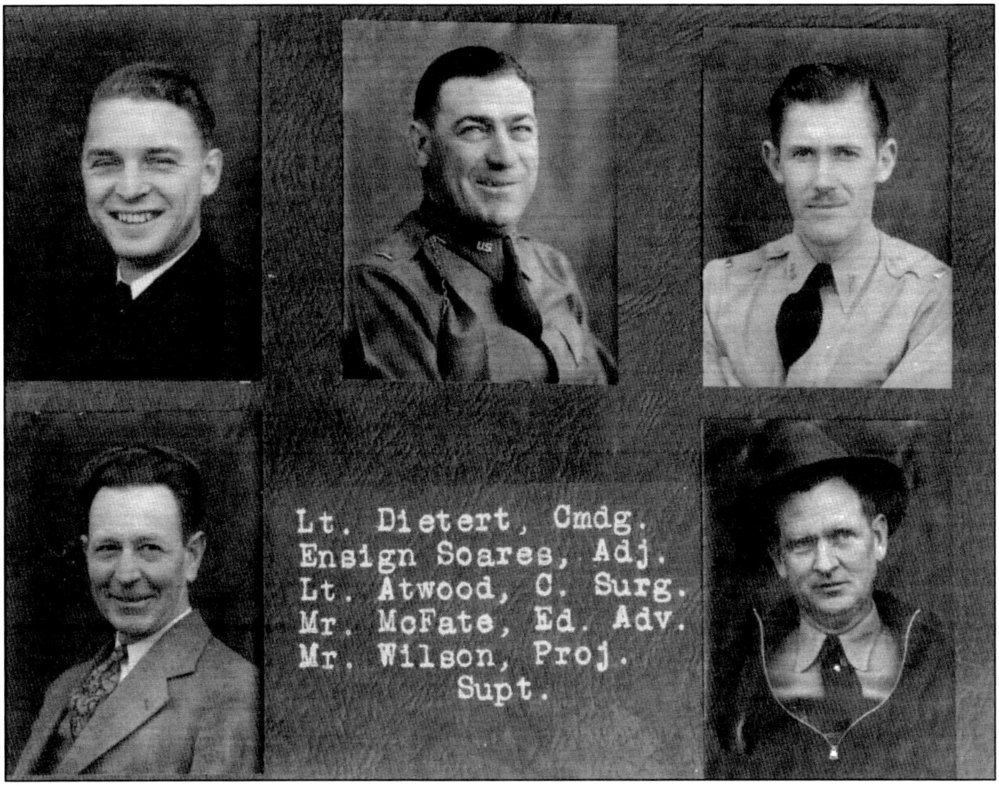

There were several leaders who served as the Army overhead (above). The commanding officer was Lt. Milton E. Dietert, and the adjutant was Ens. Glenn J. Soares. They received the men who were arriving daily from Texas. The camp surgeon was Clarence S. Atwood, and the educational advisor was Roy L. McFate. McFate was responsible for educating the men in arithmetic, English, writing, shorthand, spelling, first aid, and general science. Other units were added as the camp saw fit. McFate was hired about four months after the camp was established, so the men played catch-up with their education when he arrived. The men were taught after a hard day at work (below).

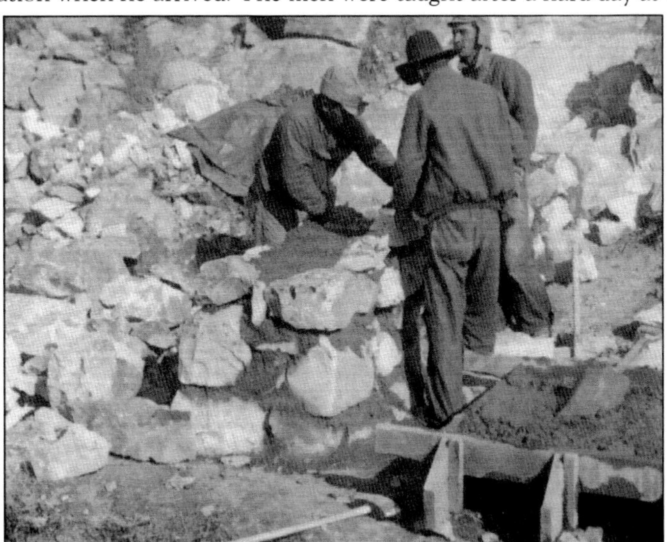

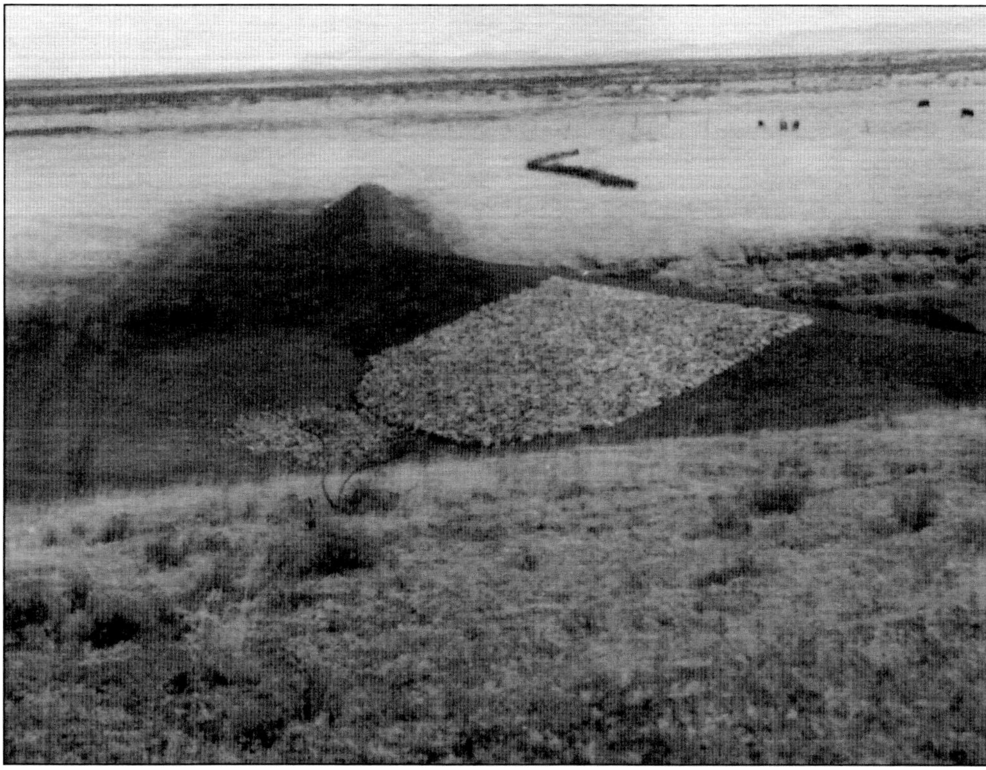

The Division of Grazing, created by the Department of the Interior, was in charge of the Mirage camp. A lot of their work took place at the foothills of Cooke's Peak, north of Deming. This was ideal, because the camp was several miles from the base of the mountain. Both of these photographs were taken in this area. Horses were used to assist the men construct the dams (below). The earthen dams that were built remain in the area today (above).

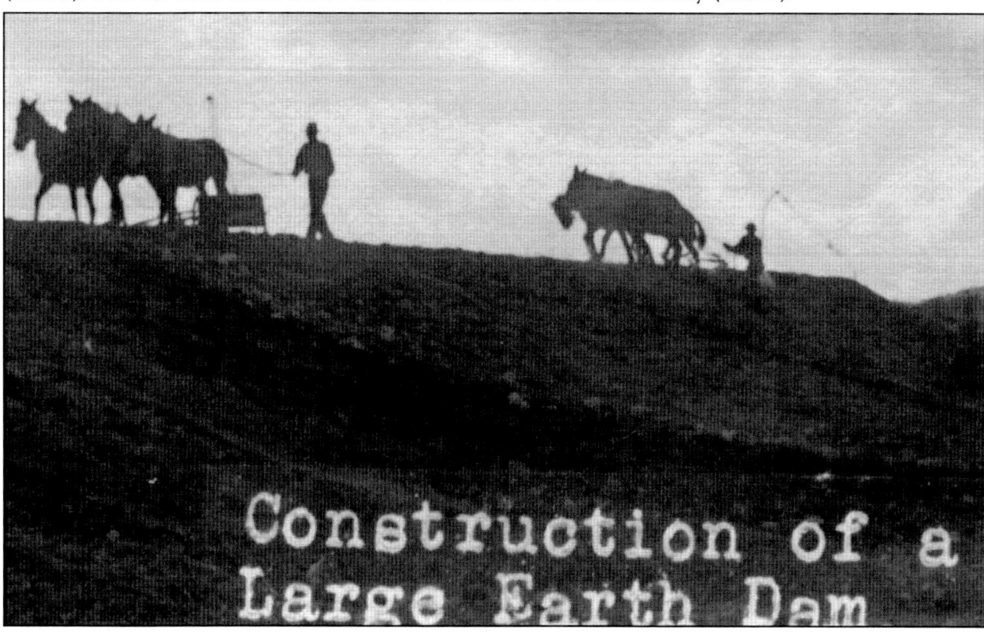

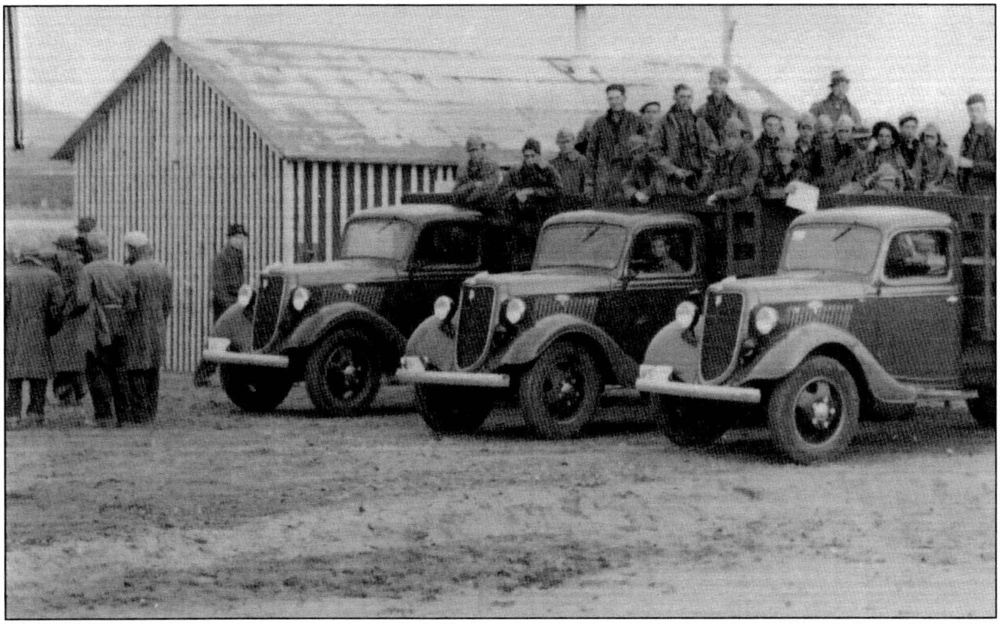

About a dozen uniform vehicles transported the young men of the Civilian Conservation Corps to their work sites and into the town of Deming, if necessary. Not only did the men work near Cooke's Peak, which was near their campsite, but they also traveled to the Florida Mountains, southeast of Deming. At an area known as Spring Canyon, in the Florida Mountains, the men constructed watering tanks. Rocks, gravel, and dirt had to be hauled to many of the locations for the work that they were engaging in and to complete many projects. Rocks and gravel were also hauled from Cooke's Peak to beautify the camp at Mirage.

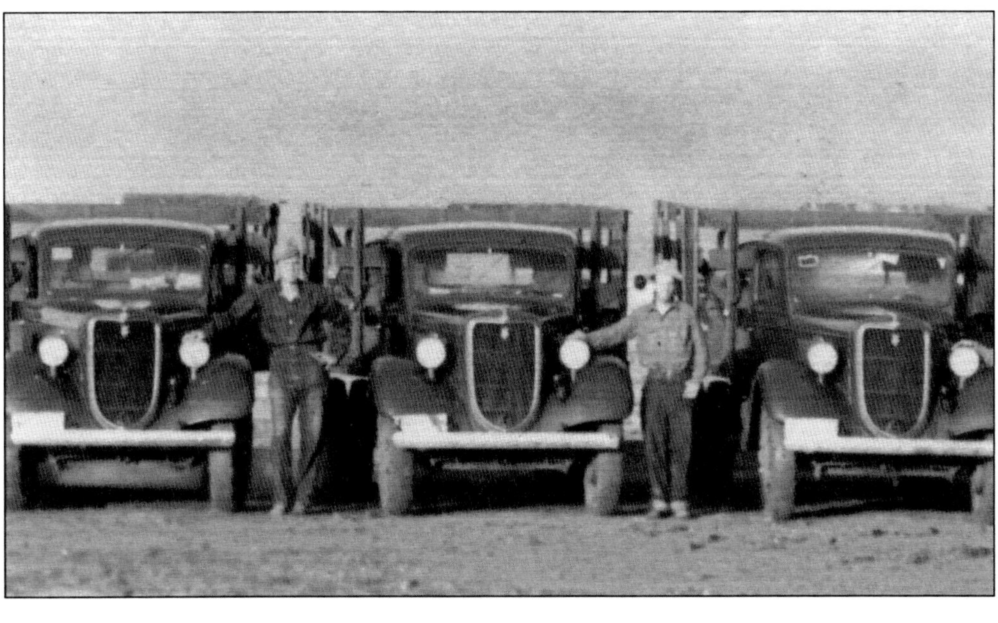

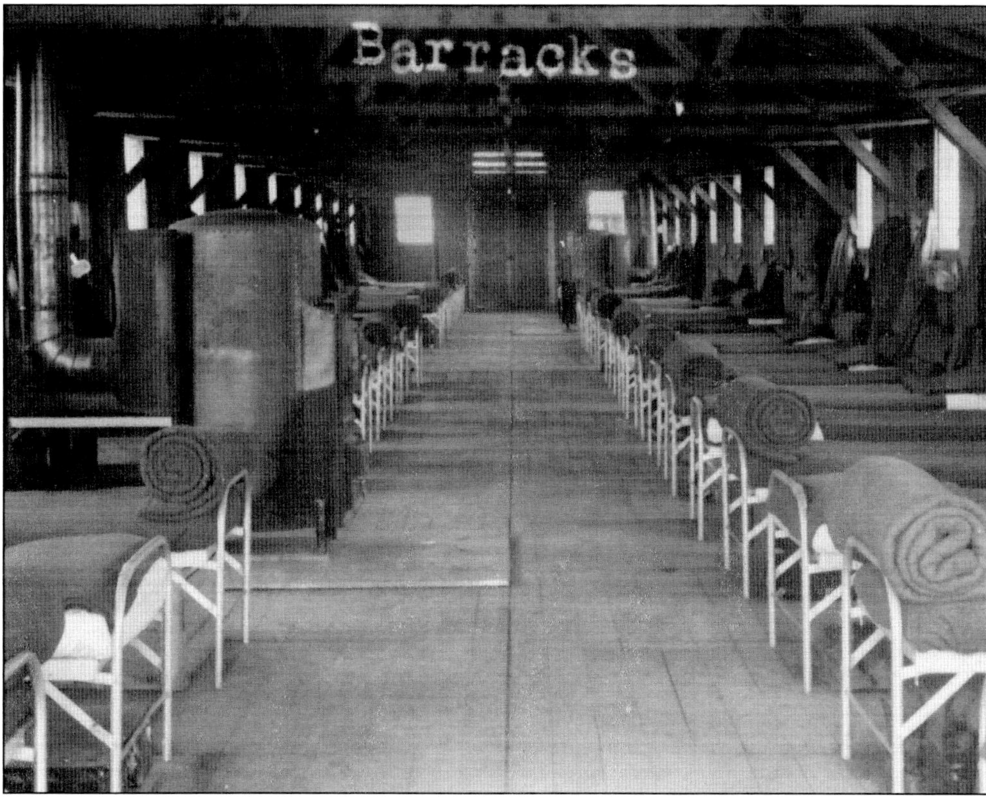

After working to better the land around the Deming area and playing active games in the large recreation hall, the young men of Mirage were able to rest in their barracks (above). While the building was standard with no fancy amenities, each man had his own bed (below). Fortunately, they did not have to sleep in tents. Heating units were present in the barracks as the men worked into the winter months. Also, the camp's basketball team joined a local league and played other camps as a diversion in the winter. All that is seen today at the site are the remnants of a rock chimney.

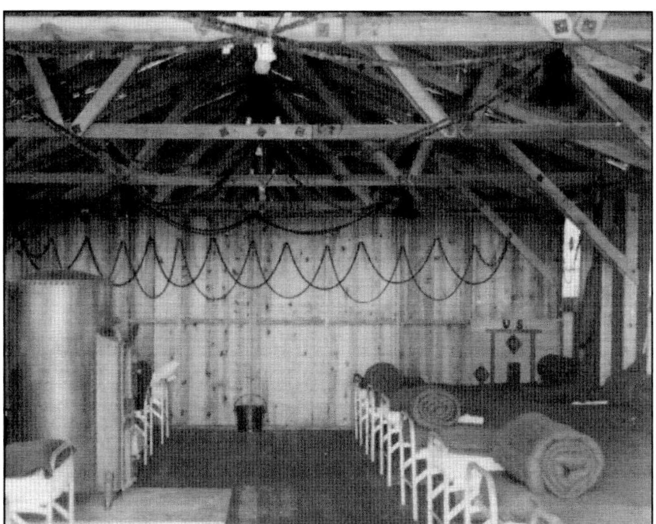

Eight

Deming Army Air Field and World War II

The construction of the Deming Army Air Field began in March 1942 in the area known today as Industrial Park, located southeast of downtown Deming. The Deming Army Air Field housed a bombardier training school for enlisted young men during World War II. After their training was completed, they were commissioned as either second lieutenants or flight officers. In December 1942, the Deming Army Air Field was completed, with its first training class beginning in January 1943. This class graduated on March 6, 1943. By December 24, 1943, there were 800 civilians working at the airfield. One out of every three women working in the field was the wife of an enlisted man, cadet, or officer. About 8,000 men were trained in Deming during the war.

While men were training at Deming Army Air Field, other men from the community enlisted in the Army to fight in the war. Deming men were enlisted in the 200th and 515th Coast Artillery Anti-Aircraft Regiments—the New Mexico Brigade. After eight months of training at Fort Bliss in El Paso, Texas, the men were transferred to Fort Stotsenburg, in the Philippine Islands, in September 1941. Many of the men believed that they would be home to celebrate Christmas; unfortunately, they were forced to become prisoners of war and take part in the Bataan Death March. While 53 Deming men were liberated after the war, 39 died.

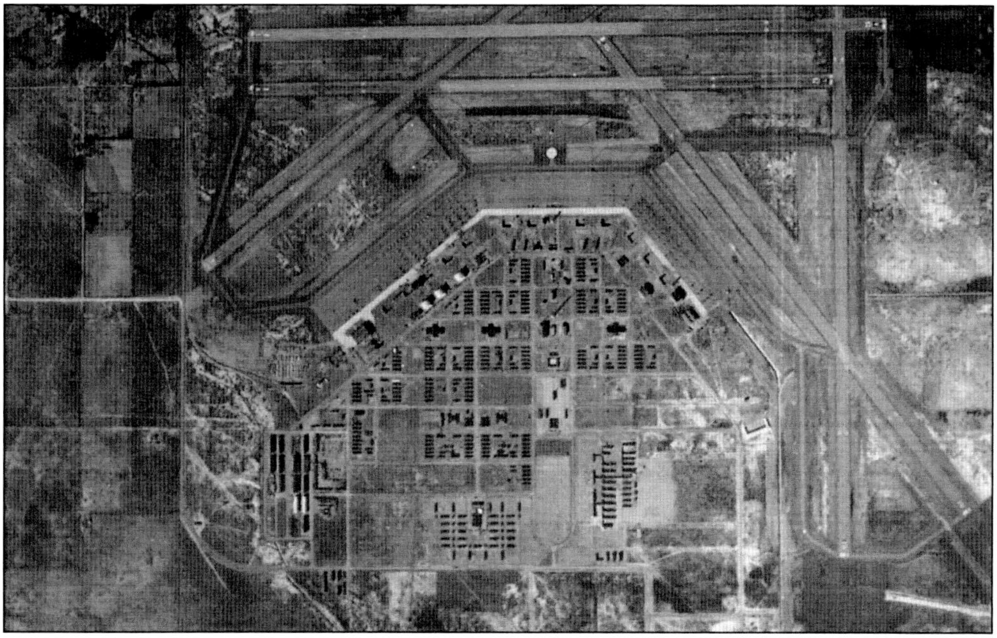

This aerial photograph shows the enormity of the Deming Army Air Field, located southeast of Deming during World War II. The construction cost of the airfield exceeded $5 million. The Arizona Construction Company was awarded the contract for building the runways. Another $3 million was used for the construction of buildings by Lee Moore and Thomas W. Hanson of El Paso, Texas.

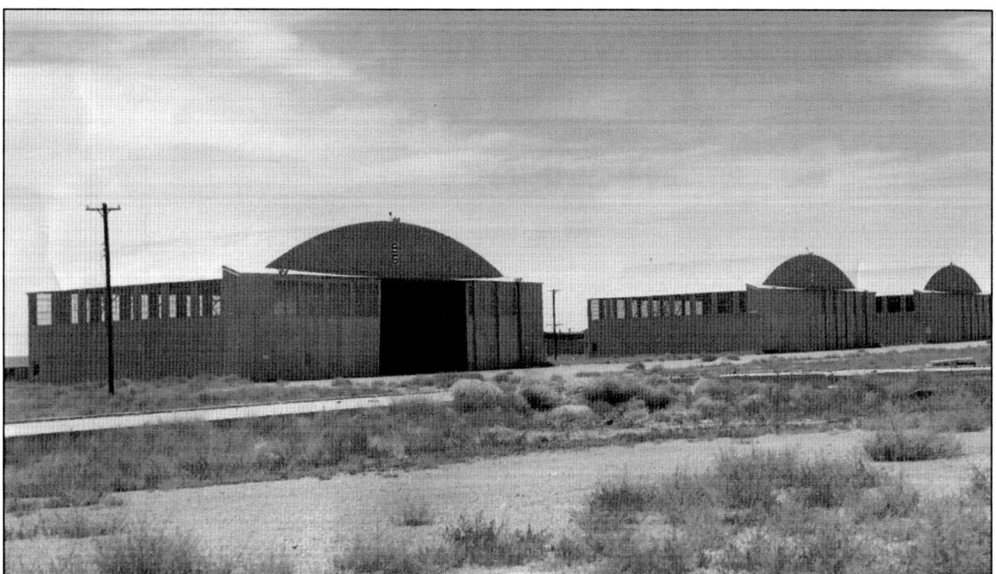

The three large hangars are the identifiable markers in any photographs of the airfield at this time. They were used to house simulators that the men used to train. These three hangars still remain in Deming today. Over the years, they have been leased to various organizations. The summer of 2007 found many stars inside the hangars filming scenes for *Indiana Jones and the Kingdom of the Crystal Skull.*

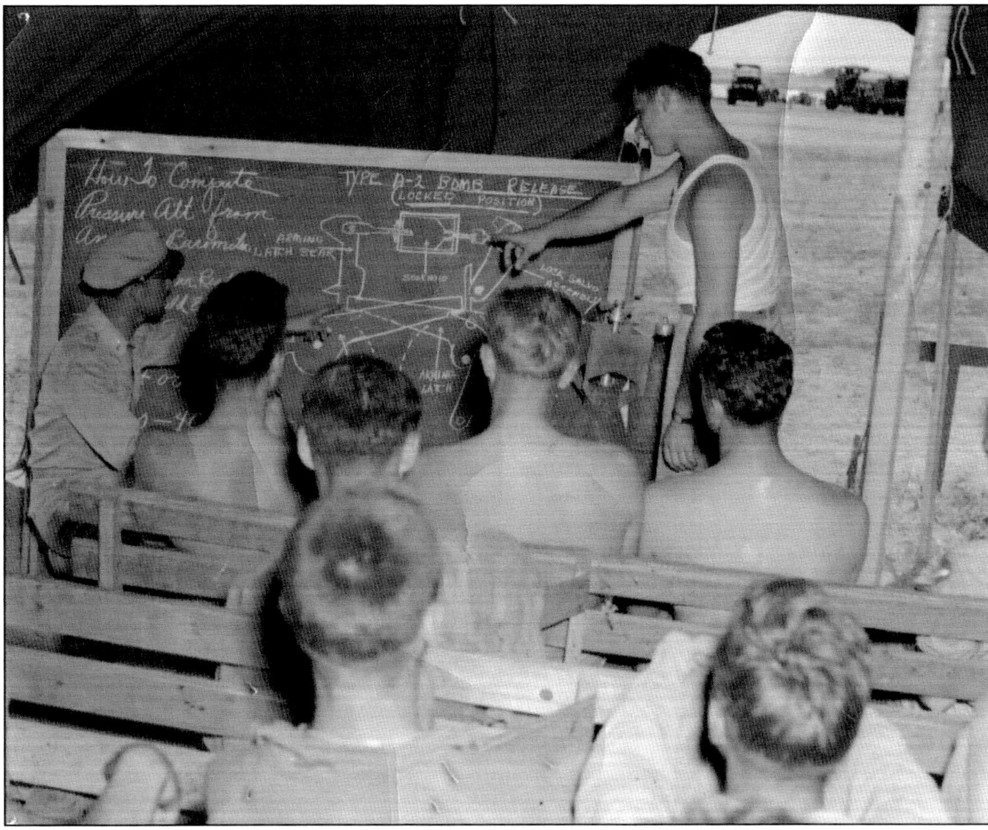

Training at Deming Army Air Field was rigorous and lasted between 12 and 18 months. The men were arranged into groups of 150 to 200 students. This number was then broken up to make the class sizes smaller. All students were first instructed in bomb theory and use of the Norden bombsight in ground school. Classes were held in buildings and tents. Many students went to the training classes without shirts, as the summers were quite warm for the boys who came from across the country (above). Other training included bivouacking, as demonstrated by a class of men in June 1944 (below).

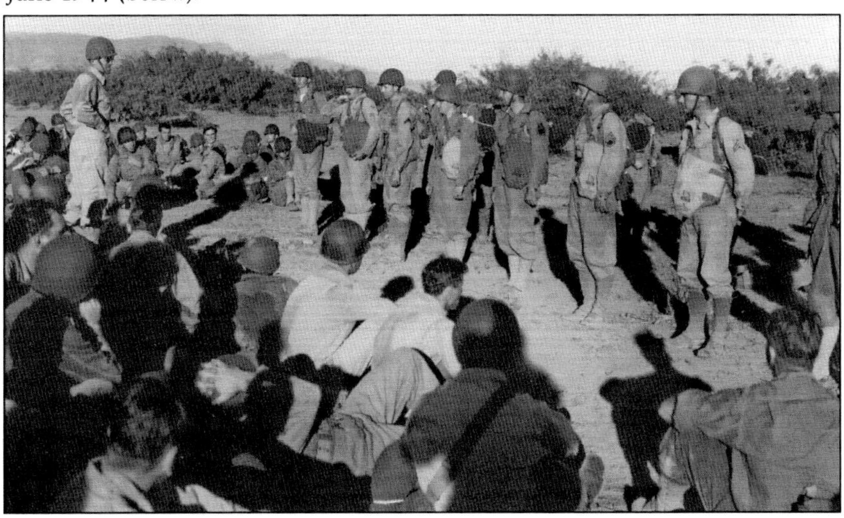

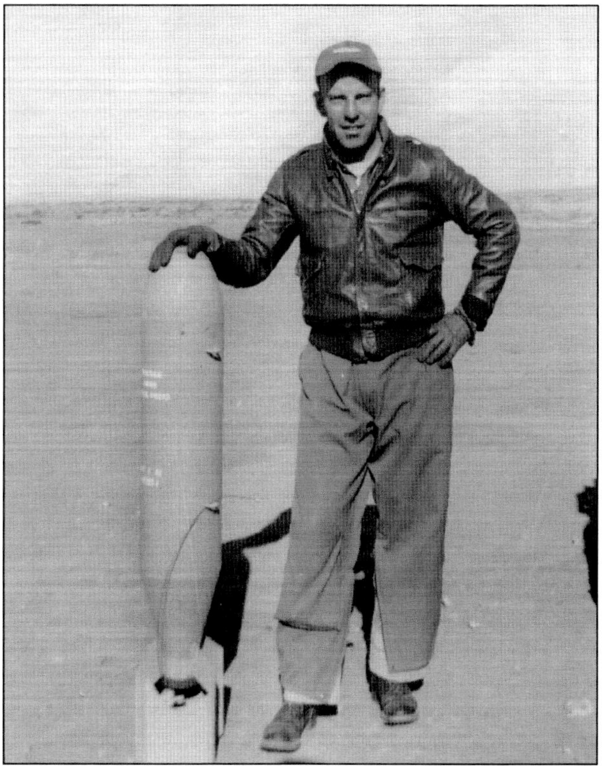

Richard S. Carolus stands with a bomb at Deming Army Air Field in February 1944. Bombing altitudes were from 4,000 to 10,000 feet. Pilots were scheduled for two or three flights per day. An instructor had one, two, or three cadets on each flight. Saturdays and Sundays were rest days for the men.

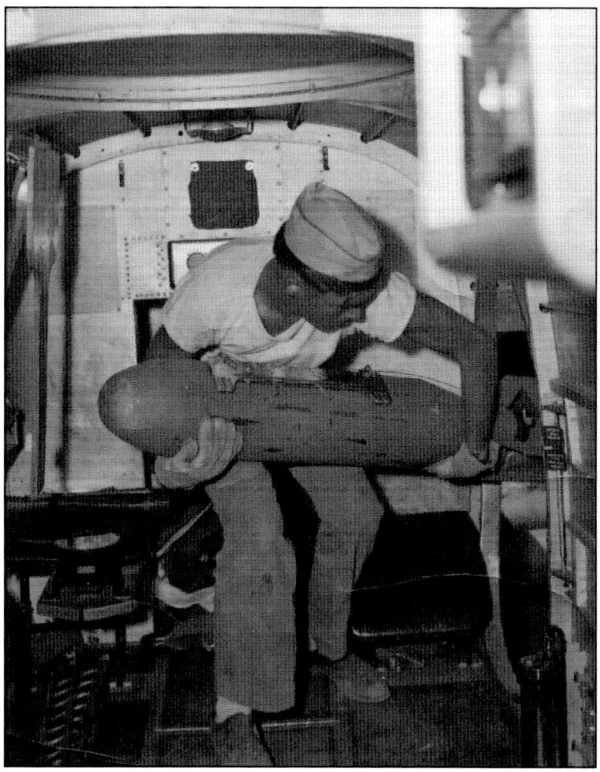

Jack Martin loads the plane before training. The bomb bay had enough room for at least 12 practice bombs that sat in racks in the bay. Every new pilot had to complete a pilot bombardiering course. Seven hours of bombing simulations plus dropping 10 practice bombs with an instructor present were required.

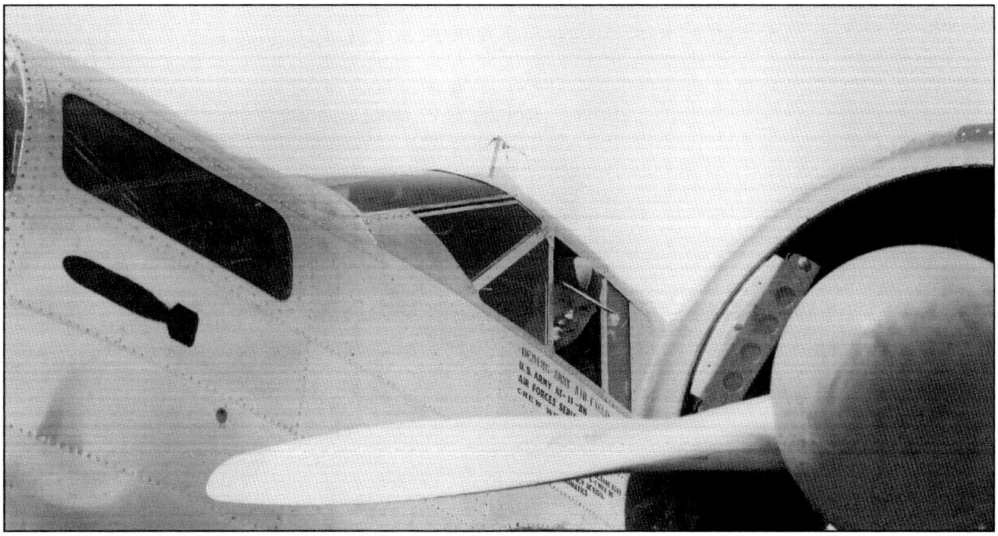

The Beechcraft AT-11 aircraft was used as an advanced trainer until 1948. The AT-11s were nicknamed "Kansans." The Norden bombsight, which the AT-11s were equipped with, was one of the most important technological advancements to come out of World War II. Carl Lucas Norden's bombsight was created before the war, but its use in World War II made it well known.

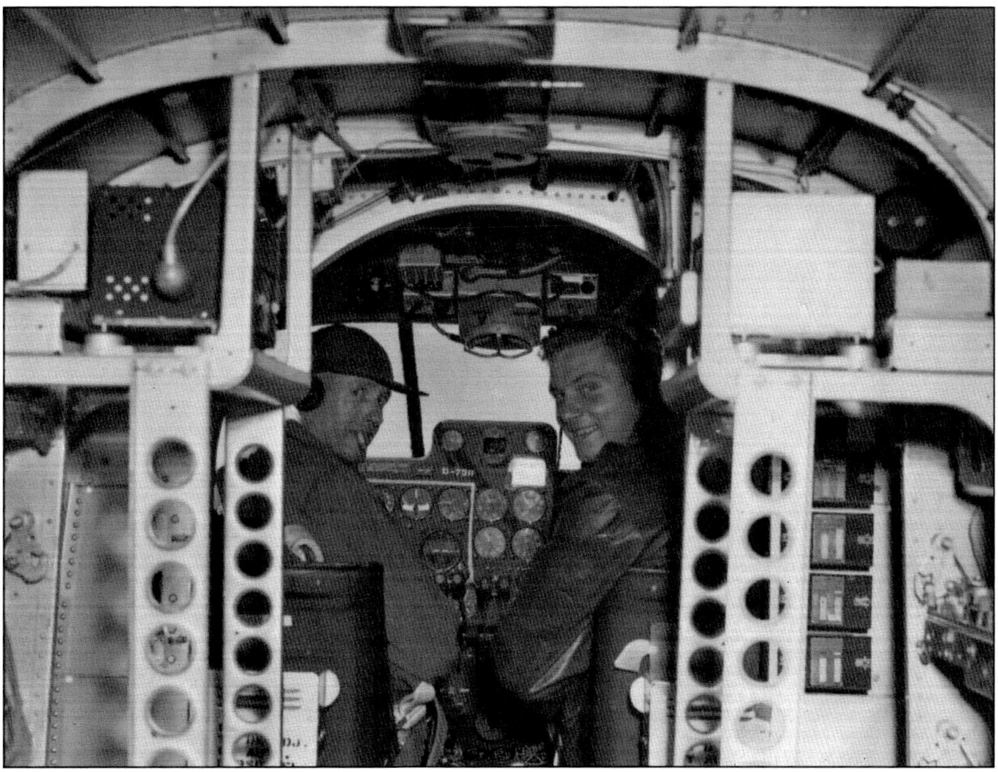

Major Smith (left) and Jack Martin are sitting in the small cockpit of an AT-11 plane ready to log a few hours dropping practice bombs. The small cockpit seated only two. The bombardier instructor, Smith, occupies the copilot seat. Two additional bombardier cadets could fit behind the cockpit seats.

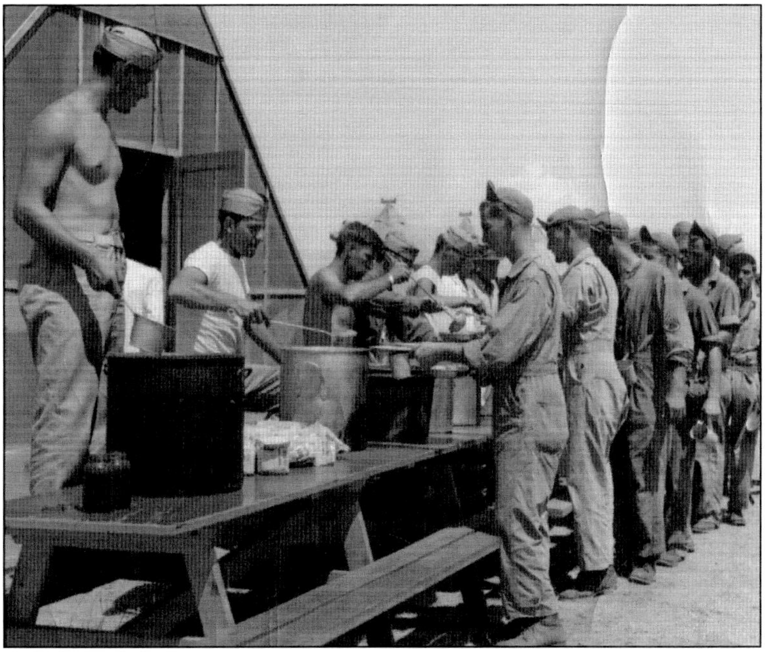

Young men walk through a line outside to receive their portion of food. The requirements for the training school were that the men had to be between 17 and 27 years old. Seventeen-year-olds were encouraged to enlist as aviation cadets and go on reserve status until they were 18. At age 18, the young men could apply for training as pilots, bombardiers, and navigators.

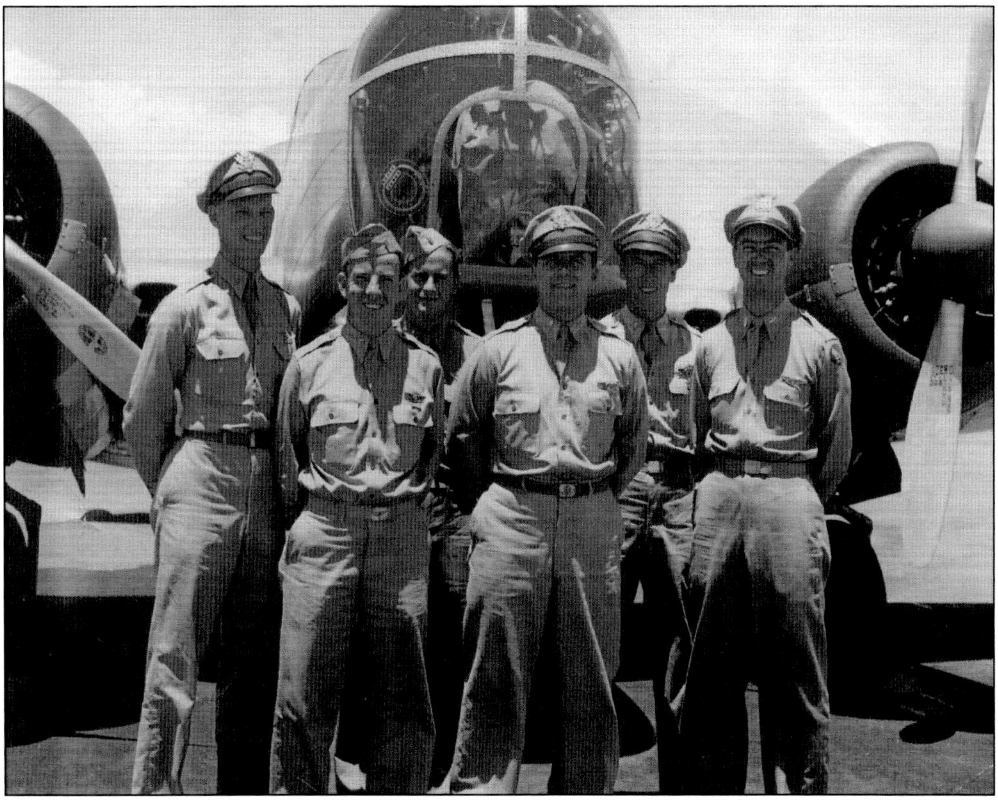

A group of men stands in front of an AT-11 at Deming Army Air Field. From left to right, they are (first row) Carolus, Neilson, and Mooney; (second row) Jack, Hambley, and Chapman. Nearly 8,000 men trained at the Deming Army Air Field.

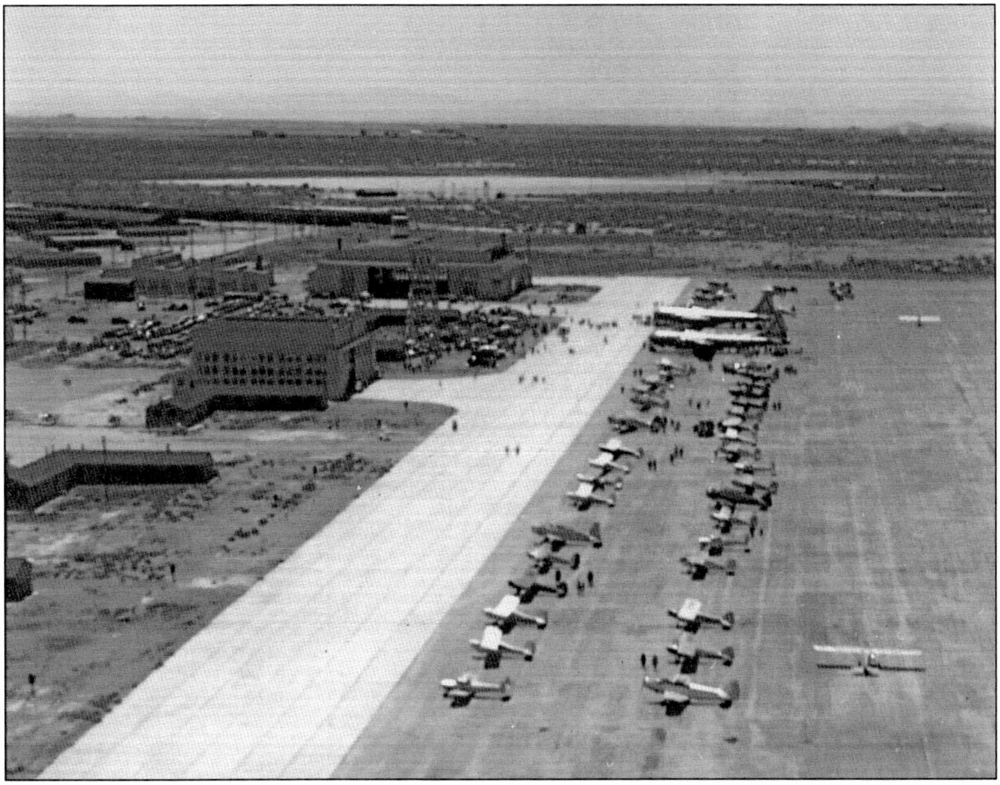

In July 1946, the Deming Chamber of Commerce joined the fight to keep the Army airfield in Deming. The chamber offered its support, as it felt that Deming could continue to support Army Air Reserve personnel. The men needed to log 80 hours of flying time per year, which was the chamber's case in pleading to keep Deming's field active. Unfortunately for the local economy, the airfield closed down. The federal government transferred the Deming Army Air Field to the Village of Deming. Planes sit on the flight line (above) as Deming residents look around their new airfield (right).

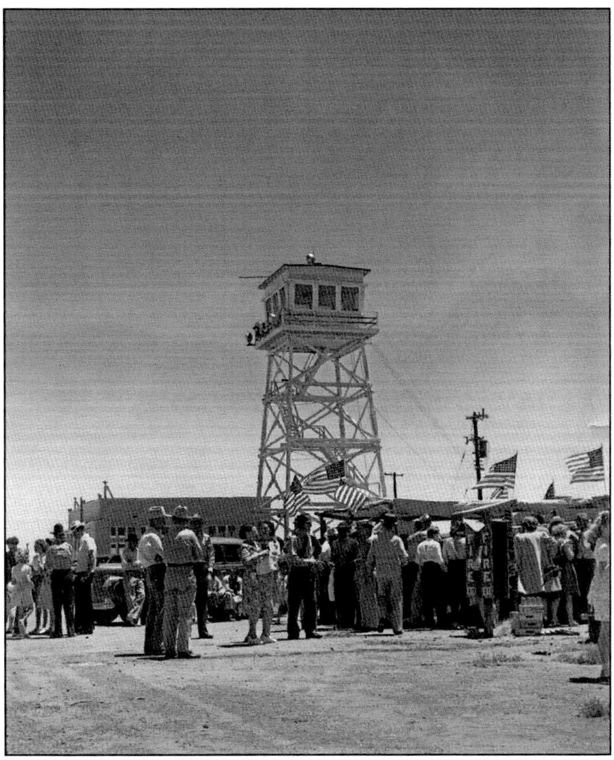

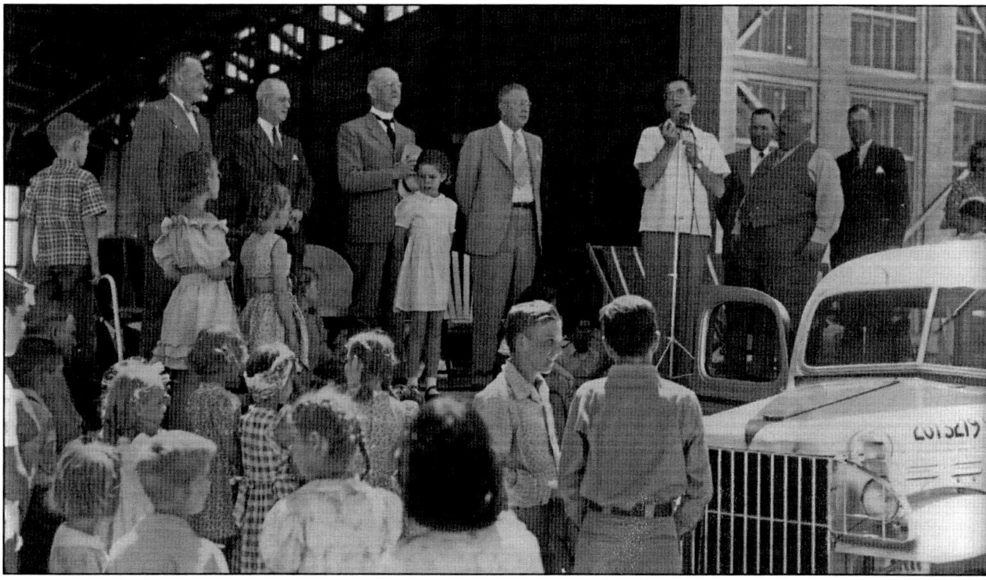

Officials at the June 1, 1947, ceremony are, from left to right, William B. Sloan and John A. Skeen of the War Assets Administration; Rev. G. W. Ribble of the Episcopal Church; Judge A.W. Marshall, who gave a short history on Deming; Robert Canavan of KROD radio of El Paso; Mayor Tom C. Getzwiller; Baron Auriemma of the Salvation Army; and G.W. Patterson, manager of the Deming Chamber of Commerce.

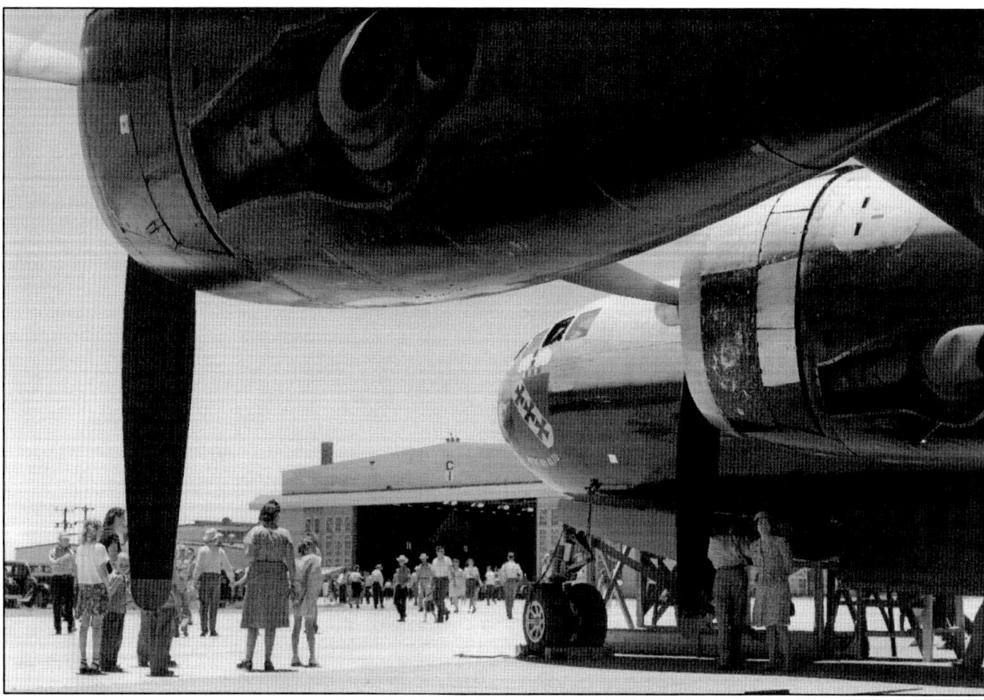

The dedication and celebration for the Deming Air Park, or Municipal Airport, began at 10:00 a.m. on June 1, 1947. The event concluded at 4:00 p.m. Invitations were sent out to 500 out-of-town guests who were connected to the event or part of the government. At least 2,000 people were expected in total.

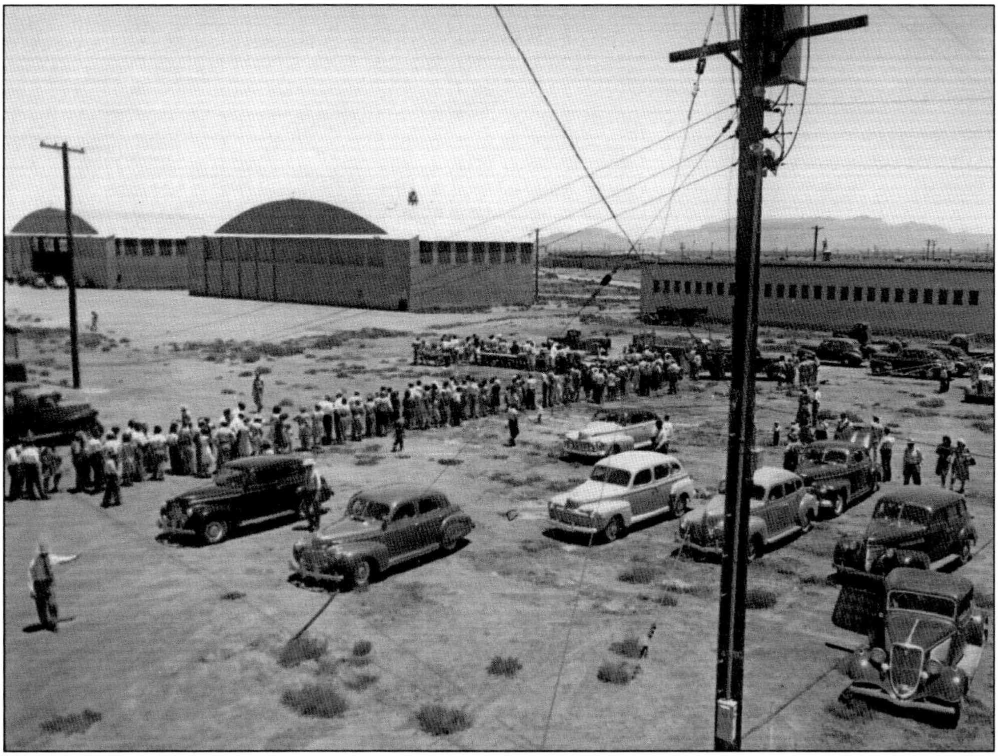

A large barbecue meal was prepared and served to the guests in attendance. Enough food for 1,500 people was brought to the airpark in anticipation of the large crowd. After the people made their way through the large buffet of food, they could eat picnic-style in the surrounding area.

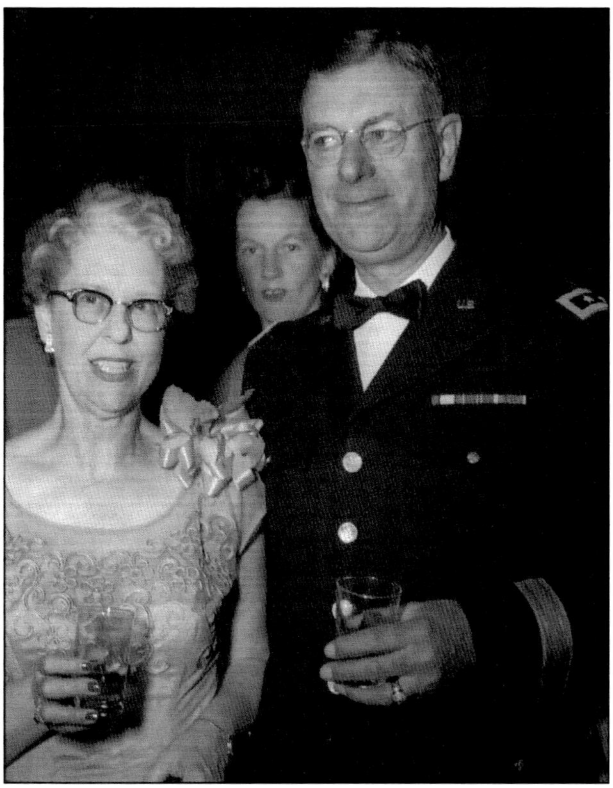

Maj. Gen. Charles Gordon Sage and his wife pose for a photograph at the National Convention of the Adjutants General in Santa Fe, New Mexico, in February 1954. Major General Sage was the commander of the 200th Coast Artillery in the Philippines and received a Distinguished Service Medal for meritorious service. Prior to the war, Sage was the publisher of the *Deming Headlight*.

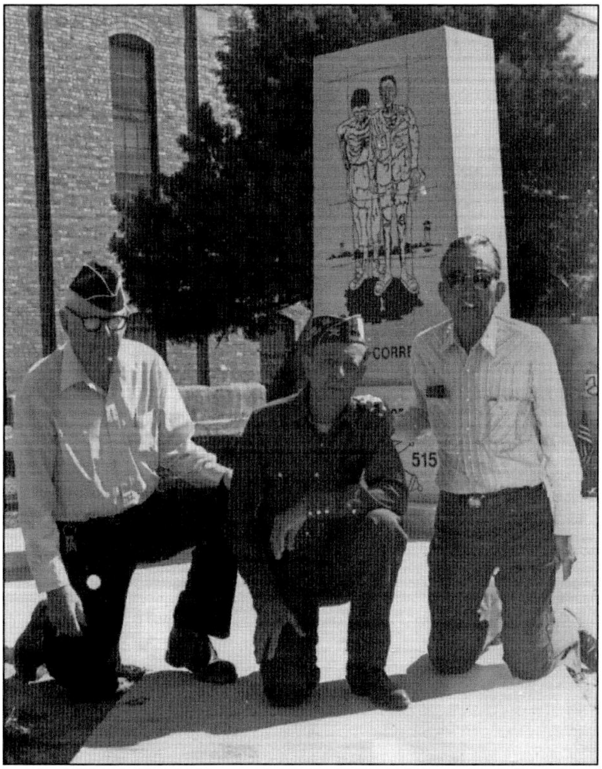

The special dedication for the large Bataan-Corregidor Monument, which is located in front of the Deming Luna Mimbres Museum, was held on April 19, 1991. The last surviving men of the Bataan Death March from Deming at the time are, from left to right, James W. Donaldson, Frederico S. Almeraz, and Lee R. Pelayo.

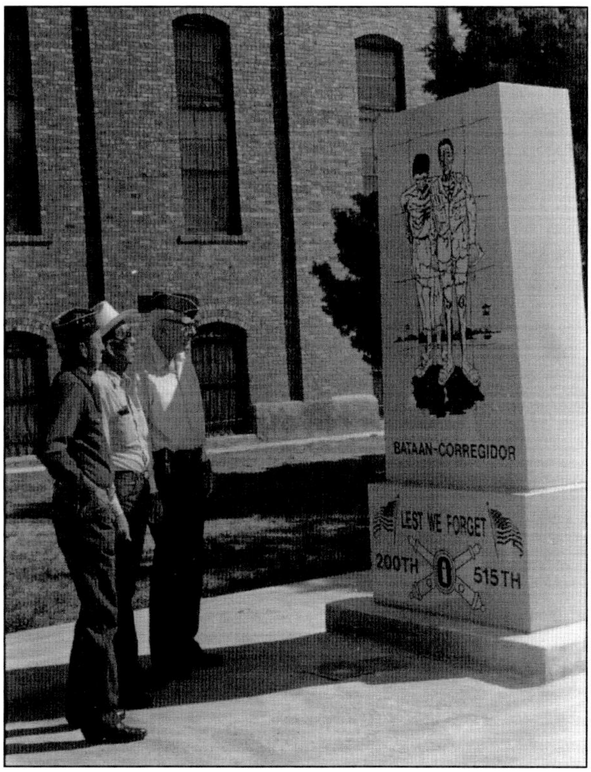

Bataan Death March survivors, from left to right, Frederico S. Almeraz, Lee R. Pelayo, and James W. Donaldson stand in front of a $14,000 monument to their struggles at Bataan-Corregidor. The monument was made possible by a small group of Deming residents who were interested in honoring these men. The group set a fundraising goal of $14,000, but by the time it completed its activities, $15,000 had been collected.

Nine

Highway and Interstate Bring Business and Tourists

The highway system that ran through Deming has significantly impacted how the business sector has operated. At three different times, the highway moved its route through Deming, and the center of the business sector changed with it. US Route 80 came through Deming's Spruce Street with the early automobile age in 1925. Businesses filled the city blocks. In 1950, Route 80 was moved to Pine Street, which gave each direction of traffic two lanes.

Route 80 was replaced in the 1960s with the bustling Interstate 10. This interstate moved the highway through Deming from Pine Street to Railroad Avenue. Road crews began surveying the streets of Deming in September 1961 for the proposed interstate. It was recommended in March 1962 that the highway pass through Deming between Railroad Avenue and Cedar Street. The green light was given to construction crews on May 9, 1963. I-10 continues to bring people who choose to relocate to the area and tourists looking for some delicious Mexican food or a stop at the large Deming Luna Mimbres Museum.

The interstate brought a new boost to the local economy in the 1960s. A division of Triple S Land Corporation, Deming Ranchettes, was a real estate development firm that was established in 1960s. This company sold parcels of land called "ranchettes." It bought 4,200 acres of land from the May Ranch, and about 80 percent of the land was sold as part of this development campaign. The ranchettes were sold to the public starting at half-acre tracts and were located within 10 to 20 minutes of Deming.

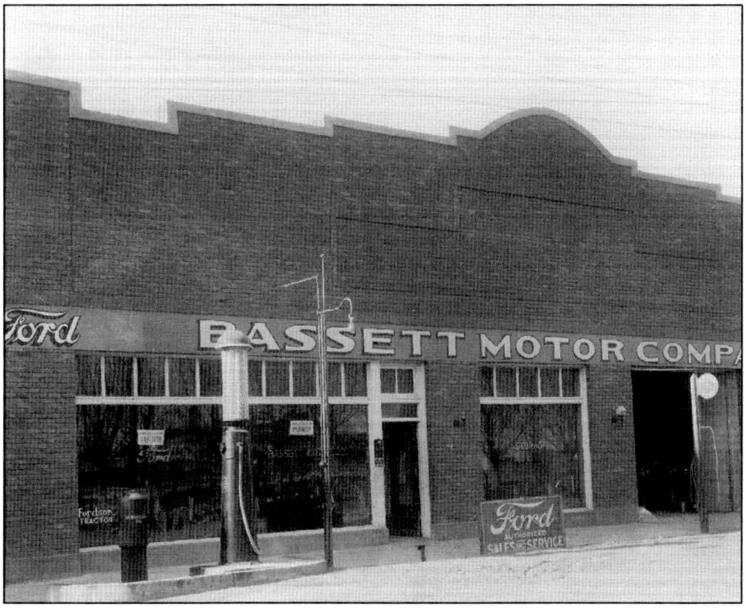

Bassett Motor Company was located at 110 East Railroad Avenue and later moved to 300 East Spruce Street. The Ford automobile agency was previously run by James Kerr and Fred Sherman and known as the Park Garage. In 1921, C.C. Bassett moved from Silver City, New Mexico, to manage the store.

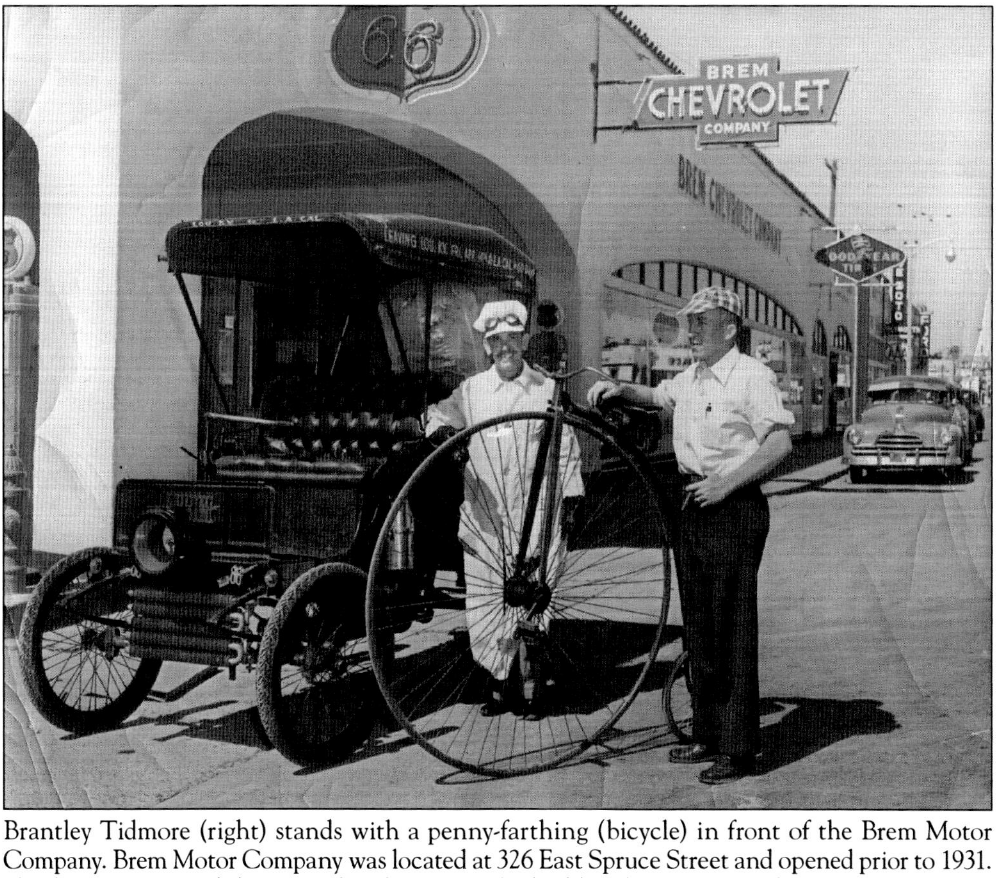

Brantley Tidmore (right) stands with a penny-farthing (bicycle) in front of the Brem Motor Company. Brem Motor Company was located at 326 East Spruce Street and opened prior to 1931. Fletcher Brem owned the expanding business. The building became a Sinclair service station in 1941. Brem owned several stations in Deming.

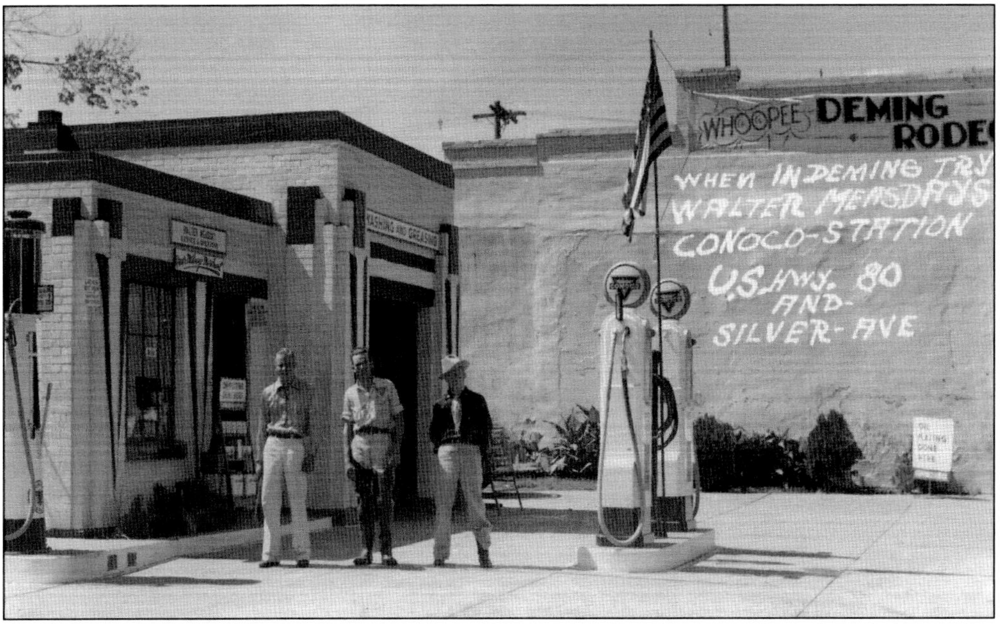

Standing in front of the Measday Conoco Station at 122 East Spruce Street, from left to right, are Lawrence Measday, T.N. O'Kelly, and Walter Measday. Walter began leasing the building in 1937, when this photograph was taken. The structure was formerly owned by John Bell. Lawrence, Walter's son, took over the lease in 1940 so Walter could focus his effort on his Goodrich store across the street.

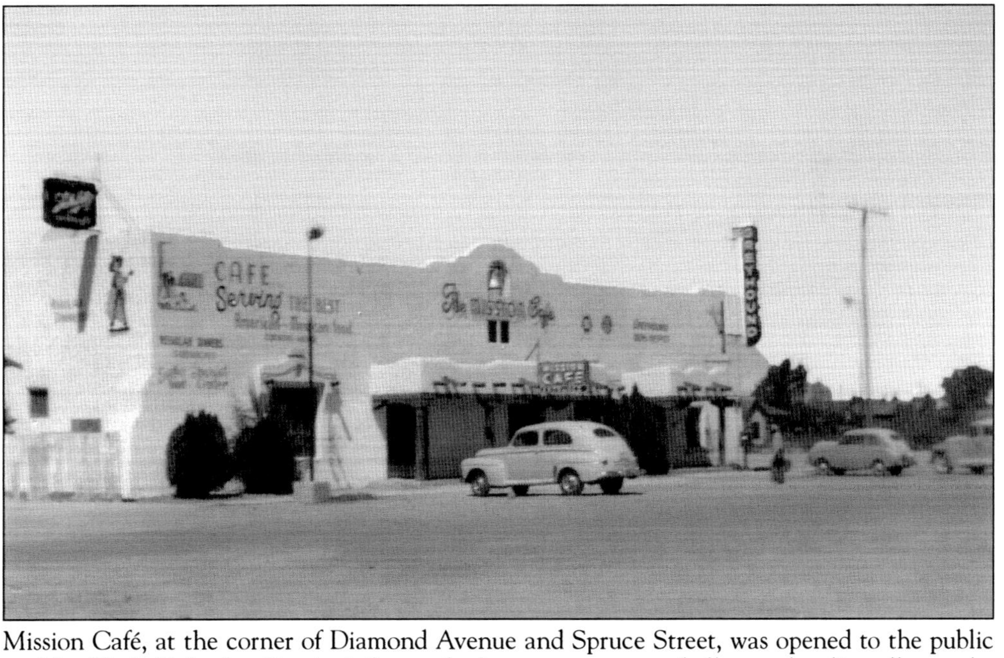

Mission Café, at the corner of Diamond Avenue and Spruce Street, was opened to the public on May 25, 1940, by Joe Garcia. It featured a lounge, restaurant, ballroom, bowling alley, and a Greyhound bus station. Garcia closed the business, and Ben Franklin Craft Store and Safeway occupied the structure before it became the Garcia Civic Center. Today, Marshall Memorial Library uses the large building.

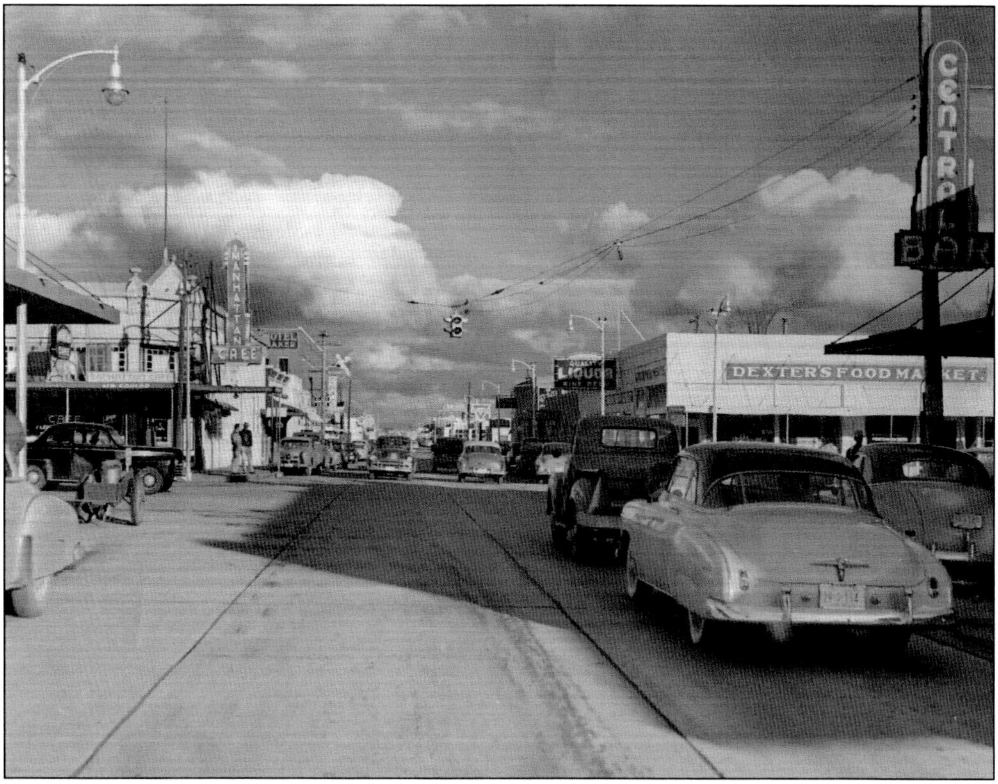

This is the corner of Spruce Street and Gold Avenue. The Manhattan Café and Hotel Baker can be seen on the left, while Central Bar and Dexter's Food Market are on the right. The photographer is standing on Spruce Street facing east in between the Mahoney Building (left) and Central Bar (right). Bill Mihaus opened the Manhattan Café in 1937.

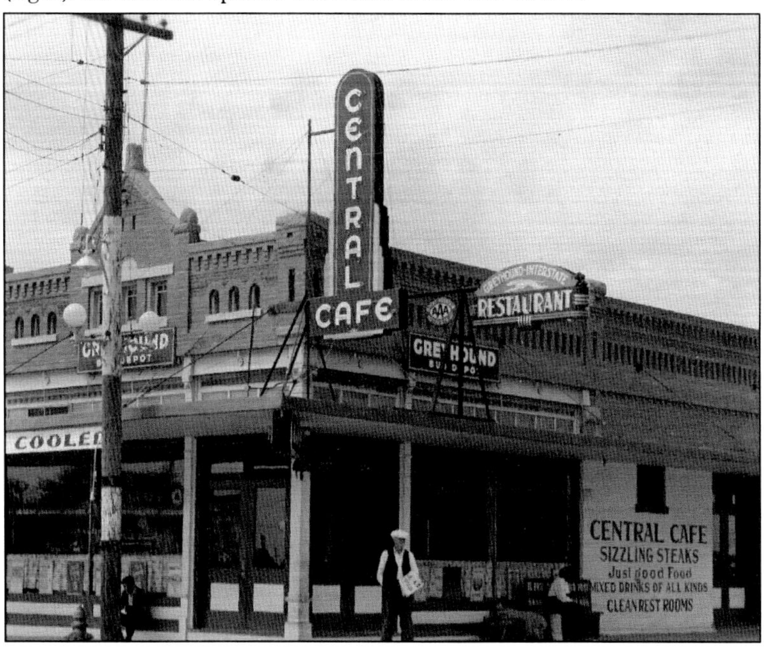

Central Café and Bar operated for at least 30 years in Deming. It was located on the southwest corner of Spruce Street and Gold Avenue. The large bar was mahogany-backed. Many locals held gatherings and groups held meetings there. Travelers along US Route 80 often stopped in for a delicious meal or a drink.

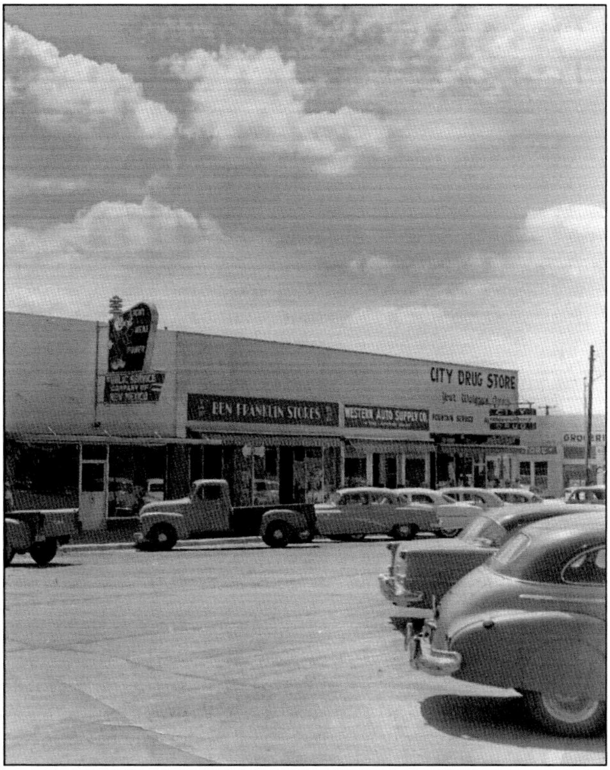

These are the businesses that were on the east side of Gold Avenue. They are, from left to right, Public Service Company of New Mexico, Ben Franklin Stores, Western Auto Supply Company, and City Drug Store. City Drug Store occupied the corner after the Manhattan Café closed. Western Auto Supply Company began on Iron Street and moved to the location on Spruce Street in November 1941.

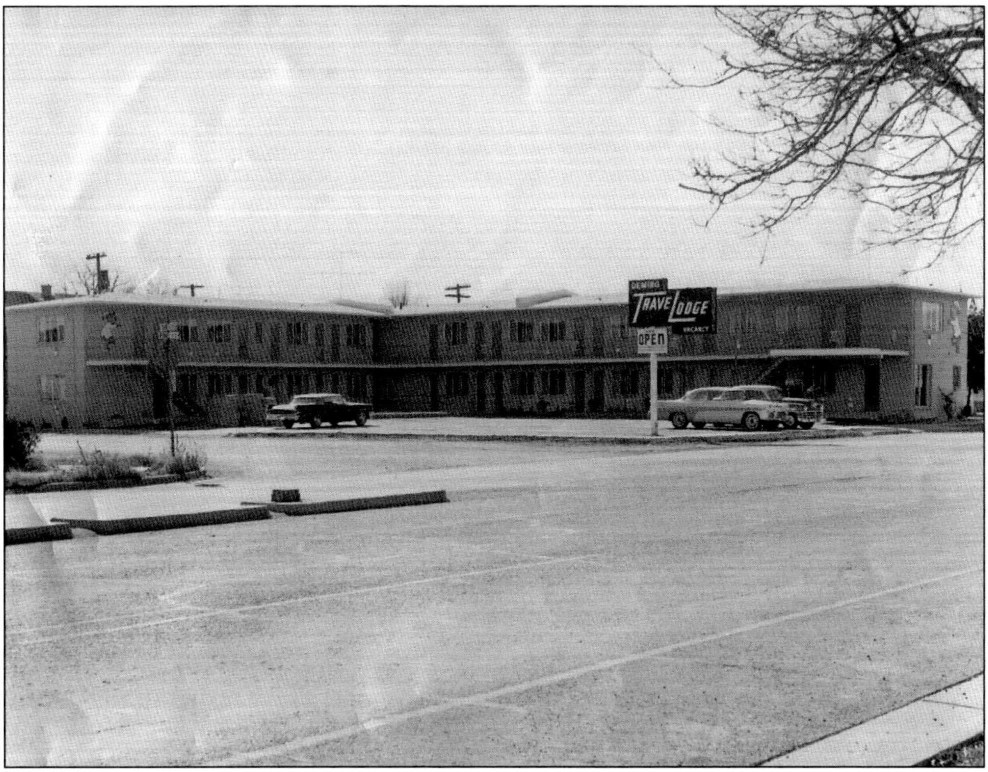

Travel Lodge Motel was a large two-story structure built in 1958. It was located at 500 West Pine Street. At that time, Ralph Zabrist and his wife operated the motel. The metal bars that wrap around the building have the letters *TL* on them, representing the name of the business. Today, Deming Motel occupies the structure.

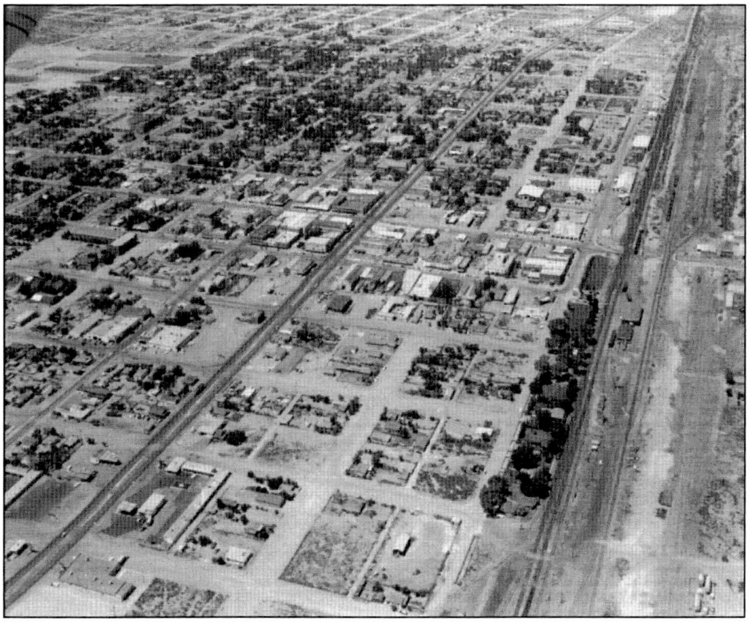

This aerial photograph of Deming was taken in 1959. The broad streets running north and south are named for minerals, while the streets running west and east are named for trees. Deming's original plan was similar to what westward settlers claimed resembled Colorado Springs, Colorado, in the 1880s.

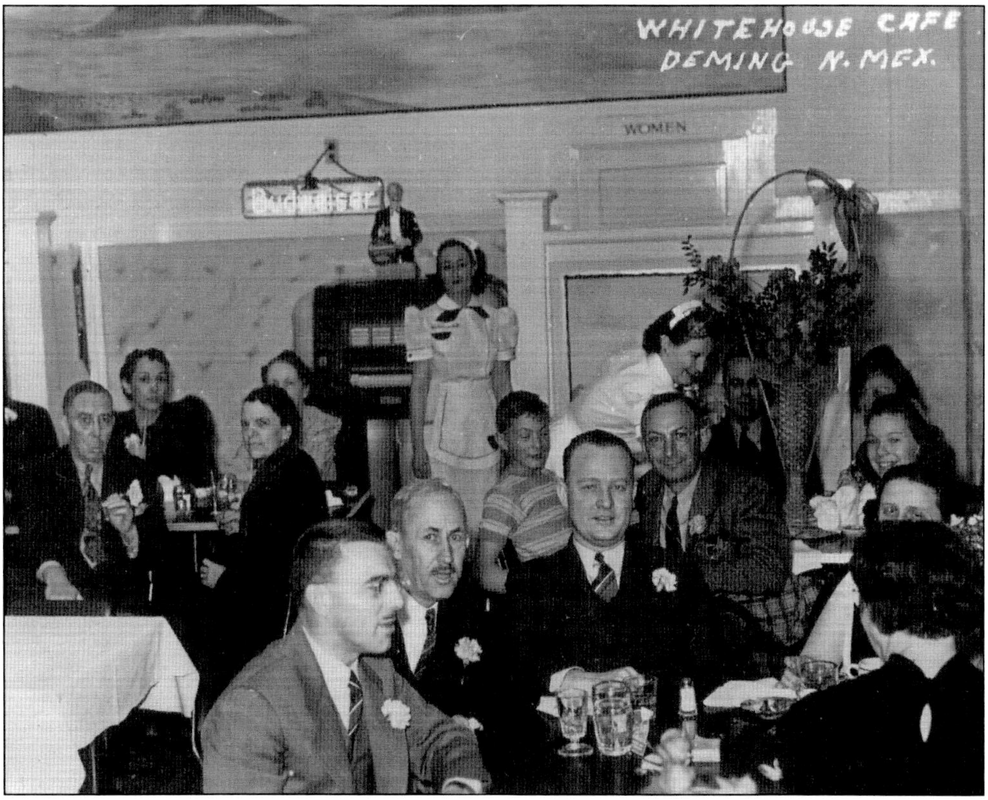

The White House Café, located at 116 West Pine Street, used to house the Clark Opera Company. Prior to moving into the theater building in 1954, the café was located in a building at 119 East Spruce Street. William Jarvis owned the café, which began prior to 1931, until 1963, when he sold it to Richard Sainz.

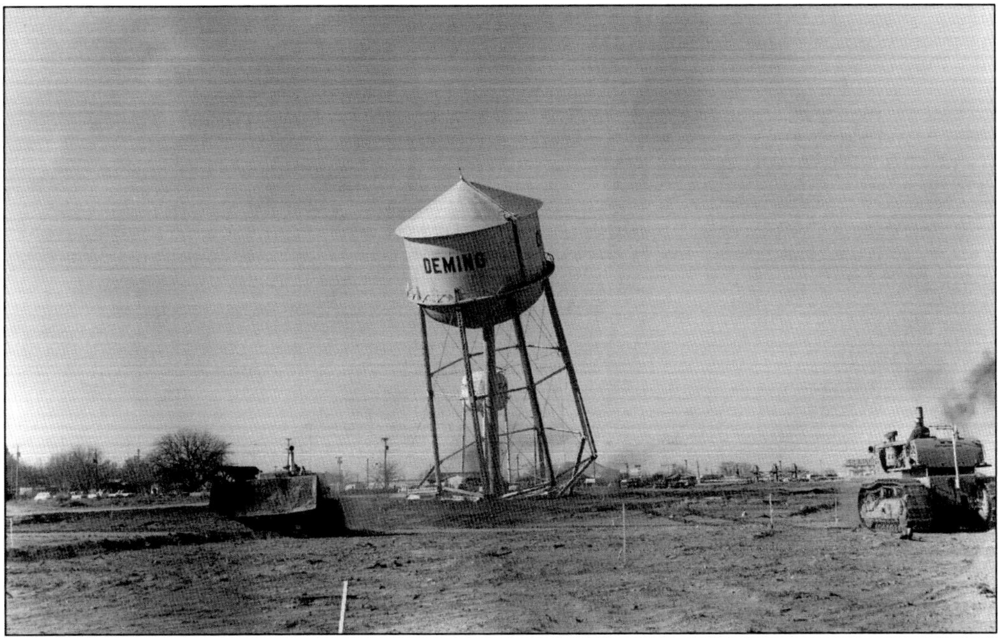

The old water tower (foreground) on property in west Deming is taken down in 1963 on account of the interstate coming through town. A larger tower (rear) replaced it. Shortly after the new water tower was put up, the city council voted to paint it blue instead of leaving it as the factory aluminum.

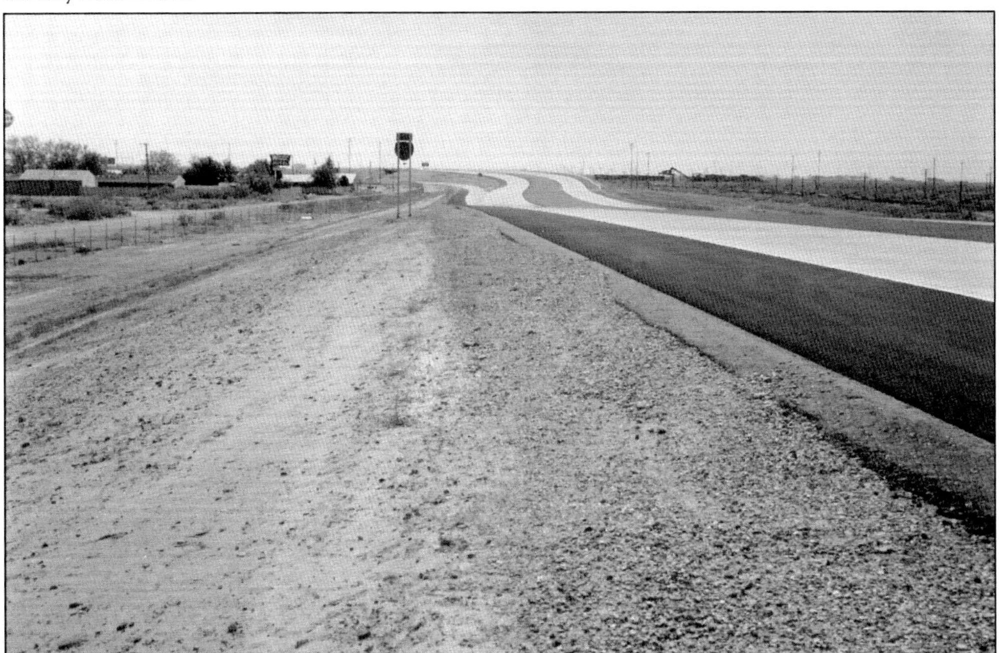

Many businesses had to close their doors and relocate. Deming Coca-Cola Bottling Company, Foxworth Galbraith Lumber Company, Harris Electric, and Dunne's Automotive all found new homes in Deming. Several business owners, such as the proprietors of the Park Hotel, chose not to relocate. There were also many residential properties along the path of the interstate.

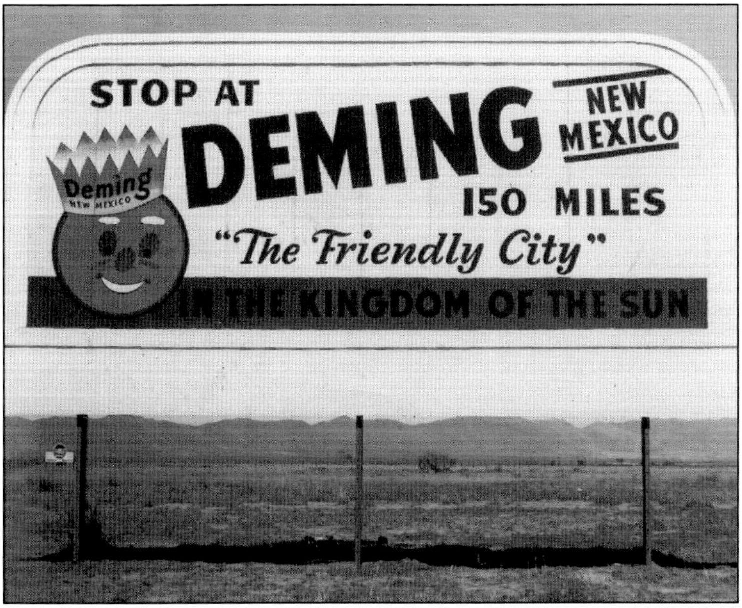

This large billboard advertising Deming, "The Friendly City," greets people passing through on Interstate 10. "The Kingdom of the Sun" was Deming's slogan during this time. A Deming radio station's call letters also reflected the slogan in 1948. The call letters were KOTS (Kingdom of the Sun).

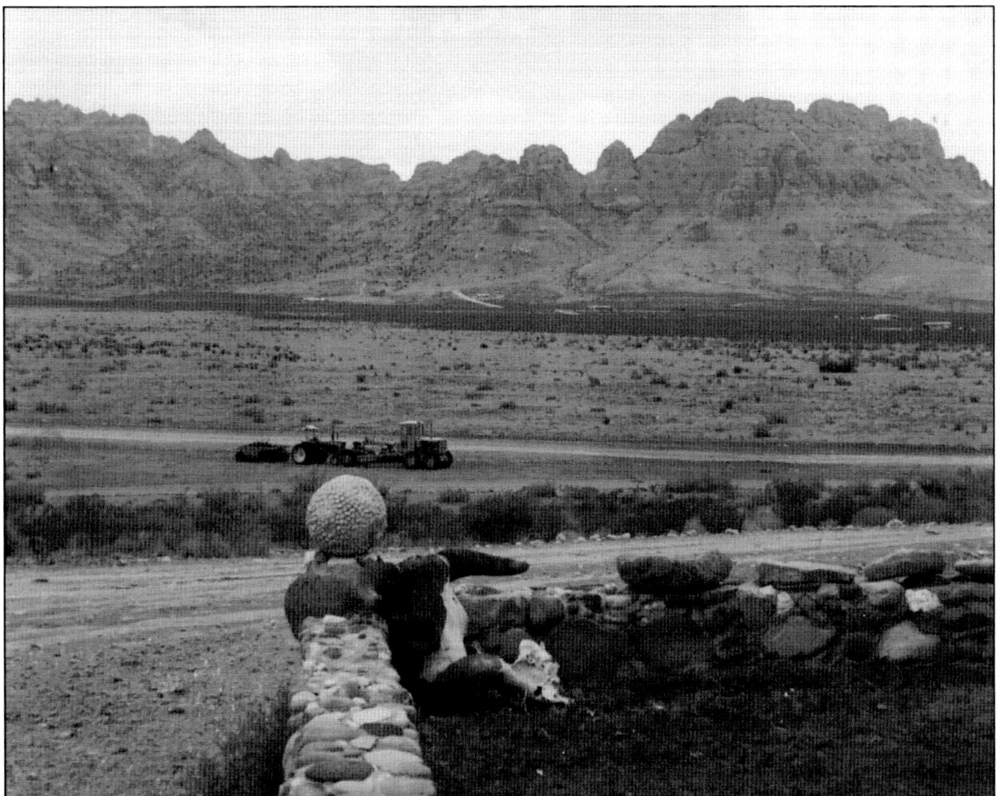

The majestic Florida Mountains rise over construction at Deming Ranchettes. A division of Triple S Land Corporation, Deming Ranchettes was a real estate development firm that was established in the 1960s. Harold Schwartz, Hank Schlasberg, and Larry Serlin came together in 1961 and were joined by realtor Carter Kirk in 1965.

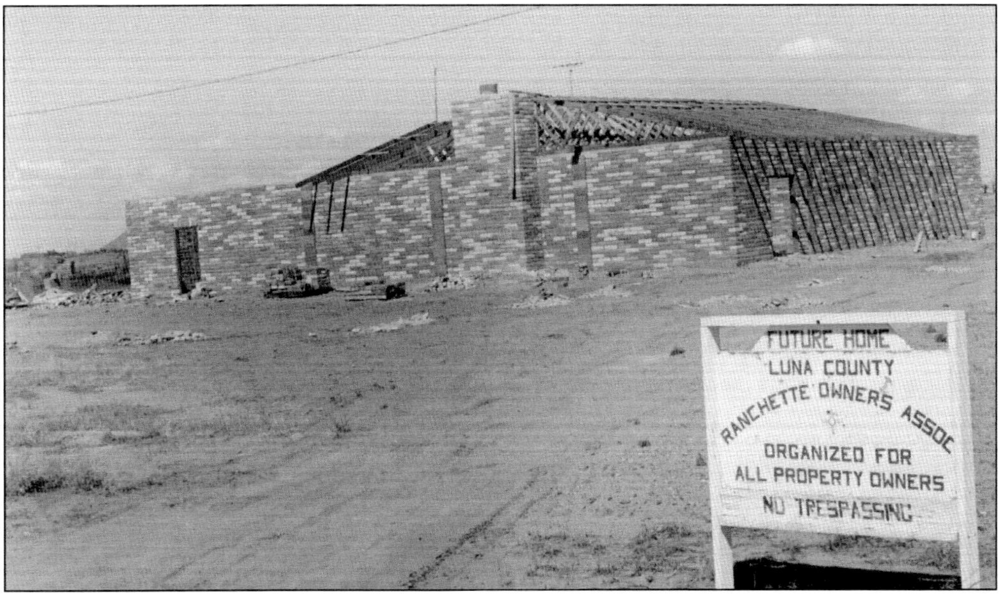

Due to the success of the Deming Ranchettes advertising campaign, people were flocking to the town. Luna County ranked third for population growth among the 32 counties in New Mexico during this time. The Luna County Ranchette Owners Association (LCROA) was organized, and a building was erected off of Rockhound Road, southeast of Deming.

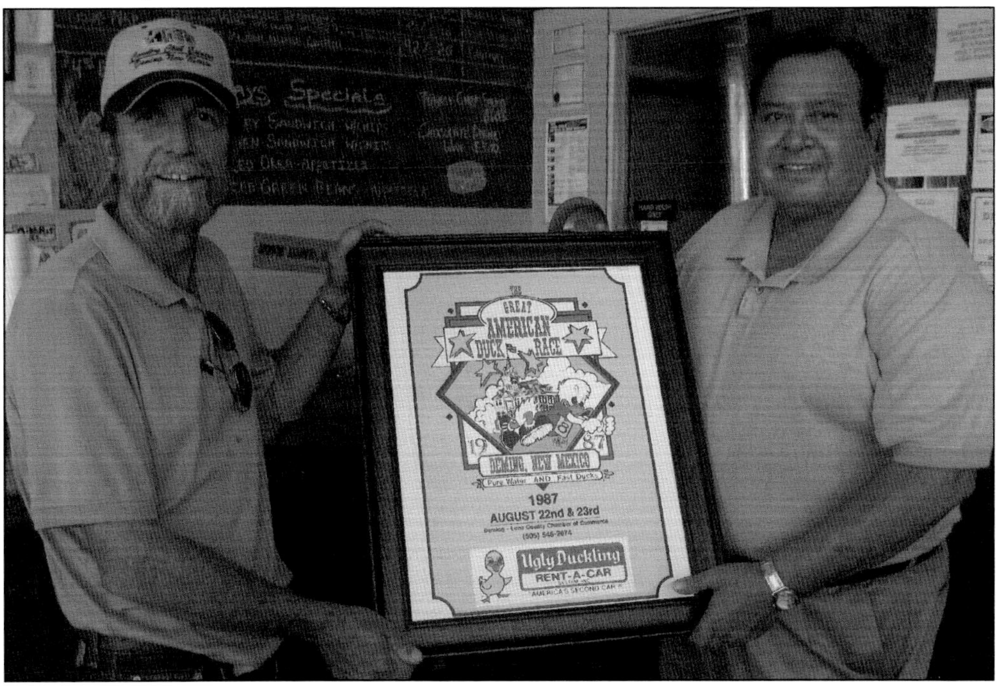

The Great American Duck Race began in 1980, after a group of friends met over after-work drinks to brainstorm ways to boost tourism. The promoters grew to include Harold Cousland, William McKinley, Joe "Butter" Milo, Bernie Green, Jim Reedy, Jim Worthan, and Steve Marlowe. Reedy (left) and Milo (right), photographed at the Mimbres Valley Brewing Company, are the only two originators left in Deming. (Courtesy of the author.)

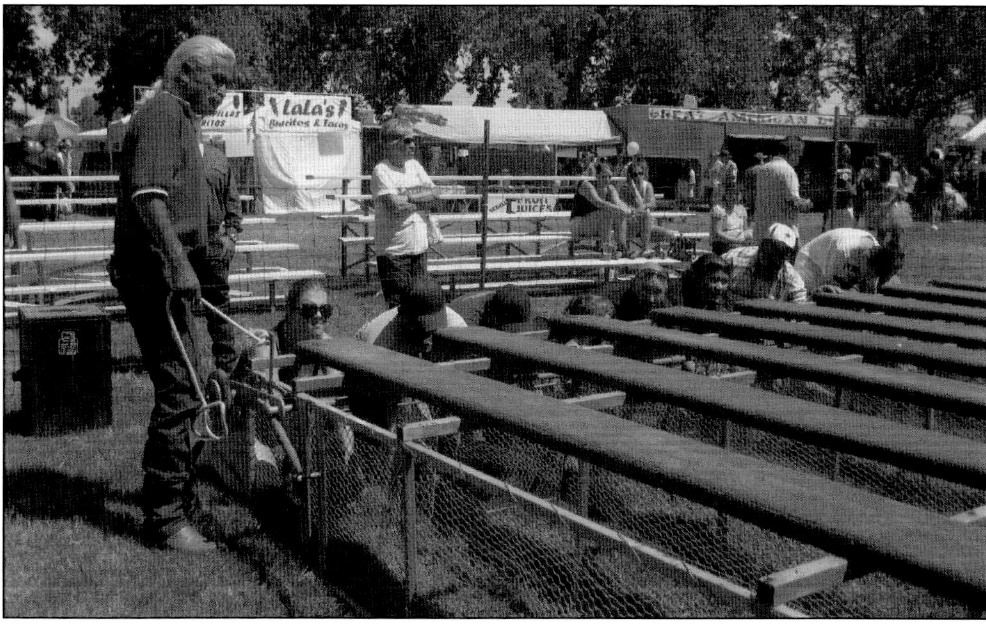

The ducks used in the races are rented for $5 per race. One duck is put in each of the eight lanes on the track. The duck wrangler, Steve Smith (left) releases the gate, and the ducks waddle to the finish line. The first duck to get there wins. Winners compete in quarter- and semifinals to find the grand champion. (Courtesy of the author.)

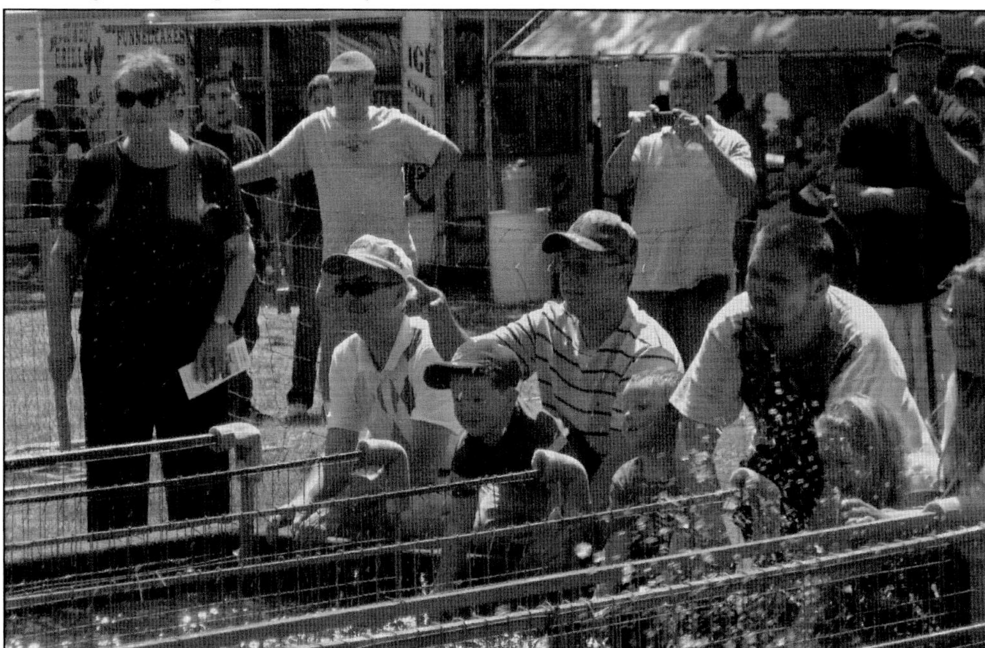

A few years ago, a wet track was also added. The idea of racing ducks down eight lanes remained the same, but splashing water at the ducks added to the fun. Several small children are accompanied by their parents to see their ducks off the tracks. The Great American Duck Races are held on the fourth weekend in August. (Courtesy of the author.)

Ten

FAMOUS FOLKS LIVED IN DEMING

What do Charlotte Thurmond, Nacio Herb Brown, and Ray Cash all have in common? A famous Texas gambler, a brilliant musical composer, and a devoted father to one of the most well-known country singers have all lived in Deming, New Mexico. Thurmond lived in Deming for 53 years, while Nacio Herb Brown resided there for only eight years. It is unknown the total time that Cash was in Deming—most likely one year.

Charlotte Thurmond was known elsewhere as Lottie Deno, a famous female Texas gambler. Deming residents knew her as "Aunt Lottie." She was a very active member of the community after her arrival to Deming in 1881. While it was often whispered that Thurmond had an exciting past, it was overlooked due to her kindness and generosity.

Nacio Herb Brown, composer of the famous song "Singin' in the Rain," was born in Deming on February 23, 1896. He was raised by a musically inclined family and learned to play the piano and violin. Brown was eight years old when his father was offered a deputy sheriff position in Los Angeles, California. His family moved there because of his father's career. Brown went to school and became a famous composer but never forgot his hometown.

After he enlisted in the Army, Johnny Cash's father, Ray Cash, was stationed at Camp Deming under the command of Gen. John J. "Black Jack" Pershing in 1916. Cash told stories to his sons about sleeping with one leg in the United States and the other in Mexico waiting for Pancho Villa to appear. Cash returned to Deming in 1981 for its Centennial Celebration honoring the establishment of the town.

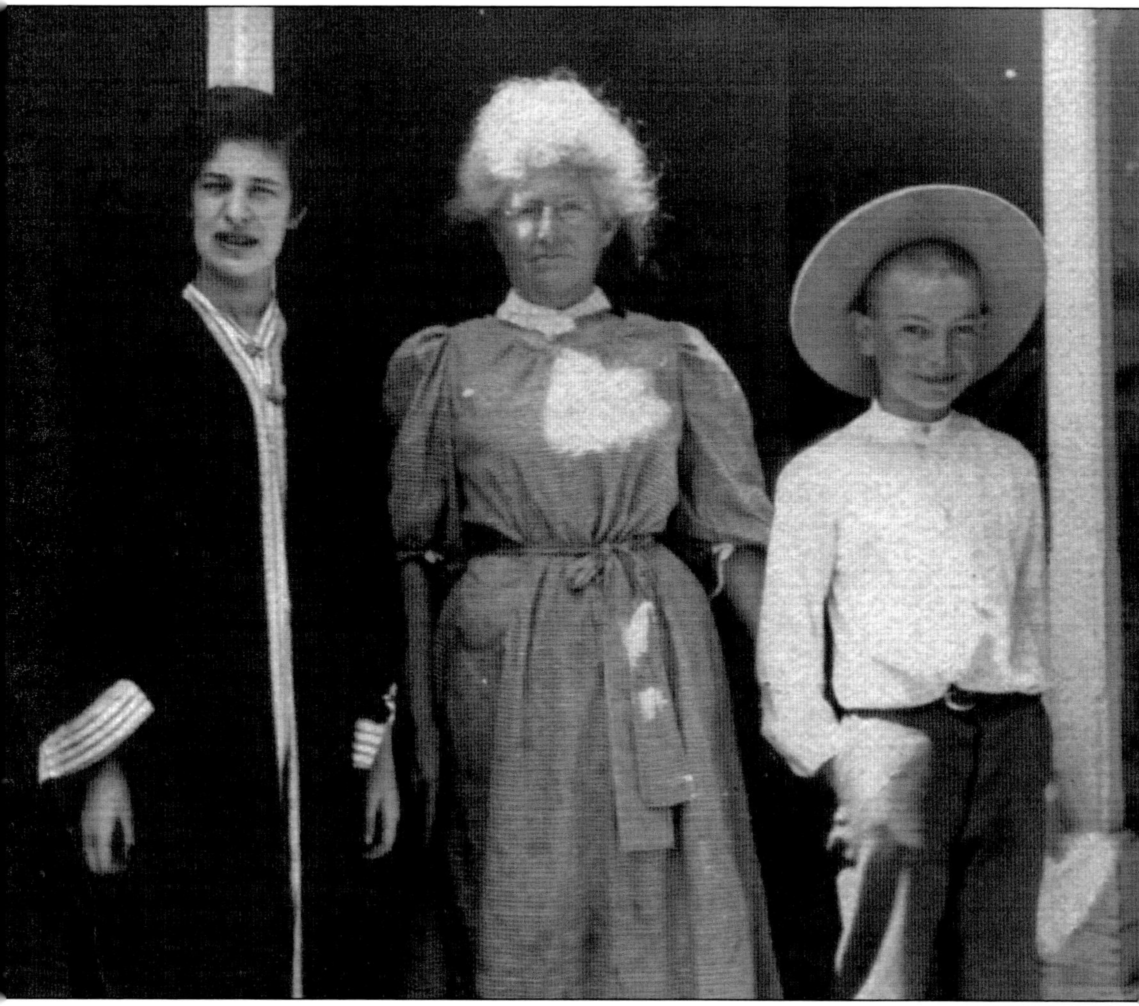

Charlotte Thurmond (center) is standing between Lillian Lindauer (left) and Herman Lindauer. Thurmond was born Carlotta J. Thompkins and used to play with her father's slaves on the family plantation when she was younger. Her father was a member of the Kentucky Congress. After he passed away in the Civil War, she moved to Detroit, Michigan, and became a gambler in a private club. She supported her mother, who was in a wheelchair, and her younger sister until her mother's death. Then, she moved to San Antonio, Texas, and gambled for one year. Afterward, she occupied herself by conducting poker games at University Club. It was run by three Thurmond brothers, one of whom, Frank, became her husband in 1866. They moved to Deming in 1881.

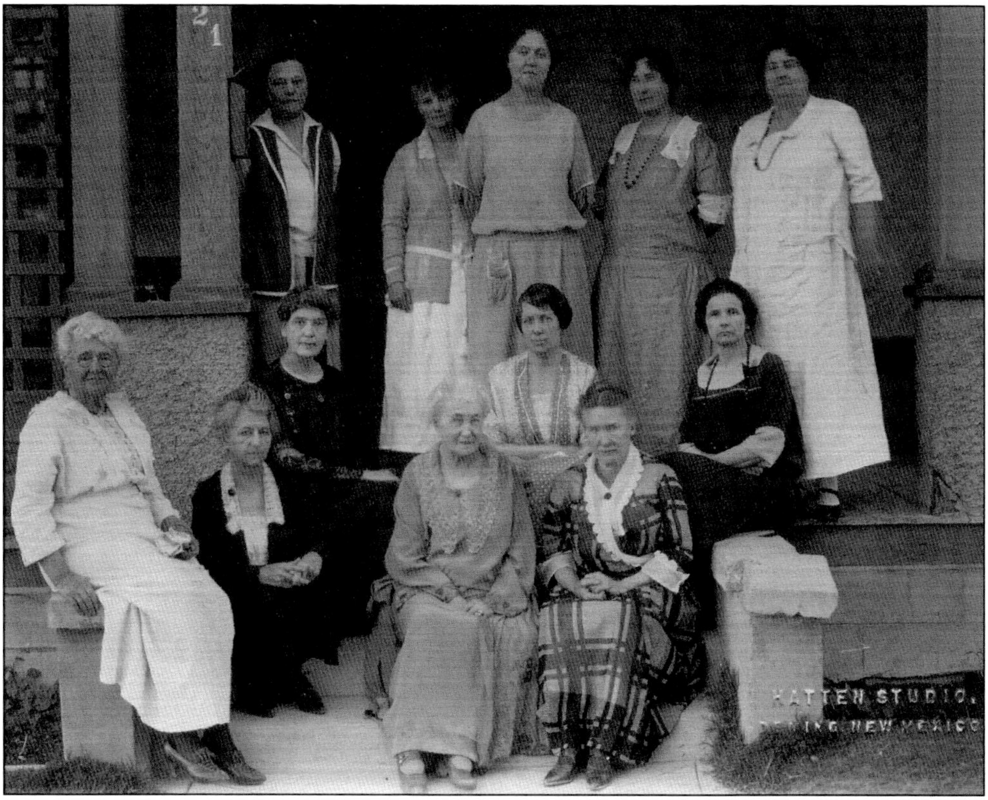

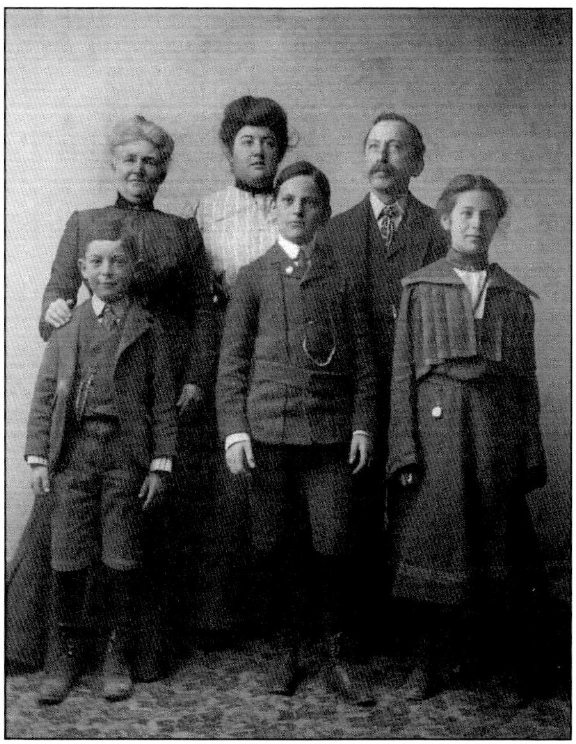

Charlotte Thurmond was the organizer of the Golden Gossip Club in 1912. The group of a dozen wives of local businessmen met weekly to play bridge and other card games, knit, and sew while they discussed all of the things that needed care in Deming. In the image above, from left to right, are Charlotte Thurmond, Ellen M. Holt, ? Rogers, ? Shepherd, Mary L. Donaldson, Edith E. Pollard, Cora L. Steed, Kate E. Moir, Mary E. Bickford, May Schoepf, Doll W. Jordan, and Ella Mahoney. Membership was exclusive, and a spot was opened only when a member died or moved. The Sigmund Lindauer family became very close to Thurmond. In the image at right, from left to right, are Herman and Bertha Lindauer, Charlotte Thurmond, Samson, Sigmund, and Lillian Lindauer.

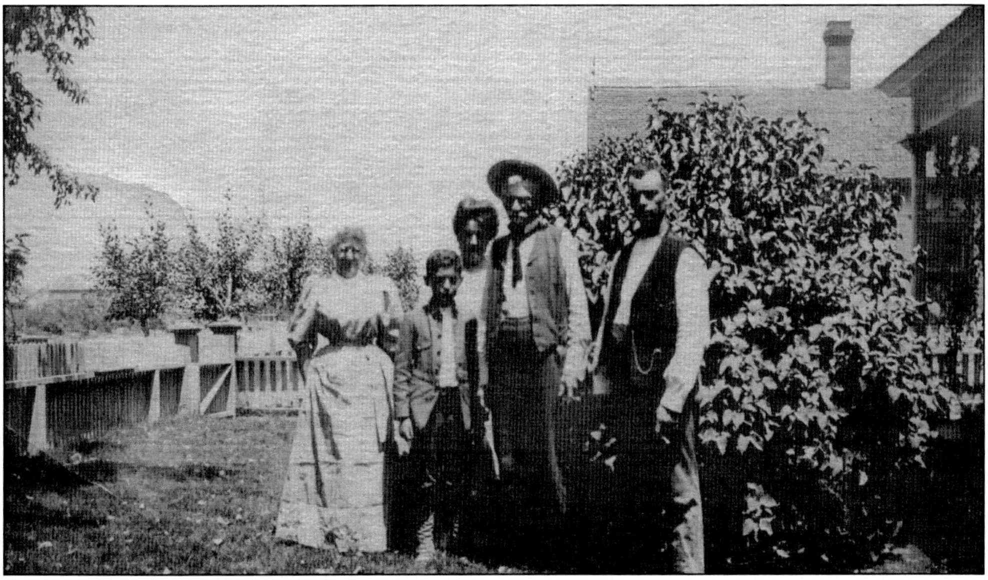

This photograph was taken prior to 1908 with, from left to right, Charlotte Thurmond, Herman and Lillian Lindauer, Frank Thurmond, and Samson Lindauer. Frank owned a ranch outside of Deming. He passed away in 1908 from cancer of the mouth. Colorful stories were told of him. He is buried in Mountain View Cemetery in Deming, New Mexico.

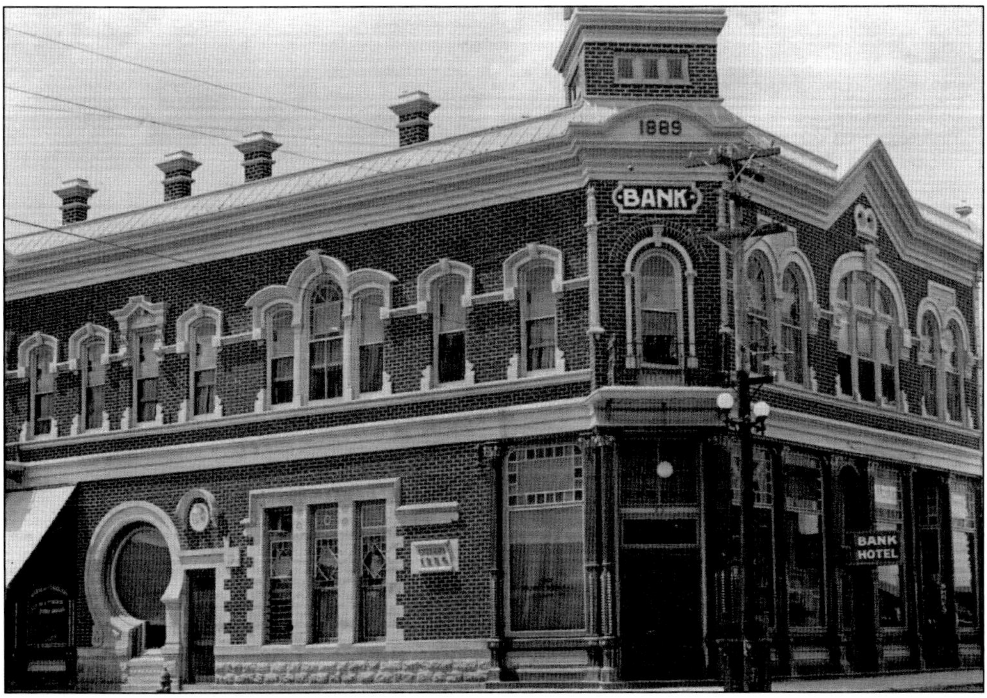

There was a period where the Bank of Deming was closed by a bank examiner. During that time, Frank Thurmond demanded that he be able to withdraw his $1,110 on deposit. Since all payments were pending investigation, Thurmond pulled his Colt .45 six-shooter and received his money quickly. He was arrested, but his case was dismissed in territorial court, and the money that he attempted to withdraw from the bank was returned the him.

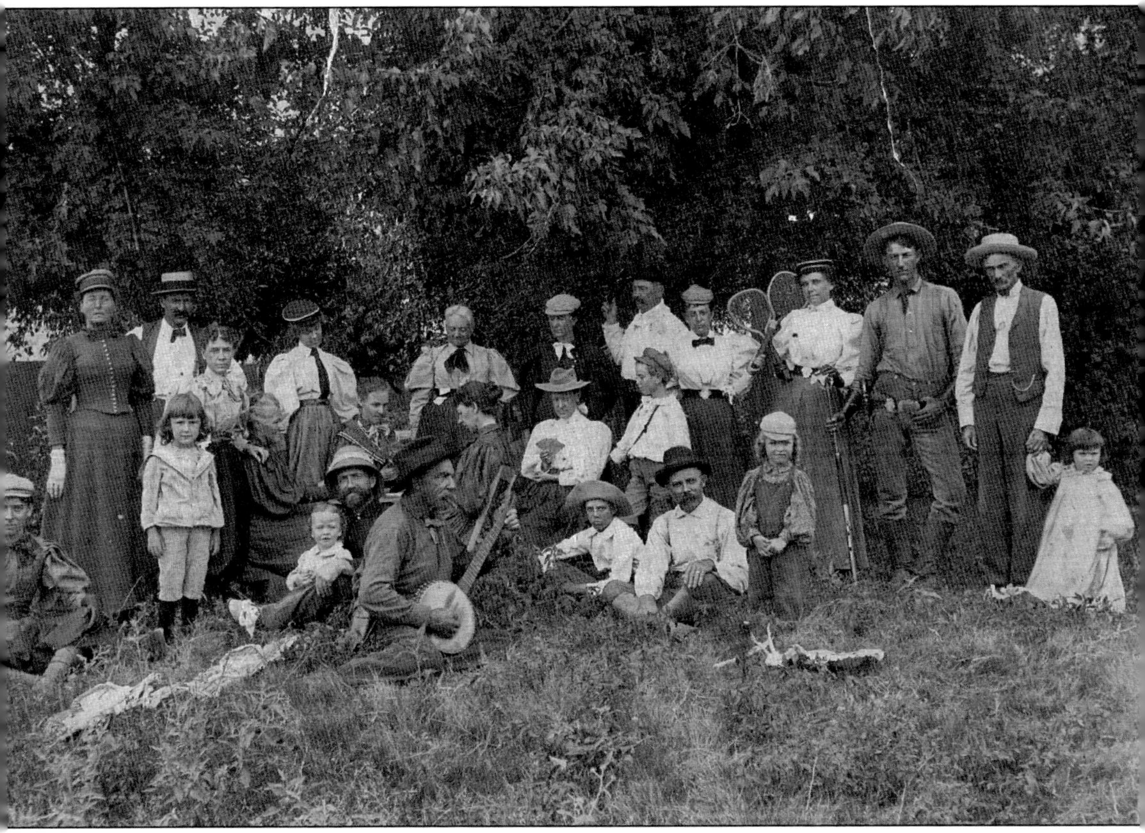

It was very common for friends to gather on the Gila River north of Deming for hiking and camping trips. This image includes, from left to right, (sitting in the first row) unidentified, Helen Swope (baby), Dr. Swope, ? Gilbert (with banjo), Ralph Byron, and Dr. Byron; (sitting and playing cards) Charlotte Thurmond, ? Swope, Anna Gould, and Marie Gould; (standing around card players) Louis Brown and Mary Lou Swope; (standing in second row) ? Gilbert, Newton A. Bolich, ? Bolich, Alice G. Smith, May Bolich, ? Congdon, Belle Congdon (with racket), Allie Beals (with racket), Butch Smith, Frank Thurmond (holding child's hand), and Esther Bolich.

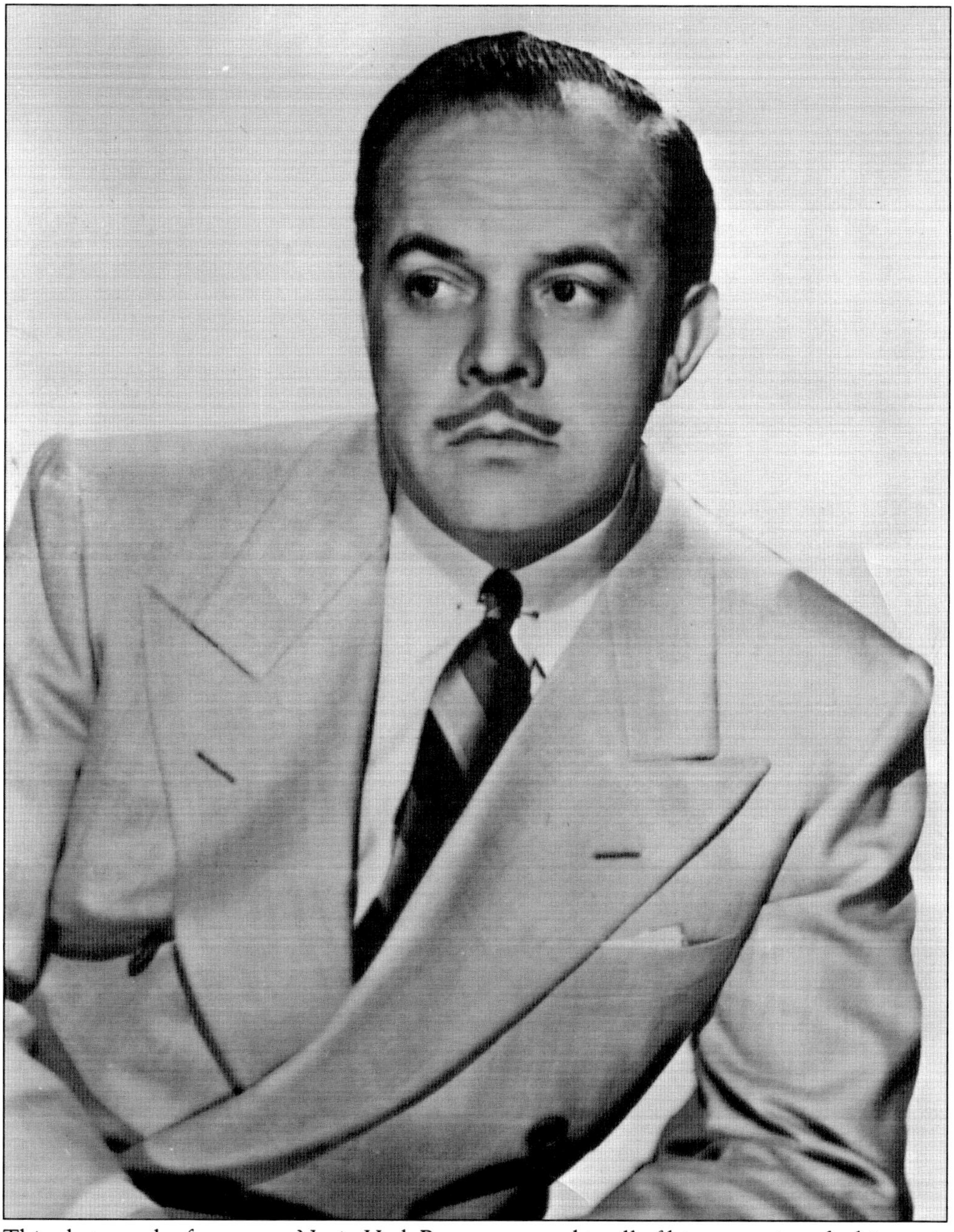

This photograph of composer Nacio Herb Brown was used in all of his promotions for his music and events. Though Brown only spent eight years of his young life in Deming, the community was always very proud of his accomplishments and claimed him as its own. After Brown graduated from high school, he attended the Southern Branch of the University of California (now UCLA), where he earned a degree in business. Brown teamed up with Alice Doll, a vaudeville singer, as an accompanist. This is how his music career began. Brown intended on retiring in Deming, but he died before he could return to his hometown. He passed away at age 68 on September 28, 1964, of cancer. He is buried in Inglewood Park Cemetery in Inglewood, California. He was the father of three children.

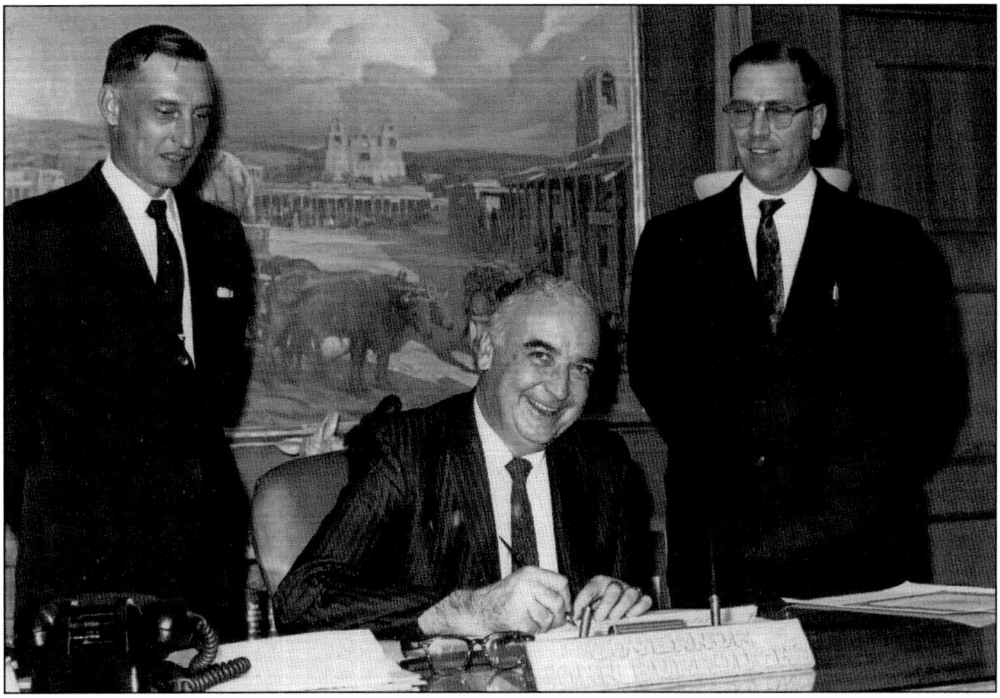

Nacio Herb Brown returned to Deming in February 1960 to celebrate his birthday with folks from his hometown. Two Deming men went to the capitol at Santa Fe, New Mexico, to witness the signing of an official proclamation at the governor's office. In the image above, New Mexico governor John Burroughes (center) signs the Nacio Herb Brown Day Proclamation as Robert Tobey (left) and Robert Beckett (right) happily watch him. Below, Governor Burroughes (center) hands the Nacio Herb Brown Day Proclamation to Robert Tobey (right) as Robert Beckett watches. Radio stations around the area featured Brown's music on Nacio Herb Brown Day.

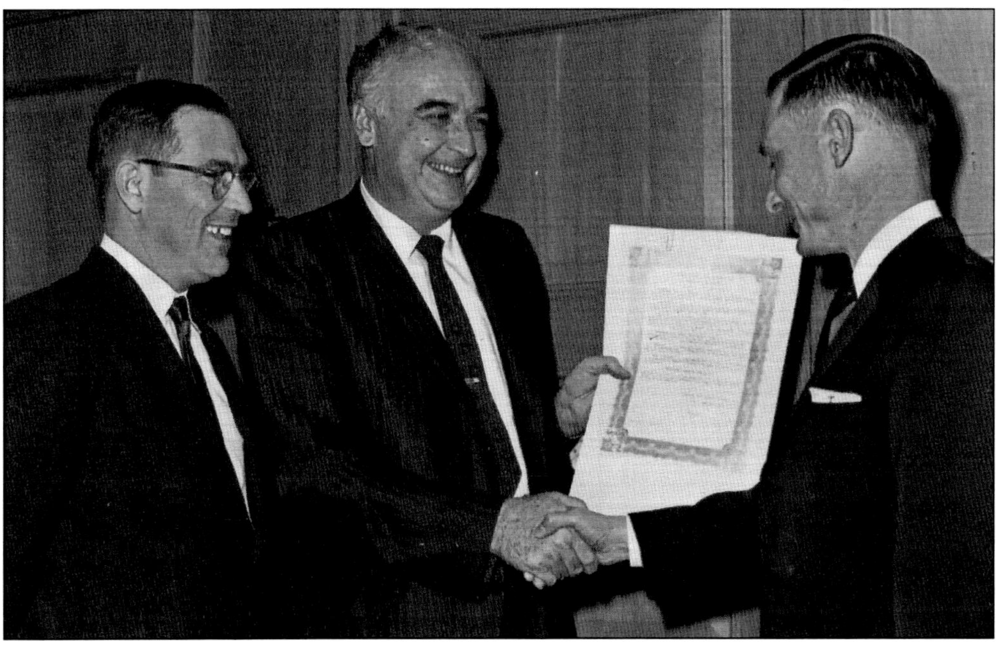

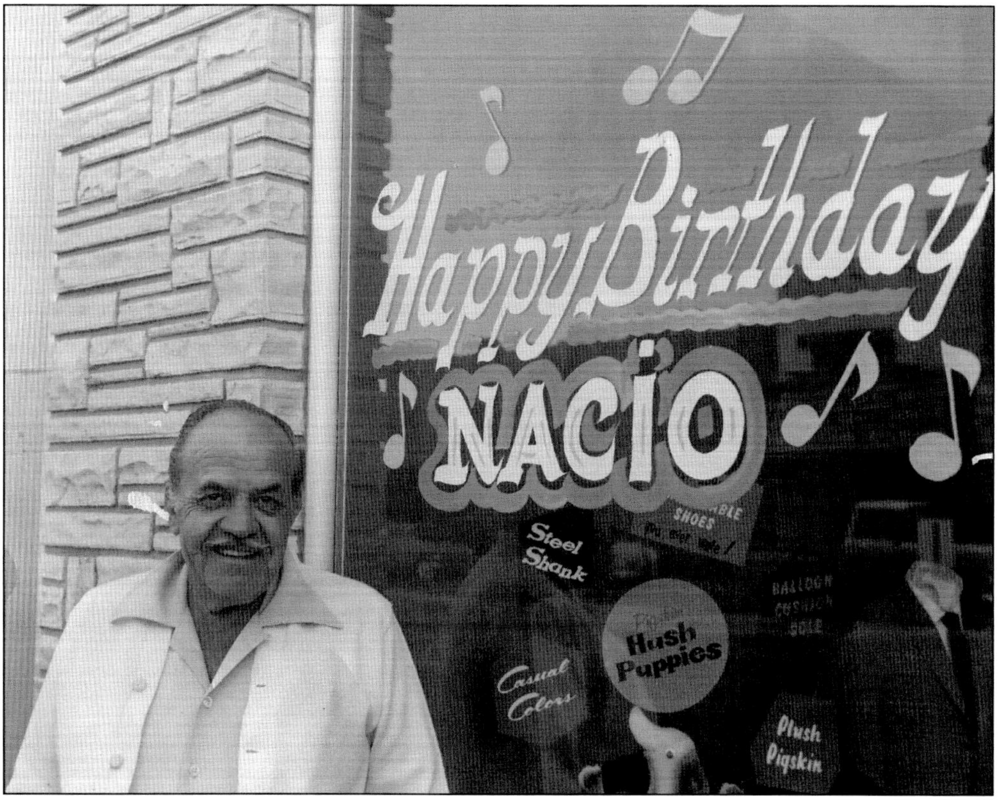

Nacio Herb Brown stands in front of a store window on Pine Street that advertises, "Happy Birthday, Nacio" (above). Deming mayor Adrien D. Graveline (left) speaks at the microphone and reads the plaque aloud at Brown's birthday ceremony (below). R.J. Hodson (right) stands next to Nacio Herb Brown (center). A large "Welcome Home" banner hangs in the background above the Deming High School Wildcat Band. In return for this gesture by the community and the state, Brown wrote the "Deming High School Wildcat Fight Song" and the "Deming High School Alma Mater," which are still played by the high school's band today.

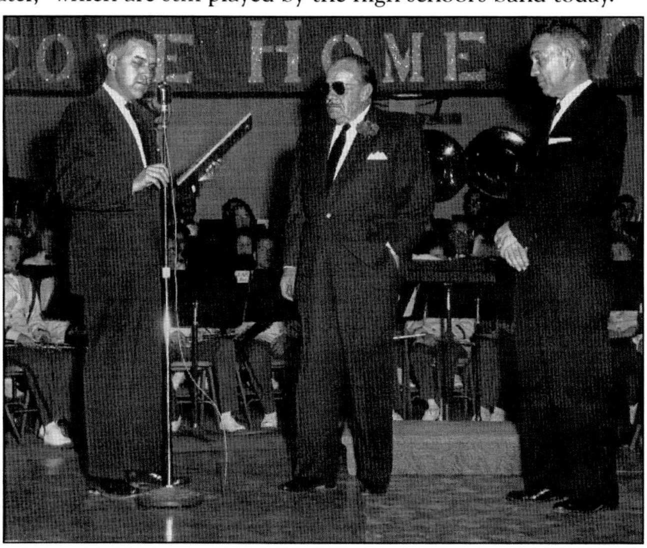

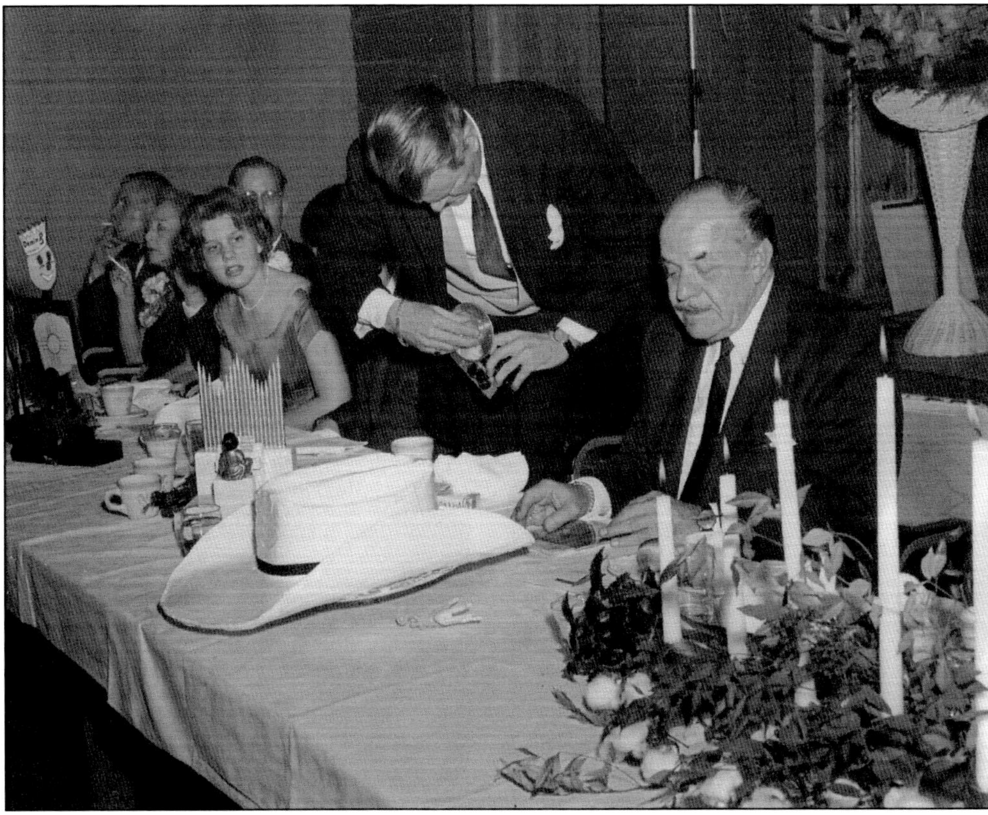

An unidentified man stands on as Nacio Herb Brown admires his homemade cowboy-hat birthday cake in February 1960 (above). The theme for the large reception was everything Deming and New Mexico. The City of Deming logo, which represents the Kingdom of the Sun, and New Mexico's Zia symbol adorn the table as decorations. Several prominent Deming women pose to take a photograph with Brown (below). In this image are, from left to right, Mary Mahoney Carney, Esther Brisley, Nacio Herb Brown, May Schoepf, Carolyn Marshall, Carrie Clarkson, and Susannah Tidmore. The women made him feel like a king at his homecoming celebration.

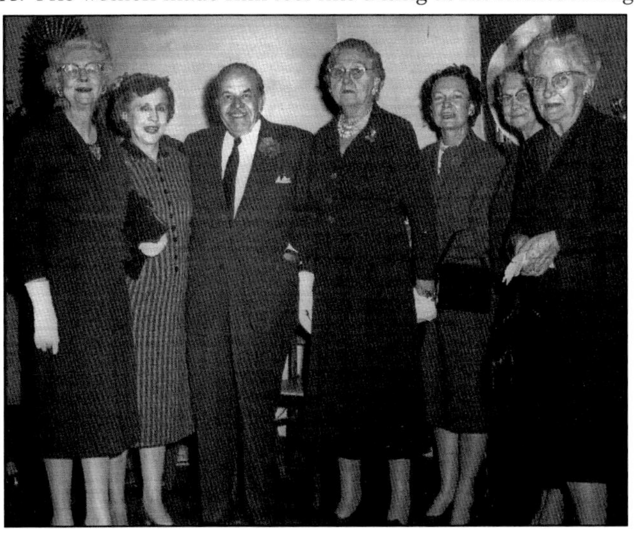

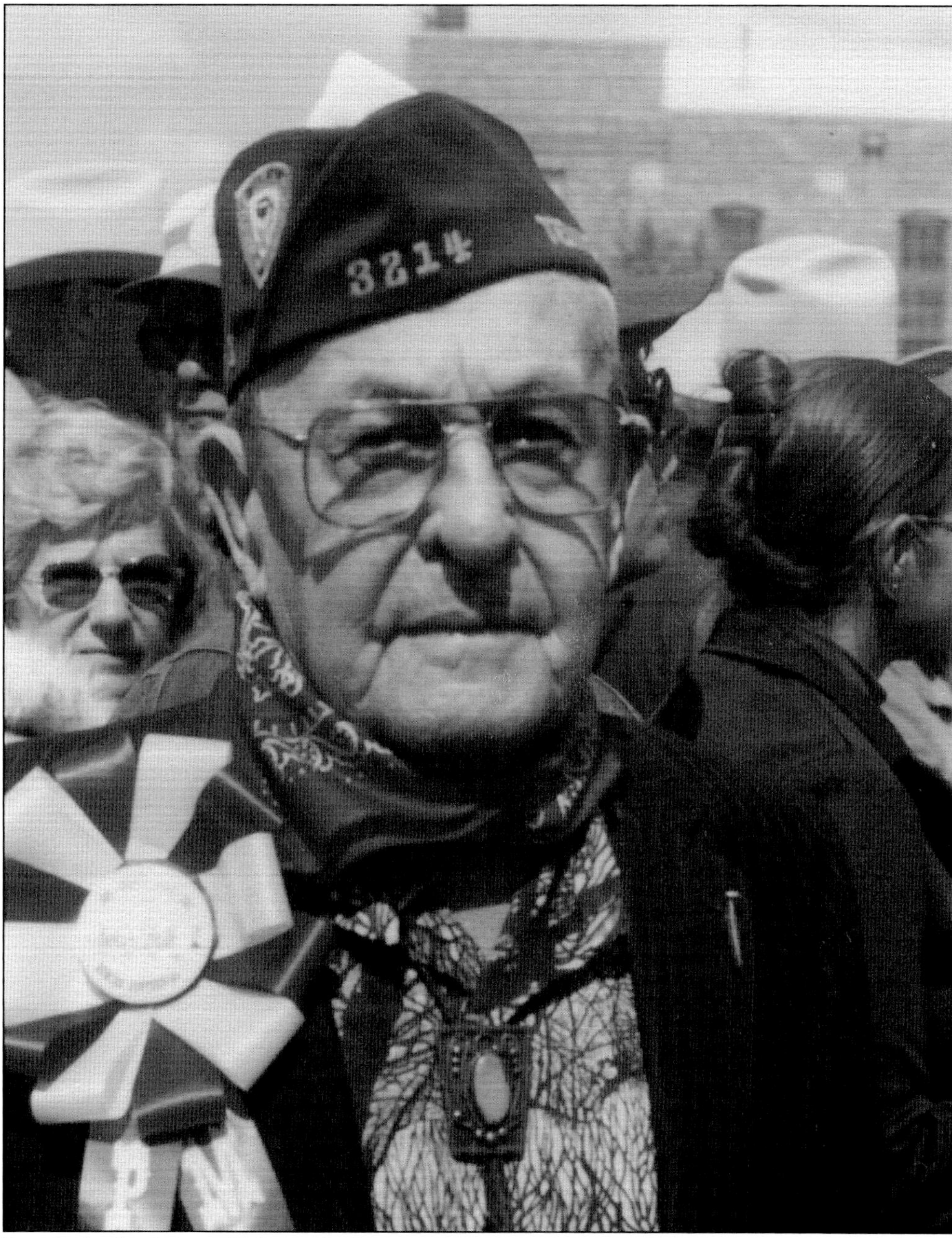

Ray Cash, the father of Johnny Cash, was married on August 18, 1920, to Carrie Rivers. Johnny was the fourth of their seven children. The entire family grew up picking cotton. One trying time for the family was when Ray and Carrie's son Jack died due to an accident where a table saw sliced through his body. Jack stayed alive until he saw his family. The day after they buried him, the family went back to work in the cotton fields—each grieving the loss of a son or brother. The Cash family were hard workers. Ray is credited with teaching his children a work ethic. He was stationed in Deming during the Mexican Revolution and died in Hendersonville, Tennessee, four years after this 1981 photograph was taken.

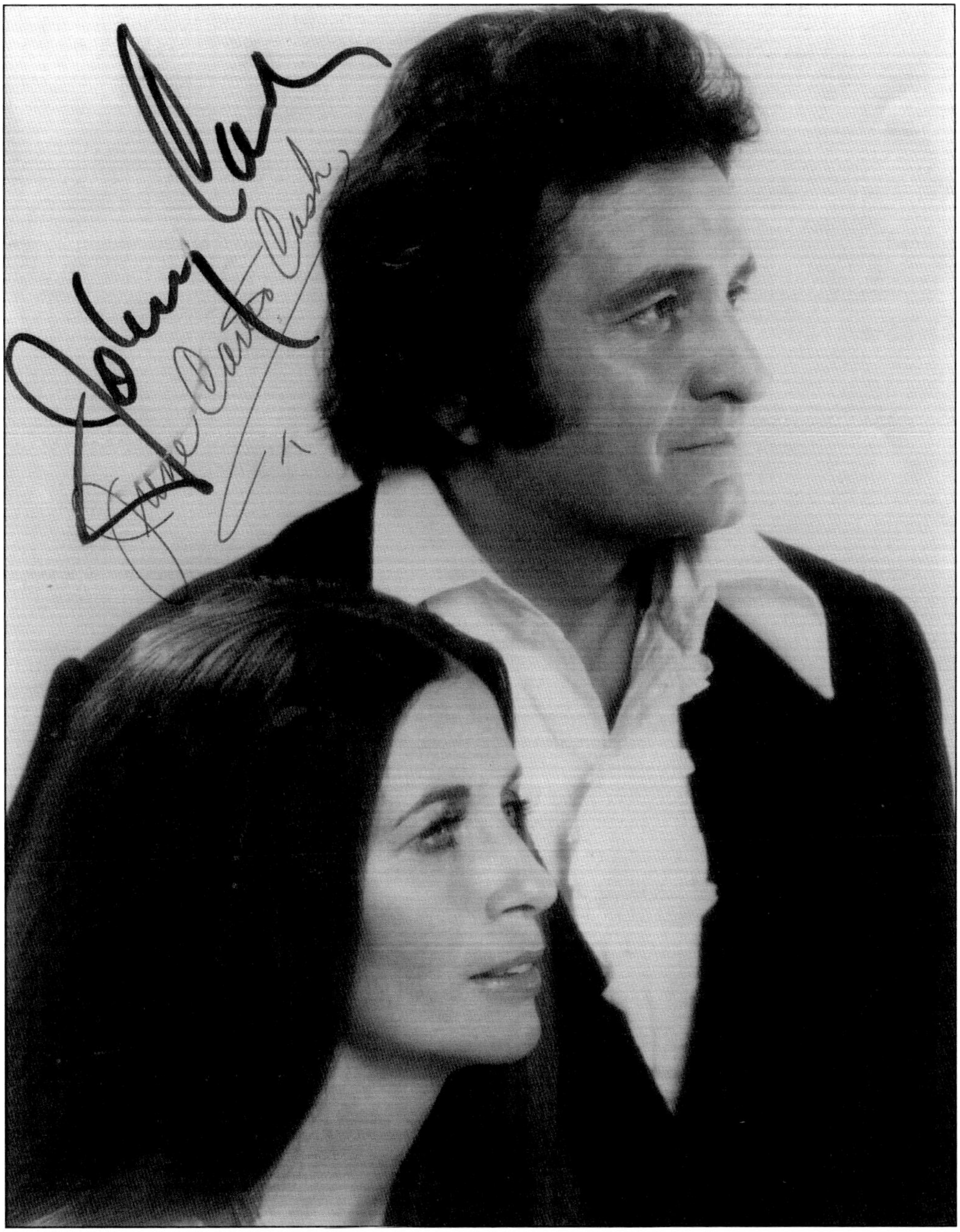

Cash: The Autobiography, written by Johnny Cash with Patrick Carr, states the following about Ray Cash: "Daddy, the youngest son and only child still at home, was just fifteen at the time, but he supported my grandmother until her death three years later, after which he enlisted in the army. His first posting, in 1916, was to General John J. Pershing's command in Deming, New Mexico, and he was under Pershing when Pancho Villa came through and burned Columbus. I remember him telling me that for three nights he lay with his head in Mexico and his feet in Texas, waiting for Villa. Villa never came; Pershing had to go looking for him." Johnny was born on February 26, 1932, as John R. Cash. He was married to Vivian Liberto before marrying June Carter.

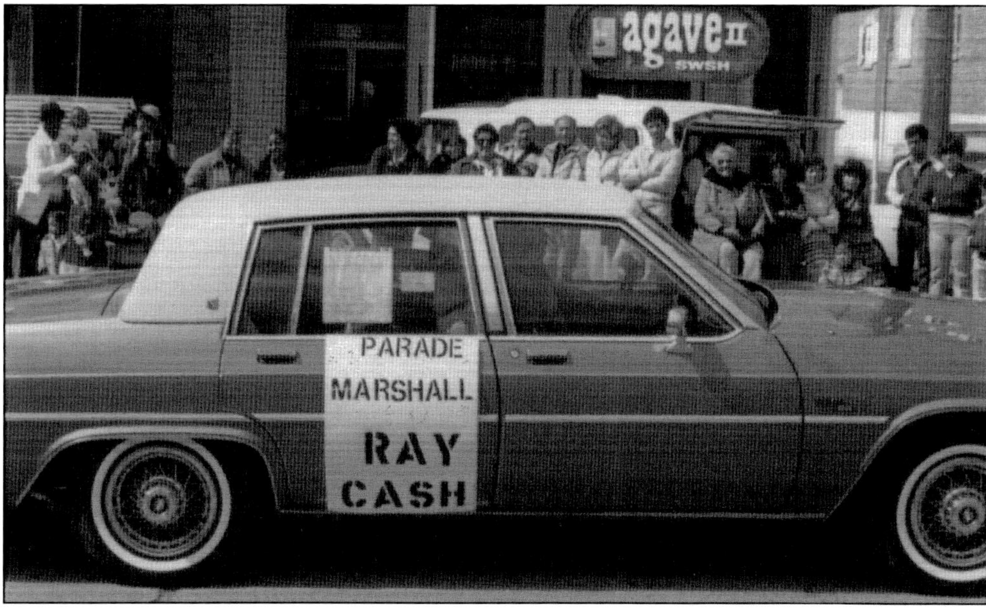

Ray Cash serves as the grand marshal of the Deming Centennial Celebration in 1981 (above). Centennial Celebration Committee members were seeking someone who knew Deming to be the marshal of the parade. Johnny Cash was seen on television talking about his father's service in Deming, which caught the locals' attention, so they invited Ray Cash to join them, probably wishing that his son, Johnny, would come as well. During the parade, the oldest man and woman living in Deming were honored. Carl Schultz and Fate McKeyes Wells ride together in a 1930s Ford in the Centennial parade (below). Wells was born in Deming on February 24, 1892.

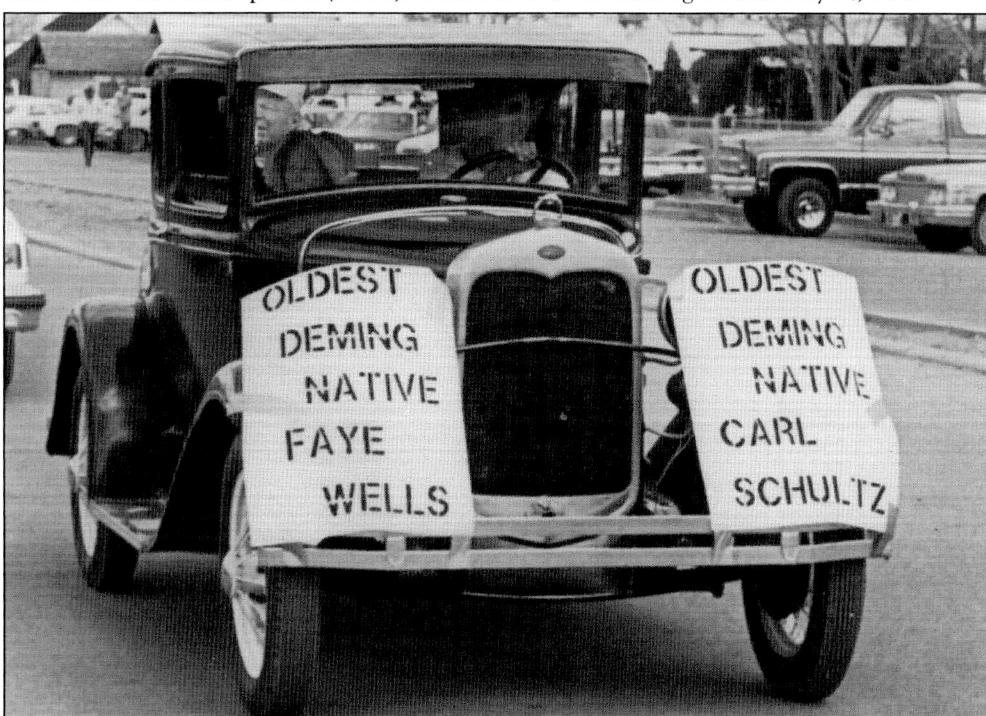

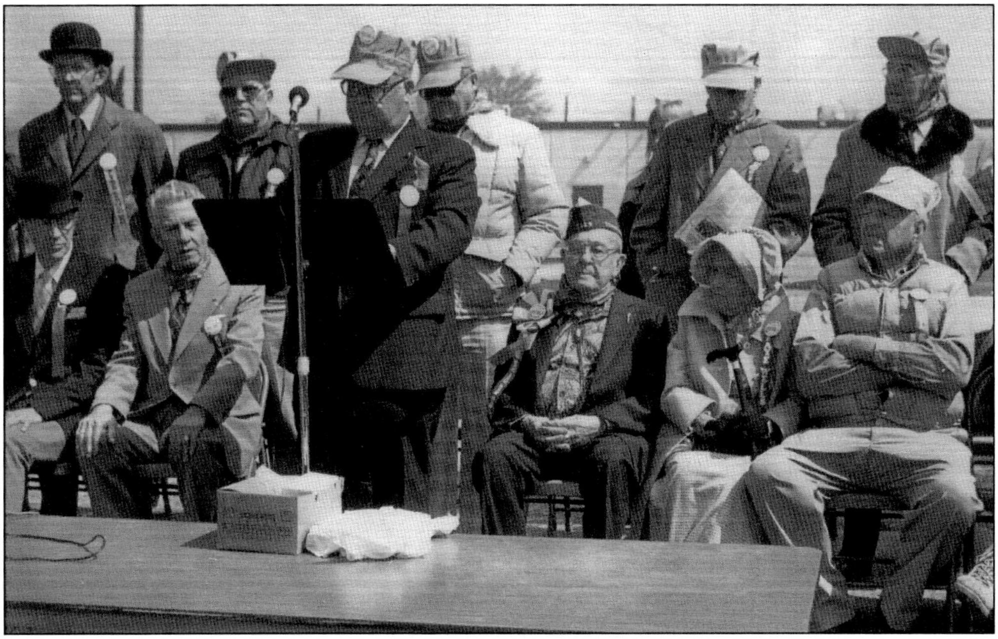

Above, from left to right, (standing) Richard Noyes, Robert Beckett, Mayor Lloyd Pratz (podium), Rep. Von Rue Crawford, former mayor Tom C. Getzwiller (holding paper), and former mayor Adrien D. Graveline; (sitting) Marcus Burr, Roy Cash, Ray Cash, Faye McKeyes Wells, and Carl Schultz are involved in the Centennial Celebration. Below, from left to right, Mayor Lloyd Pratz, Ray Cash, Faye McKeyes Wells, and Carl Schultz are present at the Centennial Celebration for the city of Deming in March 1981. Mayor Pratz presented Ray Cash with a key to the city of Deming. This bronze key was the first one ever given to anyone. Mayor Pratz said, "This is, after all, only the beginning—for I know and you know that the next 100 years are going to be even better!"

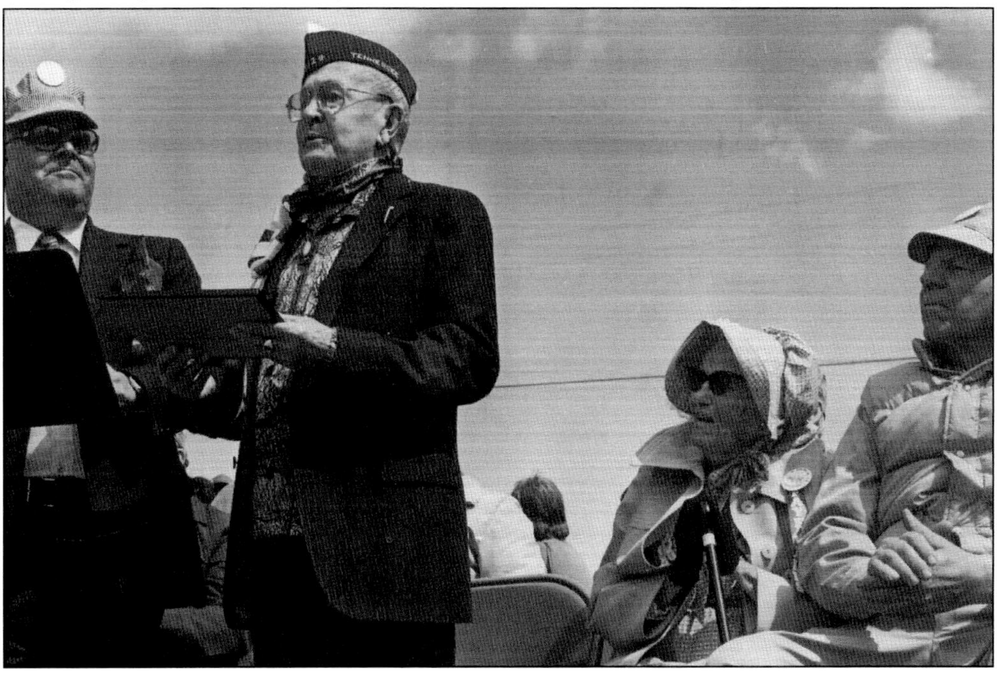

Bibliography

Borneman, Walter R. *Rival Rails: The Race to Build America's Greatest Transcontinental Railroad.* New York: Random House, 2010.

Deming Headlight, various articles, 1901–2011.

Greene Charles W., ed. *Business Directory of New Mexico and Gazetteer of the Territory for 1882.* Santa Fe: New Mexican Printing and Publishing Company, 1882.

History of New Mexico: Its Resources and People, Vol. 2. Los Angeles: Pacific States Publishing Company, 1907.

Hunter, J. Marvin. *The Story of Lottie Deno: Her Life and Times; The Story of the Mysterious Aristocrat Who Became a Lady Gambler and Female Dared.* Bandera, TX: 4 Hunters, 1959.

Luna County Historical Society, ed. *The History of Luna County.* Deming: Luna County Historical Society, 1978.

Matson, Eva Jane. *It Tolled for New Mexico: New Mexicans Captured by the Japanese, 1941–1945.* Las Cruces: Yucca Tree Press, 1994.

Ormsby, Waterman L. *The Butterfield Overland Mail.* San Marino, CA: Huntington Library, 1942.

Parker, William Thornton and Ed Bartholomew. *Annals of Old Fort Cummings, New Mexico: 1867–68.* Fort Davis, TX: Frontier Book Company, 1968.

Reyher, Charles R. *Memoirs of a B-29 Pilot.* Bennington, VT: Merriam Press, 2008.

Swartley, Ron. *Fort Cummings and Massacre Canyon: Rugged Duty in the Old Southwest.* Silver City, NM: Frontier Image Press, 2004.

INDEX

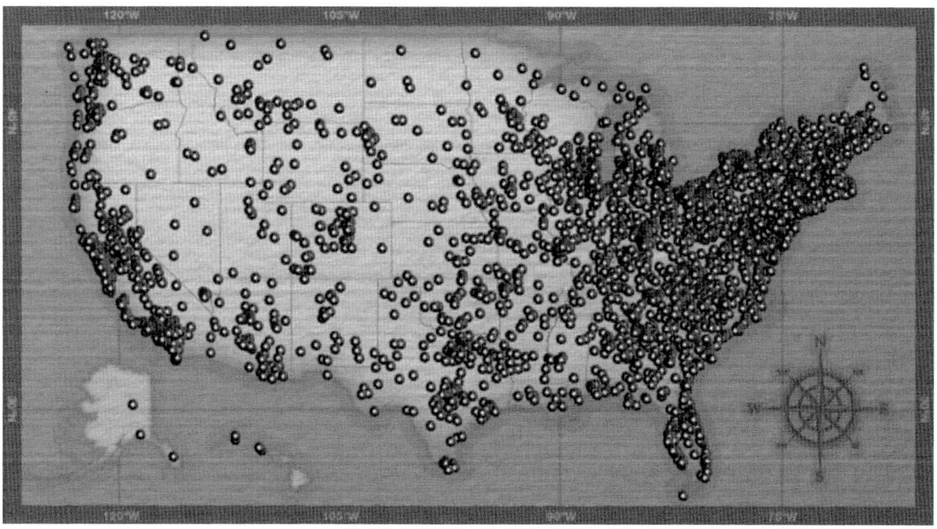